D1580014

Specific Phobias

CLINICAL APPLICATION OF EVIDENCE-BASED PSYCHOTHERAPY

A Series of Books Edited By

William C. Sanderson

In response to the demands of the new health care environment, there is a movement in psychology (and in all of health care) toward defining empirically supported treatment approaches (i.e., treatments that have been shown to be effective in controlled research studies). The future demands of psychotherapy are becoming clear. In response to pressures from managed care organizations and various practice guidelines, clinicians will be required to implement evidence-based, symptom-focused treatments.

Fortunately, such treatments exist for a variety of the most commonly encountered disorders. However, it has been extremely difficult to disseminate these treatments from clinical research centers, where the treatments are typically developed, to practitioners. More often than not, the level of detail in treatment protocols used in research studies is insufficient to teach a clinician to implement the treatment.

This series, *Clinical Application of Evidence-Based Psychotherapy*, will address this issue. For each disorder covered, empirically supported psychological procedures will be identified. Then, an intensive, step-by-step, session-by-session treatment application will be provided. A detailed clinical vignette will be woven throughout, including session transcripts.

All books in this series are written by experienced clinicians who have applied the treatments to a wide variety of patients, and have supervised and taught other clinicians how to apply them.

Social Phobia:
Clinical Application of Evidence-Based Psychotherapy
Ronald Rapee and William C. Sanderson

Overcoming Shyness and Social Phobia:
A Step-by-Step Guide
Ronald Rapee

Specific Phobias:
Clinical Applications of Evidence-Based Psychotherapy
Timothy J. Bruce and William C. Sanderson

Cognitive-Behavioral Treatment of Depression
Janet S. Klosko and William C. Sanderson

Marital Distress:
Cognitive Behavioral Interventions for Dysfunctional Couples
Jill H. Rathus and William C. Sanderson

Specific Phobias:
Clinical Applications of Evidence-Based Psychotherapy

Timothy J. Bruce, Ph.D
William C. Sanderson, Ph.D.

JASON ARONSON INC.
Northvale, New Jersey
London

Production Editor: Robert D. Hack

This book was set in 11 pt Bodoni by FASTpages of Montebello, NY and printed and bound by Book-mart Press, Inc. of North Bergen, NJ.

Library of Congress Cataloging-in-Publication Data

Bruce, Timothy J.
    Specific phobias : clinical applications of evidence-based psychotherapy / Timothy J. Bruce, William C. Sanderson.
        p.   cm.
    Includes bibliographical references and index.
    ISBN 1-56821-883-4 (alk. paper)
    1. Phobias—Treatment. 2. Behavior therapy—Decision making. 3. Decision support systems. I. Sanderson, William C. II. Title.
    [DNLM: 1. Phobic Disorders—therapy. 2. Phobic Disorders—psychology. 3. Behavior Therapy—methods. 4. Evidence-Based Medicine.   WM 178 B887s 1998]
    RC535.B78   1998
    616.85'2250651—dc21
    DNLM/DLC
    for Library of Congress   97–42371

Printed in the United States of America on acid-free paper. For information and catalog write to Jason Aronson Inc., 230 Livingston Street, Northvale, New Jersey 07647-1726. Or visit our website: http://www.aronson.com.

We dedicate this book to each of our families:
To Lori, Logan, and Madeline, and to Lynn, Kristen, and Billy.

Contents

Preface

The history of exposure-based treatments for specific phobia is a shining example of the scientist–practitioner model in action. Few other treatment approaches have been developed under the scrutinous eye of empirical validation. As a result, few other psychotherapies are as uniformily endorsed for treating specific disorders as are exposure-based treatments for specific phobias.

Modern exposure-based treatments reflect the formative learning theories that guided their development, as well as recent advances, particularly in cognitive science, that continuously influence them. In this book, we have tried to describe an application of exposure-based psychotherapy for specific phobias that reflects these influences while remaining true to the evidence base that supports them.

Chapter 1 overviews the highlights of this historical development and discusses how it has influenced the ways exposure-based treatment is applied. Chapters 2 through 9 detail a session-by-session application of an exposure-based treatment and follow clinical vignettes of a patient undergoing this treatment. Chapter 10 discusses special issues, such as relapse prevention and medication management.

The chapters detailing the session-by-session application of the therapy have been organized around session goals. Each session's goals are outlined at the beginning of the chapter. Then, key concepts and clinical considerations for accomplishing each goal are discussed under that heading. The clinical vignettes are woven throughout these sections to depict how particular goals might be accomplished.

The book is written for students learning different approaches to psychotherapy and for those practitioners interested in application of evidence-based approaches. We hope you find it helpful.

Acknowledgments

Each of us would like individually to acknowledge those persons who directly or indirectly helped bring about this book. First, thank you to Dr. Michael Moskowitz at Jason Aronson for allowing us the opportunity to publish the book. Thanks to Bob Hack at Jason Aronson for your accomplished and amiable editorial direction. Thank you to Dr. Shelley F. Gregg for your thorough and thoughtful comments on earlier drafts of the manuscript. Also, thanks to Dr. Sy Saeed, Acting Chair of the Department of Psychiatry and Behavioral Medicine at the University of Illinois College of Medicine for your personal and professional support of this project. Special thanks to Shellee Abraham—your tireless efforts and patient attention to detail in putting this book together are sincerely appreciated. Thank you to the generous educators who were instrumental in my professional development: Drs. David Barlow (whose ideas are reflected throughout this book), Jerome Cerny, Gale Christianson, Richard Heimberg, Donald Jennerman, Robert Klepac, James Mancuso, William Simmons, and the late Karl Wedemeyer. Thanks to friends and colleagues including Dan Abrahamson, Eric Curton, Cindy Dodge, Charlie Kennedy, my co-author Bill Sanderson, David Spiegel, and Les Stratford. Thanks to the supportive gang at UICOMP. Thank you to Doris and the late Martin Lamb. Thank you to Tom and Judy Tyler, and to Dana, Andy, and Ben for everything. To my late father, Thomas Joel Bruce, which you could have been here to share this one. Thank you to Ray and Sue Jordan. Loving thanks to Lori, Logan, and Madeline for your patience, support, and love. And finally, thanks to all those who've allowed me into your lives to try to help.

—TJB

First, I would like to acknowledge the individuals who have been directly involved and have had a significant influence in my professional development: David H. Barlow, Aaron T. Beck, Susan G. O'Leary, and Jeffrey Young. I would also like to acknowledge T. Byram Karasu, Chairman of the Psychiatry Department at Albert Einstein College of Medicine, who provided me with the opportunity to be productive in my academic endeavors. Numerous colleagues have served as collaborators, advisors, and friends over the years, including Tim Bruce, Janet Klosko, Alec Miller, Lata McGinn, Ron

Rapee, Jill Rathus, and Scott Wetzler. Finally, I would also like to acknowledge the many patients I have treated who have provided the motivation and challenge to evolve as a psychotherapist.

—WCS

1

Butterflies and Boys

There was a little boy who was afraid of butterflies when he first saw them. He thought butterflies had small, sharp teeth, or maybe a stinger like those terrible bees he had learned about recently, the ones that had made his father say the bad words after they had stung him. He noticed that his father now wore shoes while outside, insisted everyone else wear them too, and kept an eye out for bees.

Bees were bad, but butterflies were worse. You couldn't predict their actions. Unlike other bugs that were slow and easy to outrun or squash if you sensed attack, a butterfly could flit around faster than your hand could block it. It could land on your face, maybe even bite your eye. He knew this because in a clover field recently, he'd encountered what seemed like a battalion of them. He had barely escaped.

After that, the little boy felt fear when he saw butterflies, a gripping kind of fear, the kind that makes your insides shake. His urge to retreat to the house was undeniable. So he did, and felt safe. He didn't go out for a few days. Even though all the good stuff to play with was in the backyard, so too were the butterflies.

Mom and Dad noticed their son's reluctance. "Oh, nothin'," the little boy replied when asked what the matter was. He was ashamed and embarrassed too, but also too scared to be persuaded by those feelings.

The next sunny day Mom insisted that the little boy go play in the backyard. It wasn't long before his apprehension returned. He walked through that yard as a soldier does a minefield. And when, inevitably, a butterfly hopped from one nearby bush to another, the boy ran to the house. He was crying now and couldn't hide it any longer. It was the butterflies. Dad, unaware of the seriousness of the situation, casually assured his son that butterflies were harmless. "Maybe to Dad they are," he thought, "but not to me."

After some discussion, a plan was drawn: get to know the butterflies. The encyclopedia was first. The little boy learned about these glorified caterpillars. It surprised him to read that they were not carnivorous and even helped plants to prosper. There was no record of homicide here. "Maybe they're okay," he thought uncertainly.

This was only the beginning, though. He had to see for himself that butterflies really meant no harm. So Dad caught one while the boy watched from a distance. "Hmmm, no bad words, no quick release; Dad seems okay; maybe they really *are* okay," he hoped.

Then the moment of truth arrived. While Dad held the butterfly, the little boy touched it. "Wow, it's fragile," he thought. It actually seemed scared. He felt sympathy. "Why don't you hold it?" asked Dad. And sympathy vanished. Fear was back, and with a vengeance. The little boy's heart raced as fast as his mind: "Uh oh, I can't, maybe, no, all right." Reluctantly, he took the butterfly in his cupped hands and began to realize that it was not harming him. It was fear and excitement, laughter and tears. He held that butterfly for some time. "They're okay," he thought with a new found certainty. "Dad," he said, "can I name him Henry? I think he'll like that name."

For the next few days, the little boy got to know butterflies. He read more about them, drew elaborate pictures, and caught and released at least a dozen. Butterflies were fine now.

We all appreciate that distinguishing what is safe from what is harmful is a natural and necessary aspect of adapting to life. It is a balancing act of sorts. It requires us to assess threat and our abilities to manage it. Sensing threat engages the body: attention narrows; breathing quickens; muscles tense. The body naturally prepares us to flee or fight, to reestablish safety. And when safety is sensed, the body calms.

When threats are real, this process is adaptive. It can help us, as it probably did our ancestors. Yet, for several reasons, with some objects and situations some of us overestimate threat and doubt our capacity to surmount what seems dangerously insurmountable. Soon things that pose a manageable risk (or none at all) can distress and disable. They become the objects and situations of phobia.

DEFINING A SPECIFIC PHOBIA

According to the *Diagnostic and Statistical Manual of Mental Disorders* (1994, fourth edition (DSM-IV), a specific phobia is an anxiety disorder characterized by "a marked and persistent fear of a clearly discernible, circumscribed object or situation . . . exposure to the phobic stimulus almost invariably provokes an immediate anxiety response" (p. 405). Phobic fear is reliably bound to a particular object or situation (the phobic cue). It is not free floating, nor does it attack unexpectedly, as in panic disorder. It emerges when one engages the phobic cue in thought or action.

Phobic fear is disproportionate to the actual threat posed by the phobic cue. Although an encounter with the phobic object or situation may involve some risk of pain, discomfort, or even an element of danger, it is typically remote, manageable, or both. For example, feeling fear as one stepped onto the ledge of a window 20 stories above the ground would be quite proportionate to the moderate likelihood of falling under those circumstances. It would also be adaptive if it led one to crawl back inside. Fear felt while sitting at a table in that same 20th floor room, however, would be disproportionate to the low likelihood of falling. Phobia sufferers struggle between moments when they can realize that their fears are unfounded (usually when they are outside the presence of the phobic cue) and times when they seem anything but (typically upon exposure to the phobic cue). For those sufferers, that insight is usually abstract, unconvincing, and not sufficient to change their phobic reactions.

Physiological sensations common to fear typically accompany phobic reactions and include increased rates of respiration and heartbeat, muscle tension, weakness, nausea, and, with some phobias, even fainting. The intensity of these sensations can range from a diffuse feeling of discomfort to a severe situational panic attack. These feelings are often most intense immediately before or upon initiating an encounter with the phobic object or situation, and will eventually weaken upon extended exposure to the phobic cue (see this chapter, page 17).

It is natural for patients to seek safety from a phobic object or situation through escape or evasion. When phobic encounters are endured, it is often with great caution, distress, and uncertainty. Some sufferers will approach a phobic object or situation only when accompanied by something that makes them feel safe (a *safety signal*, or what most patients call their *crutch*), such as a trusted person, an escape plan, or even a medication. Safety-seeking (ie, coping through avoidance) can be obvious or subtle, as when patients simply still themselves, keep their distance, or avert their attention from the phobic object or situation. All forms of avoidance stem from phobia sufferers' biased tendency to overestimate threat and underestimate their actual ability to cope, but precludes them from learning that; thus, they perpetuate phobic fears.

Many people live with their phobias, never seeking to overcome them. If avoidance does not cause distress or disability, there is little reason to change it. It usually is not until social, occupational, or medical demands force sufferers to face their fears that those fears become a problem, pushing some to seek treatment. Specific phobias are some of the most prevalent mental health phenomena in the general population, but not in the clinical setting—a fact suggesting that many sufferers cope through avoidance.

SUBTYPES OF SPECIFIC PHOBIAS

The *DSM-IV* subdivides specific phobias into five types. The object of fear and avoidance distinguishes these types, but they show other noteworthy differences as well.

Animal Phobias

Animals and insects are the objects of these fears. Examples include spiders, snakes, dogs, and, in the case of our fearful little boy, butterflies. Animal phobias typically begin in childhood, particularly between ages 5 and 9. They occur more often in females than males. Indeed, animals and insects are the most prevalent of all phobic cues in females. In most cases, these childhood fears are transitory and overcome through experience with the feared animal, as with family pets. Some more persistent bugs and animals can be avoided for a lifetime without distress or disability, for instance, spiders and snakes. Unfortunately, some animal phobias interfere with a child's ability to live his or her life, and warrant intervention. Such was the case of a 7-year-old girl whose fear of gerbils and hamsters convinced her that she could not go to school, because "they live there and could get loose."

Natural Environment Phobias

Sufferers of this type of phobia fear environmental phenomena such as darkness, deep water, heights, or storms. Avoidance of these situations can be quite disabling. For example, those fearful of thunderstorms can spend so much time tracking the weather and rearranging schedules that it prevents them from attending to other priorities. Like animal phobias, natural environment fears tend to begin during childhood, but can emerge at any age. Males fear heights more than any other phobic cue; it is second for females, behind animals and insects.

Blood, Injection, and Injury Phobias

The sight of blood, injury, or other situations where the body is subject to invasive medical procedures triggers these types of fears. Individuals with fears of blood, injection, or injury have been known to avoid medical and dental procedures necessary to maintain their health, secure a job, or even be married. They may avoid watching certain television shows, for example, that depict medical procedures or violence. Some are unable to attend to their children's injuries. More than a few medical student sufferers have had to interrupt their training to overcome this disability.

Blood, injection, and injury phobias tend to begin in childhood, again often between ages 5 and 9. Evidence shows that they tend to run in families more than the other phobic subtypes. Interestingly, brief fainting or near fainting episodes are more common in this type of phobia (as many as 75 percent of patients in some studies) than in other phobias where fainting is rare. A specific coping technique has been developed that helps manage this unique physiological reaction (see Chapter 4).

Situational Phobias

This type of phobia includes fears of specific life tasks and circumstances such as flying, driving, or taking elevators. Claustrophobia is the well-known situational phobia of enclosed places. Situational phobias may arise in childhood or develop later in life. As discussed further in this chapter, situational fears characterize another common anxiety disorder, panic disorder with agoraphobia, sometimes making differential diagnosis difficult.

Miscellaneous Phobias

The fifth diagnostic subtype of phobia is a catchall category of other phobic objects and situations. Fears found here include vomiting, choking, loud sounds, certain foods, and more obscure phobias such as "space" phobia (Marks 1981), in which the sufferer fears falling down if walls or other means of physical support are unavailable. Although residual in the classification system, these phobias are no less distressing or disabling than others, nor do they require a different type of treatment.

DISTINGUISHING THE SPECIFIC PHOBIA: DIFFERENTIAL DIAGNOSIS

It can be challenging to differentiate a specific phobia from phobic-like phenomena occurring in other anxiety or mental disorders, or even from normal fear in children. It is important to do so, though, partly because anxiety disorders differ in their response to treatments, both psychological and pharmacological. A key to differential diagnosis is identifying the focus of patients' fear that motivates their avoidance.

Panic Disorder with Agoraphobia (PDA)

In PDA, fear is focused primarily on suffering the consequences of an unexpected panic attack. Sufferers of PDA require a history of recurrent (at least two) unexpected panic attacks (which typically can be found near the onset of the disorder). Most patients have many of these attacks. Unexpected panic attacks are not bound to a specific object or situation as in specific phobias, but rather come "out of the blue." As a result of that unpredictable threat, patients begin avoiding objects, situations, or activities that they fear could provoke another attack and possibly leave them vulnerable to some level of incapacitation, embarrassment, or worse. Targets of this agoraphobic avoidance include crowded stores, driving alone, exercising, eating certain substances, as well as almost any situation from which patients feel escape is not readily available. As PDA develops and the anxiety becomes increasingly bound to avoided objects or situations, its clinical picture resembles that of specific phobias.

Fear of flying, for example, can be a feature of PDA or a specific phobia. In the former, patients avoid flying for fear that they could suffer the consequences of an unexpected panic attack while in a situation where escape is not readily available—a plane at 30,000 feet. In a specific phobia of flying, the possibility that the plane will crash is often the primary focus of fear. Collateral evidence supporting the specific phobia would include patients' collection of newspaper clippings of recent plane crashes, their research into airlines' safety records, and their up-to-date knowledge of current weather conditions.

A clinical feature that can confuse the distinction between a specific phobia and PDA is that sufferers of either may show fear of the physical sensations they experience. This is a key feature of PDA. Having had unexpected panic attacks and fearing their return, PDA sufferers typically become hypervigilant to bodily sensations they fear may signal an impending attack. In a sense, the sensations themselves become phobic cues. Sufferers of PDA often fear that the sensations of panic attacks will result in catastrophic consequences like a heart attack, stroke, or even insanity. This is why many avoid substances such as caffeine, exercise, or other activities that would provoke feared sensations. In specific phobia, persons phobic of heights, for example, typically fear falling. They may also fear the sensations of weakness that accompany their phobic reaction because it makes their primary fear of falling seem more likely. Even though both disorders may share this clinical feature, and it may be a consideration in treatment planning, it is not diagnostic. The differential diagnostic task involves examining the history for an unexpected panic attack and avoidance motivated by fear of future attacks (PDA) versus a reliably elicited fear of a specific object or situation where a fear of sensations may be part of that clinical picture (specific phobia).

Social Phobia

Although both are phobias in name, the DSM has separated social phobia from specific phobias since 1980. Sufferers of either disorder may avoid the same situations, though, obscuring their differences. Being embarrassed, humiliated, or otherwise negatively evaluated is the focus of social phobic fears. Patients avoid situations where they believe those consequences are possible. These may include social interactions (formal or informal, small or large), public speaking, or even using a public restroom. These same situations may be avoided in specific phobias, but for different reasons. For example, patients may avoid a medical appointment because they fear the examiner's scrutiny and possible negative evaluation (social phobia), being hurt by an invasive procedure (blood, injury, or injection phobia), or feeling trapped or confined in a small examination room (claustrophobia).

A more difficult diagnostic challenge presents when patients with specific phobias fear the embarrassment of reacting fearfully in front of others. For example, claustrophobic patients, who primarily fear being confined, may also fear that people will think they are crazy or weak for being so fearful. In those cases, the fear of embarrassment is secondary to the primary fear of confinement and supports the diagnosis of a specific phobia. When a patient's specific phobic concern persists after the possibility of scrutiny has been removed, hypothetically or not, it usually supports the primacy of the specific phobia.

Post-Traumatic Stress Disorder (PTSD)

Patients with PTSD often fear stimuli associated with the trauma and react to them with fear and avoidance. Those features can be mistaken for specific phobias, particularly those developing from an aversive experience. Trying to differentiate the two disorders based on the nature of the precipitating stressor is chasing a red herring. Although the nomenclature highlights the extreme severity of the traumatic stress precipitating PTSD, some stressors that result in a specific phobia (e.g., a life-threatening auto accident) can be difficult to differentiate on that basis alone.

In PTSD, phobic behavior occurs in the context of a larger syndrome that differs from that characterizing a specific phobia. The syndrome includes features such as intrusive recollections of the trauma (e.g., nightmares or flashbacks), dissociations, and emotional numbing. In addition, there is often a generalized, nonspecific sense of heightened arousal in PTSD that extends beyond encounters with feared objects, whereas in specific phobias anxiety outside the presence of the phobic cue is usually anticipatory of an encounter with it. These syndromal features occurring with the phobic behavior suggest a diagnosis of PTSD rather than specific phobia.

Other Mental Disorders

According to the *DSM-IV*, hypochondriasis can be differentiated from the specific phobia of contracting a disease (a miscellaneous type of phobia) based on the presence of the conviction that one *has* the disease (a feature of hypochondriasis) versus the fear that one *could contract it* but does not already have it (a feature of the specific phobia).

In some of the more severe mental disorders, delusional fears may lead to phobic-like avoidance. Although specific phobias involve overestimations of actual threat and other cognitive biases, phobic fears are not products of systematized or generalized delusions. In addition, most patients suffering delusions lack insight into the unfoundedness of their fears, whereas many people experiencing specific phobias can recognize the excessive nature of their fear, even if only outside the presence of the phobic cue.

Childhood Anxiety

In children, it can be difficult to distinguish phobic fear from other displays of emotion. Children may express phobic anxiety as tantrums, clingingness, crying, or complaints of illness. Children also may not be able to identify the target of their fear, or recognize that their fears are excessive and unfounded. A good starting point is to assess whether the child's emotional outburst or avoidance occurs reliably in response to a specific object or situation.

Even if a phobia is suspected, immediate treatment may not be warranted. As discussed above, phobic fears, particularly those of animals and the natural environment, are common in childhood and often transient. Education, support, and encouragement may be all caretakers need to provide for children to overcome their fears. This is one reason why the diagnosis of a specific phobia in children has a six-month duration criterion. If fears continue to distress or impair the child beyond that time frame, then a specific phobia should be suspected and further intervention considered.

Separation Anxiety

In separation anxiety disorder, fear and avoidance develop around objects or situations that, in children's minds, could separate them from persons to whom they are attached. For example, children may have unreasonable fears that other people or activities that take parents out of their presence may result in permanent separation. Because the focus of fear revolves consistently around the theme of separation, separation anxiety disorder would be the appropriate diagnosis.

THE DEVELOPMENT OF SPECIFIC PHOBIAS

A phobia is one of the most prevalent and recognizable of human experiences. Just about anyone would admit to being "phobic" about one thing or another. Readers are probably familiar with those "Phobias from A to Z" lists that are so popular with the media, or maybe have had the misfortune of being asked what something like buggeverbaphobia means (fear of big words?). It seems anything could become the object of a phobia, however, objects and situations are not equally likely to become phobic cues. The question of why that is has been a matter of much research and fruitful scientific debate.

Why Snakes?

University of Pennsylvania psychologist Martin Seligman finds it no coincidence that many present-day phobias are of objects and situations that would have been more of a threat to the everyday survival of our earliest ancestors than to us. Examples include potentially deadly animals or insects, high or closed-in places, and even blood and injury—fainting and all. Seligman suggests that natural selection has left us biologically prepared to develop phobias more readily to these evolutionarily significant objects and situations than to others. A classic example is the electrical socket—it poses more everyday threat of harm to use than, for example, an enclosed place such as an elevator or MRI scanner; however, the latter are more likely to elicit phobic reactions.

Biological preparedness theory has been invoked to explain results from animal and human research suggesting that the learned association between fear and a prepared stimulus (1) is acquired more rapidly and is more resistant to extinction than it is to unprepared or contraprepared stimuli; (2) can be acquired while subjects are unconscious and therefore are noncognitive, irrational, and resistant to rational disputation; and (3) are selectively associated with specific responses (e.g., seeing injury causes fainting, aversion to food causes nausea and vomiting). Preparedness theory advances that phobias are not simply products of aversive conditioning to random stimuli, but rather reflections of a biological predisposition to learn and retain specific survival-relevant associations (see Seligman and Hager 1972 for review).

Preparedness theory has not gone unchallenged. Some theorists not only question whether it is the best explanation for the above-cited research results, but point to inconsistencies in the results themselves (see McNally 1987 for review). The details of this complex debate are beyond the purposes of this volume. Interested readers may want to start with the references cited.

Suffice it to say that most phobias do seem to develop in response to threats of evolutionary significance. If biological preparedness accounts for that, then it leaves us with a predisposition to develop certain types of specific phobias. Development itself, though, depends ultimately on one's experiences with the object or situation. The question then is, "What kinds of experiences can lead us to develop fear of an object or situation that is so disproportionate to the threat it actually poses?" As University of British Columbia psychologist Stanley Rachman (1977, 1978) has discussed, evidence points to some familiar influences.

Aversive Experiences

Research investigating the onset of phobias shows that many sufferers report specific aversive events associated with the onset of their phobia (Ost & Hugdahl 1981, 1983). Although the proportion of sufferers who report these experiences varies between studies, and the mechanisms through which they result in a phobia remain uncertain (Barlow 1988), most experts agree that aversive experiences such as being bitten by a dog, trapped in a confined place, or seriously hurt in an accident can initiate a phobia.

Interestingly, it is not necessary for a potential phobic object or situation to cause the aversive experience for it to become the phobic cue. Association can be sufficient. For example, one of the present coauthors, who will remain anonymous, once became violently ill due to a flu, but also unfortunately after eating his mother-in-law's famous stew. Needless to say, he has had many an awkward moment declining it since.

The nature of aversive experiences, their frequency, and their intensity all seem to influence the developmental course of a phobia. For example, some individuals develop a specific phobia after a single aversive experience. Such was the case of a patient who developed a specific phobia for rice-based chicken dishes after finding maggots in a half-eaten order of chicken fried rice. Others may develop a phobia after several mildly aversive encounters, like repeated experiences of feeling pain or faintness upon giving blood or receiving injections. Complicating the picture is the fact that, once acquired, a phobia can lie seemingly dormant for many years, only to reemerge in a more severe form when the individual reencounters the phobic object or situation. Of course, direct personal experiences are not the only source of our fears; others' trials can influence them as well.

Observational Acquisition

Observing phobic fear and avoidance is another very strong developmental influence (see Bandura 1969, 1986 for review). Examples range from observing subtle displays of apprehension to witnessing trauma. The child who watches an older sibling let go a hysterical, blood curdling scream upon noticing a spider, or who sees a parent head for high ground after spotting a mouse, is learning that those creatures are to be feared, and is picking up pointers on reacting to them accordingly. We may have forgotten watching a parent subtly avoid highway driving or flying in an airplane until we find ourselves having difficulty encountering those same situations later in life. Anyone who has ever said, "Oh, my gosh! I just sounded like my (mom, dad, teacher, etc.)" has experienced the effects of observational learning.

Instructional Acquisition

Information gleaned through any number of sources can convey the message that an object or situation is more threatening and unmanageable than it actually is and thereby influence the development of a phobia. Warnings, scary stories, and other information highlighting danger and threat, conveyed by any number of sources, are all potential means to the instructional acquisition of a phobia. The popular media are particularly notorious for overrepresenting the rare but catastrophic dangers of life.

RESILIENCE AND VULNERABILITY

Aversive encounters, modeling, and fearful messages do not guarantee the development of a specific phobia. Many plane crash survivors continue to fly. Even some practicing rattlesnake handlers have been bitten. The movie *Jaws* did not keep everyone from swimming in the ocean—okay, a few fools continued to swim. So what makes one individual more vulnerable than another to developing a phobia under the same circumstances, or the same person more vulnerable at one time versus another? From his critical analysis of the literature on the processes and origins of anxiety, Boston University psychologist David Barlow (1988) suggests that several factors, biological, psychological, and social, can affect an individual's resilience or vulnerability to the effects of potentially phobiogenic experiences.

One example relates to the family transmission of phobias. There is evidence that certain types of phobias run in families. The first-degree biological relatives of persons with specific animal phobias, for instance, are more likely than relatives of nonphobics to develop an animal phobia as well but, interestingly, not necessarily to the same type of animal. Phobias of blood, injury, and injection appear to have a particularly strong familial influence, with some studies showing that approximately two-thirds of these sufferers have a close relative with the same problem (Ost et al. 1984). One explanation for familial transmission is that phobic individuals have inherited a vulnerable physiological system, such as the propensity to faint in response to blood. That reaction may make these individuals more vulnerable to developing a blood, injection, or injury phobia in response to having blood drawn, for example, than individuals who do not experience it.

Stress, too, may precipitate the development of a phobia. Stress diathesis is a familiar notion to mental and medical health professionals. Several problems, including physical illnesses and psychiatric disorders, begin or exacerbate in response to acute or background stressors (e.g., death of a loved one, family or work conflicts, physical illnesses). Stress can make the small things seem large; events seem less predictable, less controllable. It can even weaken the immune system. As described by famed stress researcher Hans Selye (1956, 1976) years ago, the nervous system does not resist the demands of stress indefinitely. Under such demands, we may be vulnerable to develop phobias in response to experiences that would have otherwise been tolerable.

Throw into the mix of a developing phobia a person's previous experience with that particular phobic object or situation. For example, a second-time swimmer who struggles to resurface after jumping into the deep end of a pool is more vulnerable to develop a phobia of deep water, for example, than an experienced lifeguard who does the same thing after three years on the job. Interesting evidence from animal studies suggests that previous experience with control over one's environment may buffer the effects of fear-engendering experiences, whereas previous experience with uncontrollability may predispose another to fear and avoid potential threats (e.g., Mineka 1985, 1986).

Of course, there are individual differences in resilience and vulnerability. For example, many people struggle with physiological anomalies such as periods of dizziness and imbalance (e.g., Meniere's Disease) or accelerated heart rate (e.g., mitral valve prolapse) and yet do not develop phobias. The same is true of psychosocial variables. Even some victims of childhood physical or sexual abuses surprisingly do not suffer some of the emotional consequences one might expect. Suffering an aversive encounter, witnessing avoidant actions, or hearing fearful messages while vulnerable may increase a person's risk of developing a phobia but does not guarantee it. Clearly, predicting the onset of phobias is not an exact science.

The development of a specific phobia can be a complex, multifactorial process. Although much has been learned about the types of experiences and vulnerabilities that can give rise to them, ascertaining causality can be a dubious enterprise. Fortunately, it is not necessary to unravel the developmental history of a specific phobia to treat it successfully. Once established, specific phobias follow a relatively predictable and identifiable pattern of fear and avoidance that can maintain them indefinitely. Understanding that pattern is the first step toward successful treatment.

THE MAINTENANCE OF PHOBIAS

The *phobic cycle* is a name that describes the pattern of response to a phobic object or situation that serves to maintain it. Within the phobic cycle, biased fearful beliefs and associated physiological sensations are maintained by various forms of avoidant, safety-seeking behavior. In the abstract, the phobic cycle can be broken down into its component parts: the cognitive, including biased fearful beliefs; the physiological, involving sensations of anxiety and fear; and the behavioral, referring to the range of subtle and obvious avoidant behavior.

Phobic Beliefs

Phobic beliefs are biased in that they overestimate the threat posed by the phobic cue, at times catastrophizing anticipated encounters with it and often tacitly underestimating the patient's capacity to cope. Phobic patients believe that something terrible could happen to them that they will not be able to handle.

That cognitive set guides patients' encounters with phobic objects and situations in several ways. For example, they attend hypervigilantly to aspects of the object or situation that suggest the slightest hint of the anticipated threat, often ignoring reassuring signs of safety. They may misinterpret elements of the situation or their own phobic sensations as signs of imminent trouble. Even patients' memories of encounters can be selective toward those elements that support their phobic beliefs. Many sufferers also hold misinformation about phobic objects or situations that perpetuate their fearful beliefs. Once established, this biased appraisal process is usually experienced automatically upon exposure (imaginal or actual) to the phobic cue, and sometimes outside the patient's awareness (see Dombeck and Ingram 1993 for a review of cognitive theories of anxiety).

Physiological Reactions

Another aspect of the phobic cycle involves physiological sensations ranging from mild anxiety to strong fear. This reaction, generally termed the *flight or fight response*, is the body's natural response to appraised threat. Barlow (1988) draws an important distinction between flight or fight reactions that occur in response to actual threats (true alarms) and those occurring in response to a phobic overestimation of threat (false alarms). Within the context of patients' phobic beliefs, this distinction is lost and contributes to their fear. Indeed, although the phobic alarm is false in the face of objective evidence, many patients interpret its presence as confirmation that the threat they sense is real. That process, termed *ex consequentia* or *emotional reasoning* by Beck and Emery (1985), refers to the sufferer's assumption that "If I feel fear, there must be danger." As indicated previously, some patients come to fear the sensations of the false alarm as well, particularly if those sensations make the feared outcome seem more likely (e.g., shortness of breath is feared by claustrophobic patients because it makes suffocating seem more likely). Thus, phobic beliefs and the false alarm are inextricably tied into the phobic cycle.

Coping Through Safety-Seeking

This sense of impending threat leads to an undeniable and understandable urge to seek safety through escape, evasion, or outright avoidance. As discussed, safety-seeking can be obvious, as in "I'm not going to do it," or subtle. Subtle avoidance can be thought of as a multitude of ways in which patients protect themselves from fully engaging the phobic object or situation and thus challenging their fears. It may include reliance on a safety signal such as a safe person or object, overprotection, or even distraction. The overriding theme is, "There is a potential threat, so I'm not going to make myself vulnerable to it."

Although the cognitive, physiological, and behavioral components of the phobic cycle are distinguishable in concept, in action they overlap and interact in complex and varied ways. Sometimes reactions are synchronous and strong, resulting in an intensely aversive phobic experience and escape. Other times they are desynchronous and weak, as when thoughts of unlikely harm lead to mild discomfort but no avoidance. The components of the phobic cycle can play off one another in rapid sequences that can quickly spiral anxiety from low to high levels. Take, for example, the case of John who sought treatment for an animal phobia.

> John was fearful of dogs and anticipated being bitten (overestimating threat) while encountering one recently. As John approached the dog, he felt his heart race and saw his hands were shaking (false alarm). He wasn't thinking about how he was going to handle this dog (ignoring coping). Rather, he was attending to any indication that the dog was about to strike (hypervigilance toward the overestimated threat). He was keeping his distance and preparing to run, if necessary (safety-seeking). Noticing his own fear, John instantly feared that the dog

might be able to sense it too, and would attack if it did (overestimation of threat based on misinformation). Feeling his fear surge even more (false alarm), he was now convinced that the dog was about to bite (emotional reasoning). As the dog approached John nonaggressively, John lowered his chin (safety-seeking), thinking that the dog would go for his neck (catastrophic thinking based on a misinterpretation of the dog's actions). John immediately backpedaled and left (safety-seeking). Later, he concluded that he had escaped an imminent attack in the nick of time.

Safety-seeking, in all its forms, perpetuates patients' phobic fears by never allowing them to be disconfirmed through corrective encounters. Abbreviated encounters such as John's typically serve to reinforce fears, even though they provide no objective evidence that the threat was real. Similarly, endured encounters characterized by subtle avoidance usually fail to challenge and disprove patients' fears. Phobic beliefs and false alarms remain and motivate continued avoidance. Breaking this cycle is a primary goal of treating a specific phobia. Exposure-based therapies have proven very effective in doing so. Indeed, few other efforts to identify an effective psychotherapy for a particular problem have been as successful as has research supporting the effectiveness of exposure therapy for specific phobias.

EXPOSURE-BASED TREATMENTS OF SPECIFIC PHOBIAS

In its simplest sense, exposure involves putting oneself in the presence of the phobic object or situation until fears wane. As a brief history of its development reveals, however, in theory and practice exposure proved more complicated than that. Today's versions of exposure are products of several independent, pioneering lines of investigation, each of which tested a different approach and proved effective to some degree. They suggest ultimately that overcoming one's fears involves facing them.

Systematic Desensitization

It has been nearly four decades since pioneering psychiatrist Joseph Wolpe introduced systematic desensitization as a directive, present-focused treatment for anxiety-based problems (Wolpe 1958). This well-known version of imaginal exposure remains a viable, evidenced-based treatment option for many specific phobias. A detailed description of its procedures appears later in Chapter 5.

Originally, systematic desensitization involved imaginal exposure to a graduated hierarchy of fearful scenes, moving from least to most feared. During each exposure, patients imagined a feared scene. If anxiety was sensed, they stopped the exposure and began relaxing. When the anxiety quieted, the exposure was resumed. The procedure continued in this fashion until patients could progress through each item in the hierarchy without experiencing undue anxiety. Eventually it was learned that patients benefited more if they transitioned from imaginal systematic desensitization to desensitization in vivo (to actual phobic cues) or did it in vivo from the start (see Barlow and Mavissakalian 1981 for review).

Systematic desensitization was based on Pavlovian extinction (Pavlov 1927). Patients underwent repeated exposure to a feared conditional stimulus (the imagined phobic cue) in the *absence* of an unconditional response (fear); relaxation was used to preclude fear. Over repeated trials, the conditional response (phobic fear) weakened. Specifically, Wolpe (1958) conceptualized this process as one of counterconditioning: during exposure the imagined phobic cue is conditioned to a parasympathetically based response (e.g., relaxation) which is counter (i.e., reciprocally inhibitory) to the sympathetically-based phobic fear response. This is one reason why patients who underwent systematic desensitization were asked to indicate when they felt anxious—so it could be countered immediately with relaxation.[1] In blood, injection, and injury phobias, where fainting may be part of the patient's reaction to exposure, a technique called applied tension (see Chapter 5) has been used with success to counter the blood pressure drop that causes fainting (Ost and Sterner 1987) .

The efficacy of systematic desensitization became well established (see Kazdin and Wilcoxon 1976) and prompted scores of studies searching for its active ingredients. Subsequent research found that procedures such as using a hierarchy or preventing patients from experiencing anxiety during exposure were not necessary to achieve

---

1. Relaxation is not the only activity that can counter patients' phobic reactions. Eating and sexual arousal are others; however, their "clinical impracticality" is probably not lost on readers.

fear reduction. Although those procedures seemed to make exposure easier to do, prolonged and repeated exposure itself seemed to be the critical ingredient (see Mavissaikalian and Barlow 1981 for review). That conclusion was based, in part, on the success of a more direct version of exposure called flooding (see Marshall et al. 1977 for review).

Flooding

Flooding, like systematic desensitization, was done both imaginally and in vivo, and, like desensitization, the in vivo version proved more powerful than the imaginal (Emmelkamp and Wessels 1975, Stern and Marks 1973, Watson et al. 1973). Flooding involved exposing patients to their most feared objects or situations for long durations while discouraging escape and other forms of safety-seeking. This procedure proved more distressing to patients than systematic desensitization. Some patients turned down flooding in vivo, because the prospect seemed too frightening; others dropped out during the procedure. In the end, however, numerous comparative studies of flooding versus systematic desensitization in analogue and clinical populations showed that flooding produced similar results, often in quicker fashion (see Appendix 1 for supportive studies).

Other investigators have approached exposure as an arena for something different than classical extinction. Two lines of research, each emphasizing different principles of learning, have produced successful exposure-based treatment strategies shown to facilitate its delivery clinically, while not sacrificing its treatment effects.

Reinforced Practice

Reinforced practice was one such exposure strategy (e.g., Lietenberg 1976, Leitenberg and Callahan 1973) based on operant learning principles. Instead of targeting anxiety reduction per se, it focused on shaping patients successful approach behavior toward the phobic object or situation. The hypothesis was that anxiety might wane as approach behavior became more established; it did. Reinforced practice involved setting specific behavioral goals for exposure, then socially reinforcing successive approximations of those goals until the exposure was completed successfully. The success of reinforced prac-

tice, flooding, and systematic desensitization began to suggest that
while a common mechanism might be operating during exposure, it
could be engaged in several ways. A fourth approach strengthened
that conclusion.

Participant Modeling

Utilizing observational learning principles, Stanford psychologist
Albert Bandura and colleagues (e.g., Bandura 1969, Ritter 1968,
Rosenthal and Bandura 1978) developed the participant modeling
approach to exposure. It combined the use of therapist or coach modeling, rehearsal, and a graded hierarchy of exposure tasks in an effort
to make each exposure a success experience for patients. In brief, the
procedure involved having the therapist or a coach instruct and
model successful, nonavoidant execution of each exposure task.
Response induction aids (items or procedures, including safety signals, that make exposures easier to do) were used as needed to help
get patients started. Eventually, patients abandoned those aids,
toward the goal of completing exposures unassisted. Participant modeling aimed at building a patient's sense of self-efficacy (Bandura
1977): the belief that one has skills that are effective in managing the
phobic encounter, as well as the capability to use them successfully.
Numerous studies support the efficacy of various versions of participant modeling in treating certain specific phobias (e.g., Bandura et
al. 1974, 1975, Blanchard 1970, Rimm and Maloney 1969, Ritter
1969a, b).

What to Choose?

These several lines of study showed that specific phobias could be
overcome successfully when treatment involved repeated exposure to
the full range of phobic cues, preferably in vivo. Exposure allowed
for the reality testing of fears, the habituation of anxiety, and the
development of effective, nonavoidant behavior. Although each
approach differed regarding which of those changes it emphasized
and how best to accomplish them clinically, they all allowed for those
changes to take place and proved successful. Of course, the wait for
"the mechanism" continues.

In the meantime, within emerging guidelines for conducting exposure (see Chapter 6), most present day evidenced-based approaches to treating specific phobia borrow from each of the various approaches described above to tailor treatment regimens for specific patient needs. That same flexible, multimodal approach characterizes the exposure-based treatment described in this volume. While presenting a common current usage, this approach also allows us to present the range of options available to treatment providers from which they can select and adapt as needed. In the following sections, procedures used commonly to assist exposure are described.

COGNITIVE RESTRUCTURING

Clearly, cognitive biases operate in phobias. In addition, preliminary evidence has shown that change in cognitive biases during treatment of anxiety problems can predict recovery versus relapse after cognitive, cognitive-behavioral, or even pharmacologic treatments (e.g., Basoglu et al. 1994, Bruce et al. 1995, Clark et al. 1993). However, the question of how to change them most efficiently and effectively remains debated.

Some studies suggest that rational disputation alone is less effective than exposure in ameliorating specific phobic fears (e.g., Thorpe et al. 1987). This issue is essentially moot, though, since exposure is the primary vehicle of most evidence-based approaches to treating phobia. Attempts to talk people out of their phobias do not represent current practice. What remains unresolved, however, is whether specific cognitive adjuncts facilitate exposure in any significant way for specific phobias. For reasons discussed above, we have decided to incorporate efforts to assist cognitive change into the treatment described in this volume. Based on present data, however, those efforts deemphasize rationale disputation in favor of facilitating the cognitive change through exposure.

One aspect of cognitive restructuring is educational. For example, patients learn to identify and correct any misinformation they hold that supports their phobic fears. The remainder of cognitive restructuring involves teaching patients how cognitive biases play a role in maintaining their phobias, how to identify them, and how to disconfirm them through exposure.

MANAGING SOMATIC SENSATIONS

Some patients show more physiological reactivity to phobic encounters than cognitive fear or behavioral avoidance of them. Others show different response patterns. One rather sophisticated study reported a benefit to tailoring interventions so they emphasize the more salient dimensions of the patient's response (Ost et al. 1982). In that study, relaxation techniques benefited patients who were strong physiological reactors more than those who were stronger cognitive reactors. Yet those same investigators also found no preferential advantage to tailoring in a later study of different phobic patients (Jerremalm et al. 1986). To date, the intriguing question of whether tailored treatment is superior to a more multimodal approach remains unresolved. Until a consistent and superior advantage is demonstrated, the research of Ost and colleagues supports the practice of flexibly placing appropriate emphasis on problem areas within the context of a multimodal exposure-based treatment that encourages several areas of change.

As part of this effort, patients learn about the physical consequences of their phobic reactions and strategies for managing them. For example, they learn about the flight or fight response, the distinction between true and false alarms, and emotional reasoning. Concrete strategies for managing the physical sensations of phobic fear are taught and include relaxation training and paced diaphragmatic breathing for most phobias, and applied tension for patients with a history of fainting.

As discussed previously, some patients fear their own physical sensations so strongly that the sensations themselves serve as phobic cues, in addition to the primary phobic object or situation. For these and other patients, feared sensations may be targeted for exposure specifically, through some form or another of interoceptive exposure. In this procedure, patients intentionally induce feared sensations through exercises conducted in the office, home, or phobic situation. For example, patients who fear fainting due to lightheadedness are asked to systematically and repeatedly induce, then recover from, lightheadedness by breathing rapidly, then using coping strategies to calm themselves. The technique aims to reduce patients' fear of sensations while building their sense of mastery in managing them.

SKILLS TRAINING

Another optional treatment component is skills training. The decision
to train skills depends on whether it seems that phobic fear is interfering with a skilled patient's ability to complete the exposure task, or
whether the patient lacks skills necessary to conduct the exposure
successfully. For example, it is common for patients fearful of driving
to have spent years avoiding it. They may need a refresher driving
course or some assistance relearning particular skills in order to par-
ticipate in exposure. On the other hand, a patient fearful of deep
water may be a perfectly skilled swimmer but fears being unable to do
so while anxious. This latter scenario indicates an emphasis on fear
reduction and not skills training.

THE PRACTICALITIES OF TREATMENT

Length of Treatment

The treatment described is an eight-session program. This eight-session
format was chosen to balance the need to cover the range of material
with the editor's charge to present it as time-limited acute treatment. It
should not be interpreted as an empirically-derived standard for the
optimal length of treatment. In practice, some phobias will respond
rapidly to exposure-based therapy and may not need eight sessions of
treatment. Others may need more.

As discussed, the treatment is also multimodal and flexible. Elements of it can be condensed, expanded, or rearranged at the therapist's discretion. The described treatment involves a range of
procedures including assessment, education, preparation, and
imaginal and in vivo exposure techniques. How therapists decide
to modify these elements will also influence the overall length of
treatment.

Exposure therapy attempts to get patients well on their way toward
recovery while equipping them to continue independently. As such,
patients may not have made all of the treatment gains possible by the
end of acute therapy, nor is this necessary. Evidence shows that
patients can continue to benefit from exposure-based treatment after
it ends (e.g., Williams and Zane 1989).

The Timing of Sessions

Treatment sessions take place approximately weekly, but the exact spacing is flexible. For example, near the start of therapy when the primary goals are educational and preparational, therapists may want to space sessions more closely. They need only to accommodate the time necessary to complete take-home assignments. As treatment progresses and therapeutic goals emphasize independent and repeated exposure, sessions can be spaced appropriately.

Group vs. Individual vs. Couples Treatment

The present volume describes an individual treatment that encourages the use of a therapeutic coach (spouse or friend). A good therapeutic coach can provide emotional support, encourage compliance, model exposures, and facilitate long-term recovery, particularly if the coach is someone with whom patients will spend time after therapy. However, exposure has proven effective for unaccompanied patients as well.

Some phobias lend themselves to a group approach. For example, in treating flying fears, it is common for the entire group to take a plane flight together. Others are impractical to treat in groups (e.g., fear of storms). Since efficacy is similar across modalities, practicality and preference can dictate the choice.

Self-Therapy Exercises

Many patients assume that therapeutic change will occur within the therapy session and, although it may be emotional at times, is essentially a passive process of gaining insight. In exposure-based therapy, sessions serve in large part as staging grounds for the therapeutic change expected through the performance-based exposure exercises. Because self-therapy exercises are a primary arena for change, they are one of the most critical components of treatment. Compliance with them is important and may need special attention.

Early in therapy, these exercises demonstrate educational concepts and allow patients to practice newly acquired coping skills. Later in therapy, they take the form of specific exposure tasks. Self-therapy exercises are assigned at the end of each session and reviewed during the proceeding one. And although this could be called homework, the term *self-therapy* is preferred, because the thought of doing "homework" can dampen enthusiasm like little else. The fact is, however, that patients who do their homework usually do better.

The General Format of Sessions

To help facilitate a more focused and goal-directed intervention, each treatment session proceeds generally along the following format:

1. Outline the session's agenda and goals.
2. Review key concepts from previous sessions.
3. Review self-therapy exercise and other experiences that exemplify those concepts.
4. Accomplish today's goals.
5. Assign self-therapy exercises for next session.

Within this format, the patient's present status is monitored continuously. Unless other issues take precedence, therapists gently steer patients through this general course. However, if other issues begin to dominate more than a few sessions, then the therapist and patient should reconsider whether treatment of the specific phobia is appropriate at that time.

Record Keeping

Patients are asked to keep selected records throughout treatment for several reasons. Records can supplement the rather removed, in-office assessment with on-the-spot data. Those data are often more accurate than retrospective recall, which is subject to recall biases. Record keeping also focuses self-therapy exercises by directing patients to their objectives. It helps patients adopt a third-person perspective within feared situations, an approach encouraged throughout therapy. Record keeping is also a means to assess and enhance compliance, monitor outcome, and document change for the patient, provider, or third party payer.

The treatment approach outlined in this book describes the use of many different forms. Readers may have their own records or methods of recording that they find work as well. It is recommended that therapists experiment with different records and develop their own systems based on the results.

Finally, some patients have difficulty keeping records due to, for example, illiteracy, learning disabilities, or because they find it burdensome. Sometimes audiotape recording can help overcome these obstacles; sometimes nothing works. Although the advantages of record keeping outweigh its drawbacks, if patients cannot or will not keep records it will not preclude them benefiting from the treatment. Table 1–1 presents guidelines to increase the likelihood of compliance with record keeping.

Table 1-1: Measures to Increase Compliance with Record Keeping

1. Keep instructions brief, clear, and straightforward.
2. Limit and focus the objectives of the exercise.
3. Make recording convenient. Asking patients to make a brief rating, use a check mark, or record their responses on audiotape is easier than asking them to write a narrative. Those details can be discussed during the therapy session.
4. Demonstrate the use of forms and provide examples.
5. Identify the benefits of record keeping. Incentives can help motivate compliance.
6. Demonstrate the importance of records by reviewing and incorporating them into subsequent therapeutic discussions.

SUPPORT GROUPS

Support groups can be of great assistance to people suffering anxiety-related problems, particularly if used to help them maintain their treatment gains. They can offer the social support helpful in continuing practice and overcoming obstacles.

It is important to note that support groups that replace acute treatment or begin before therapeutic changes occur risk encouraging the maintenance of a phobia. It is not unusual for such groups to focus on worst experiences or inadvertently teach ways to avoid phobic objects or situations. Of course, this is understandable for patients early in therapy who are struggling with why they have the phobia, what it may reflect about them, and how to cope. Their sympathy for each other often leads them to recommend quick fixes, usually involving avoidance. Therefore, focused support groups, preferably following effective treatment, are encouraged for patients who are interested. Those wanting to join one before that time are not discouraged from doing so, but are warned about the common pitfalls mentioned.

CONCURRENT THERAPY

Although risks of concurrent therapies for the same problem are well known, specific phobias can often be treated while patients are undergoing therapy elsewhere for other problems. This type of arrangement is particularly common for patients who are in longer-term treatments for other reasons, but desire treatment of a specific phobia as well. In these cases, all parties should try to understand and honor the specific boundaries of the adjunctive treatment. An informal or formal therapeutic contract agreed upon by all parties may be useful.

AN OVERVIEW OF TREATMENT

Treatment begins with a thorough assessment of the phobia, moves through educational and preparatory initial phases, and then on to systematic and repeated exposure. The assessment is usually conducted during the first session. Initial therapy involves using the results of the assessment to help educate patients about the factors maintaining their phobia. This is where they learn about the phobic cycle and the role of exposure in breaking it. Patients then learn how to plan for exposure and use coping strategies to meet its challenges. Imaginal or interoceptive exposure, if desired, may be used prior to exposure in vivo. Initial exposures in vivo are therapist- and, if available, coach-assisted. As therapy progresses, patients learn to conduct exposures independently, overcoming obstacles to progress and building upon adaptive change. Final sessions focus on developing and practicing strategies that encourage the long-term maintenance of gains and the prevention of relapse.

2

Treatment Session 1— Assessing the Cycle of Fear and Avoidance

SESSION OVERVIEW

During this first session, a thorough assessment of the patients' specific phobias is conducted as part of (or following) an overall diagnostic evaluation. Prior to the session, patients are asked to complete the following questionnaires that examine different dimensions of their phobia: Phobic Types Questionnaire (Appendix 2); Phobic Objects, Situations, and Activities Questionnaire (Appendix 3); Methods of Coping Questionnaire (Appendix 4); Fearful Thoughts Questionnaire (Appendix 5); and Phobic Sensations Questionnaire (Appendix 6). There are many variations on these types of behavioral rating forms. Readers should feel free to use the present forms, make modifications to them, use other forms, or develop their own. It is advised to send the forms well before the appointment date, so they can be completed, returned, and reviewed prior to the session. The forms facilitate the assessment and reduce the time needed to conduct it.

At the start of the session proper, assessment goals are reviewed. Although those goals are outlined separately in this chapter for emphasis, the order and manner in which they are accomplished is at the assessor's discretion. Following the assessment, a brief orientation to the therapy is conducted and preliminary treatment goals are identified. The session concludes with the assignment of a self-therapy exercise that asks patients to record their reactions to an actual encounter with a selected phobic object or situation (i.e., a behavioral assessment). Results of that exercise can be used to accomplish some of the educational goals of the next session.

SESSION 1 GOALS AND SUBGOALS

1. Conduct a thorough assessment of the patient's phobia, empha-
    sizing the following subgoals:
    1a. Construct an initial fear and avoidance hierarchy of pho-
         bic objects and situations.
    1b. Identify the patient's methods of coping with phobic
         objects and situations.
    1c. Identify pertinent cognitive biases.
    1d. Identify the patient's primary physiological reactions and
         any fears of those.
2. Orient the patient to the goal-directed, collaborative nature of
    the therapy and the integral role of self-therapy.
3. Identify specific and realistic preliminary treatment goals and
    encourage realistic expectations for change.

CONDUCTING AN ASSESSMENT OF THE
SPECIFIC PHOBIA

The assessment takes place within a semistructured discussion of
patients' previous encounters with feared objects or situations and is
supplemented by their answers to the pre-session questionnaires.
Although methods of assessment will vary, it may help to begin by constructing a first draft of a fear and avoidance hierarchy of phobic objects
and situations. From that, the patient's methods of coping, fearful
beliefs, and physiological reactions to hierarchy items follow naturally.

KEY CONCEPTS AND CLINICAL CONSIDERATIONS
FOR ACCOMPLISHING SUBGOAL #1A—DEVELOPING
A FEAR AND AVOIDANCE HIERARCHY

Although specific phobias can be characterized in three-word phrases
(e.g., fear of heights, fear of flying, fear of driving), they may involve
multiple objects or situations that engender different levels of fear
and avoidance depending on the presence of various factors that
influence fear. For example, persons who fear driving may completely
avoid taking highways, drive occasionally on secondary streets, and

drive routinely on residential roads. Factors such as whether the road is familiar or unfamiliar, two lane or four lane, or urban versus rural may influence the patient's degree of fear and avoidance.

Why construct a hierarchy? Because identifying the range of phobic objects and situations improves treatment efficiency and effectiveness. For example, the objects and situations identified eventually become the targets of exposure exercises. A hierarchy also facilitates the identification of treatment goals and the tracking patients' progress towards them (see Outcomes Management in Chapter 10).

The following procedure will produce a rudimentary fear and avoidance hierarchy:

1. List a range of feared and avoided objects or situations;
2. Have the patient rate his or her fear and avoidance of each item on a standard scale (a 0-10, Likert-type scale is recommended); and
3. Rank order the objects and situations based on the patient's fear ratings.

Two of the pre-session questionnaires facilitate this process: the Phobic Types Questionnaire and the Phobic Objects, Situations, and Activities Questionnaire. The Phobic Types Questionnaire identifies the subtypes of phobias for which the patient seeks treatment. Then, for the primary phobia indicated, the Phobic Objects, Situations, and Activities Questionnaire details the various phobic objects, situations, and activities that are feared and avoided. Since patients often list only their most feared objects and situations, assessors may need to draw out less feared phobic cues to expand the hierarchy. Patients are asked to share in this process because it helps them learn the various factors that influence their degree of fear and avoidance.

Identifying which objects and situations to include in the hierarchy is the greatest challenge to constructing them. Although there are no hard and fast rules, conventional methods have evolved. The most common approach involves identifying the primary dimensions of the phobia that influence different degrees of fear or avoidance. Sometimes this is easy because a dimension defines the phobia. For example, in claustrophobia the degree of enclosure is the primary dimension. In height phobia, it is the degree of height. Other common dimensions include the size of a feared object (e.g., small versus large animals) or one's proximity to it.

In addition, identifying factors that the patient believes increase the likelihood of feared outcomes helps refine the hierarchy. For example, with driving phobias, again, crashing is often a feared outcome. As anyone does, patients believe that crashing is more likely under some circumstances than others. These circumstances might include the amount of traffic, the speed limit of the road, or whether it is daytime or nighttime. Varying these factors helps create a range of variously feared driving activities.

The hierarchy is a work in progress. There is no need to uncover all of these factors or every phobic object or situation during this session. As a general guideline, a 5- to 15-item hierarchy that spans the range of fear and avoidance is usually sufficient. The goal is to generate a range of activities that allows the patient to establish a new non-avoidant approach to feared objects and situations that will stay with them after formal treatment. It is important to note that items on this first draft hierarchy will be converted into specific and doable exposure exercises after patients learn the guidelines for exposure during a subsequent session (see Chapter 5). Anticipating those considerations now will simplify that conversion process later. Table 2–1 gives an example of a first and a last draft hierarchy for fear of enclosed spaces (claustrophobia). Table 2–2 shows examples of factors that can influence claustrophobic fear and avoidance.

Multiple Phobias

Some patients want more than one phobia treated. Before developing a hierarchy for each one, it helps to decide whether the phobias will be treated concurrently or successively. For example, multiple animal phobias can often be treated simultaneously. When treating successively, patients and therapists should consider which phobia is causing the greatest distress and disability, as well as which is most practical to treat first given the availability of exposures and the patient's resources. For example, a patient fearful of receiving shots and of heights might be best served by treating the injection phobia first. Those types of exposures are often easier to arrange and are usually quicker to respond to treatment than exposures to heights. If there is a more immediate need to manage heights, though, it may take precedence.

Table 2-1: Sample First Draft and Last Draft Fear and Avoidance Hierarchies (Claustrophobia)

1st Draft Rank	Object, Situation or Activity	Fear	Avoidance	Last Draft (used for exposure)
13	MRI Scan	10	10	MRI
12	Airplane	9	10	
11	Sauna	8	10	
10	Elevator at work (crowded)	8	8	MRI (watch film) Sauna (vary duration of exposures)
9	Wearing helmet	8	10	Elevator at work (crowded)
8	Wearing dust filtering mask	7	10	Elevator at work (uncrowded)
7	Watching film of person becoming anxious in confined area (e.g., *The Dirty Dozen*)	6	8	Wearing dust filtering mask (vary duration of exposures)
6	Elevator at work (uncrowded)	5	6	
5	Closet (small)	4	10	Wearing helmet (vary duration of exposures) Sitting in small closet (door closed) Sitting in small closet (door opened)
4	Closet (walk-in type)	3	4	Sitting in walk-in closet (door closed)
3	Sitting in back seat of car	3	4	Sitting in walk-in closet (door open) Sitting in back seat of car (moving) Sitting in back seat of car (parked)

Table 2-1: Sample First Draft and Last Draft Fear and
Avoidance Hierarchies (Claustrophobia) *(continued)*

| 2 | Watching film of person in confined area (e.g., *Apollo 13*) | 3 | 6 | Sitting in basement (door closed) |
| 1 | Basement | 2 | 2 | Sitting in basement (door open) |

Table 2-2: Examples of Factors that Influence Fear
and Avoidance (Claustrophobia)

Size of enclosure
Degree of perceived air exchange (e.g., windows, vents, or none)
Transparency of enclosure (e.g., glass vs. metal elevator)
Ease of escape (e.g., locked vs. unlocked door)
Light or dark
Humid or not
Weight above enclosure (cave vs. closet)
Presence of others

Clinical Vignette

Throughout this volume, a clinical vignette follows the treatment of a
patient using the procedures described. The subject of these vignettes
is Bob, a 24-year-old married Caucasian male who seeks help overcoming his "trouble with heights." Before discussing the construction
of Bob's hierarchy, excerpts from the report of his overall diagnostic
evaluation describe the history of his phobia.

History of Presenting Problem

Bob reports that he has been afraid of heights for as long as he can
remember. He denies knowledge of an aversive event associated with
the onset of the phobia, stating rather that he recalls as a child being

uncomfortable in situations such as climbing trees too high, crossing bridges, or standing on balconies. Throughout most of his life, Bob's fear has not disabled him to a significant degree. He reports that he has endured most places that were not "too high" by keeping his distance from the drop-off point or distracting himself (e.g., "never looking down"). Bob defines "too high" as situations where he believes falling could cause serious injury or death. He has avoided most of those for as long as he can remember. Situations that he has not avoided like crossing low bridges have become more tolerable over time.

After graduating from high school, Bob took several odd jobs and then enrolled in a technical training program. He graduated from that approximately three months ago and took a position as an electrician's apprentice at a grain processing factory, the major employer in the small rural town in which he lives. Bob reports that, since taking that job, he has been asked to do maintenance and repair work in high places and feels his phobia is "getting worse."

When asked to describe what happens to him in phobic situations, Bob indicates that his heart races and pounds, his breathing quickens, and his legs feel "weak." He states that when fearful he sometimes gets the feeling that he is being "pulled over the edge." He also fears that he might lose consciousness and fall, or somehow lose control of his judgment and jump. He reports that, when highly fearful, his mind "locks on" the fear of falling and that he cannot think about anything else. He typically copes by moving cautiously, using the aid of supports around him, escaping, or, if possible, avoiding the situation entirely. He states that at times he has been "frozen" by fear, and has had to wait until it calmed before he could move.

Bob indicates that the event that led him to seek treatment occurred when, to make a repair, he had to climb a 20-foot ladder and walk across a scaffolding located outdoors and on the roof of the processing plant. Halfway up, he became anxious and "froze." Bob came back down the ladder and told his supervisor, who had witnessed the event, that he was sick and needed to go home. When Bob asked his supervisor to complete the work for him, the supervisor treated Bob as though he were not sick, but fearful of heights. The supervisor halfheartedly joked that all apprentices had difficulty working on that particular scaffolding, and that Bob just needed to go back up and do it. Bob insisted that he was sick, though. The supervisor agreed to complete the job. Now Bob suspects that his supervisor knows of Bob's phobia and that his employment could be in jeopardy. Bob indicates that he does not want to quit this job because "it's one of the few that has good benefits." Realizing that he cannot continue to avoid high places and still be able to do his job, Bob decided to seek treatment.

Bob also endorses a specific fear of snakes, but said it was not distressing or disabling and not something for which he wants treatment.

He denies a history of an unexpected panic attack. Although concerned about having his fear of heights detected by co-workers, Bob denies primary social evaluative fears, and does not evidence them throughout his history. Bob denies the signs and symptoms of current depression.

He has not sought past psychological or psychiatric treatment.

Past Medical History

Bob denies past or present treatment for major medical conditions. His last physical exam was approximately three months ago for employment. The evaluation included physical exam, EKG, and lab work. Results were unremarkable.

Current Medications

No prescription medication; over-the-counter aspirin.

Psychosocial History

Bob married his spouse, Lucy, when both were 19 years old. They have two children: a boy, Lyle, and a girl, Mary, ages 4 and 3 respectively. Lucy works part-time at a dry cleaners during the day while her mother babysits the children. The couple reports financial stresses, but are satisfied with the quality of their relationship. Both Bob and Lucy are concerned that Bob's fears might cost him his current job, which is one of the few available that provides adequate medical insurance and the potential for good wages. Lucy is supportive of Bob's treatment and during the evaluation indicated that she "would do anything necessary" to help him overcome his fears.

Mental Status Exam

At the time of this exam, the patient was a young Caucasian male of average height and weight who walked into the office with a quick but otherwise unremarkable gait. He was neat and clean in appearance and dressed casually and appropriately for the season and occasion. He showed no unusual psychomotor activity. The patient appeared visibly anxious and embarrassed at times about "having to see a shrink," but relaxed as the session progressed. He seemed to be a reliable historian and was pleasant, cooperative, and easy to talk to. The patient described his mood as anxious. His affect was congruent with that mood, and was stable, full range, and appropriate. His thought processes were clear and goal directed. No specific abnormalities of thought process such as loose associations, flight of ideas, thought blocking, circumstantiality, or tangentiality were noted. He denied auditory, visual, or other types of hallucinations. Thought content offered no evidence of delusions, paranoid ideation, or obsessions, and focused on how distressing and potentially disabling the phobia has become. As for insight, the patient had some understanding of the development and nature of his symptoms simply through experience with them, but did not appear to understand why they have persisted. The patient showed no signs of gross impairment of judgment. He clearly and convincingly denied suicidal or homicidal ideation, intent, plan, and past attempts. He showed no impulsivity apart from the strong phobic impulse to escape feared situations. Regarding the patient's cognitive functioning, he was alert and oriented to time, place, and person. His immediate, recent, and remote memories were intact. Attention and concentration appeared unimpaired. His fund of knowledge seemed average and consistent with someone of his educational background.

Diagnostic Impression

Bob is a 24-year-old Caucasian male who presents with symptoms consistent with the diagnosis of specific phobia, environmental type (acrophobia—fear of heights). He meets the criteria for this specific phobia in that he experiences anxiety that is reliably bound to situations involving height. The phobia distresses Bob and is interfering with his ability to function occupationally. Medical evaluation ruled out that the reported symptoms are due to a medical condition or specific to substance use or withdrawal. Bob admits to social use of alcohol, but denies signs and symptoms of abuse, dependence, or self-medication of anxiety.

Mental status and past psychiatric/psychological history suggest no signs of psychotic conditions accounting for the fears. Bob shows no present or past history of mood disorder including manic, mixed, or major depressive episodes. He evidences no history of unexpected panic attacks or primary social evaluative fears. Bob denies obsessions, and did not evince them during mental status. He denies a history of trauma prior to the onset of his specific phobia, and does not show other features of a post-traumatic stress disorder.

During the discussion of Bob's past phobic experiences, the therapist segues to the task of constructing the hierarchy. Bob's first draft hierarchy reflects that most of the situations he fears occur at work, but are not limited to that setting. Bob reveals several factors that influence how fearful he finds particular situations, including the degree of height, the distance he is standing from the drop-off point, the availability of physical supports (e.g., railings), and whether he is indoors or outdoors. His completed Phobic Objects, Situations, and Activities Questionnaire is given in Figure 2–1.

Figure 2–1: Bob's Phobic Objects, Situations, and Activities Questionnaire

Type of Phobia __Heights_____

Please use the following scale to make your rating of *fear*:

0-------1-------2-------3-------4-------5-------6-------7-------8-------9-------10
No Fear   Mild Fear   Moderate   Strong   Severe

Please use the following scale to make your rating of *avoidance*:

0-------1-------2-------3-------4-------5-------6-------7-------8-------9-------10
No   Some   Often   Mostly   Always
Avoidance   Avoidance   Avoid   Avoid   Avoid

Objects, Situations or Activities	Fear (0–10)	Avoidance (0–10)
Junction Box on roof at work	10	10
Catwalks at work	8	7
Freight elevator at work	6	10
Balcony at office area	2	3
Roof of my house	3	3

After completing this form, please complete the Methods of Coping Questionnaire.

Therapist: Bob, I noticed on this form [shows Bob completed Phobic Objects, Situations, and Activities Questionnaire] that many of the situations you find troubling are at the grain processing plant. What different situations that you're asked to do day-to-day are likely to trigger the fear?

Bob: The ones that give me the most problem are the ladders and catwalks. The plant has metal grid floors, you know, that you can see through. So even when you're walking on them, it feels like you're not walking on anything solid. The one I hate the most is outside, near the top of the plant. There's a junction box that we need to do maintenance on. You've got to climb this 20-foot ladder and then walk across this catwalk to get to it. It has a railing that only comes up to your waist. It's really bad if the wind is blowing hard, because there's nothing to protect you from it.

Therapist: On the form, Bob, you rated those situations in the 8 to 10 range. Tell me about other situations around the plant that aren't 10s, but still cause you some concern. For example, what kinds of things do you do routinely, even though they may make you a little nervous?

Bob: I don't know. There's a balcony at work, but it's not too bad.

The therapist and patient continue this line of questioning until they get a list of situations both at work (where they are causing the greatest occupational interference) and apart from it, until a list ranging from low to high fear generally not exceeding 15 items is created. Figure 2–2 depicts the first draft of Bob's hierarchy.

KEY CONCEPTS AND CLINICAL CONSIDERATIONS FOR ACCOMPLISHING SUBGOAL #1B—ASSESSING COPING STRATEGIES

As discussed above, safety-seeking plays a critical role in maintaining phobias. It prevents patients from disconfirming their fears and gaining confidence in managing feared encounters. Eliminating it will be an ongoing therapeutic endeavor. Therefore, identifying the variety of ways that patients cope through avoidance is an important assessment task.

In contrast to a fearful individual, a person not fearful of an object or situation will approach and engage it without assistance or inap-

Figure 2–2: Bob's First Draft Fear and Avoidance Hierarchy

Rank	Object, Situation, or Activity	Fear (0–10)	Avoidance (0–10)	Confidence (0–10)
1	Climbing to circuit box on the roof of power plant	10	10	1
2	Ferris wheels (with family—more difficult)	10	10	1
3	Observation towers (next to rail—more difficult)	10	10	2
4	Looking out windows of tall buildings	8	10	3
5	Catwalks at work (outside) (inside)	 8 6	 7 3	 3 3
6	Freight elevators at work (>2–4 stories)	6	10	4
7	Driving across tall bridges	3	4	6
8	Climbing ladder to roof of house	3	3	6
9	Looking over balcony at mall (watching family do this) at mall (doing it by himself) at work	 3 2 2	 5 6 3	 6 7 8

propriate caution. It may be helpful to think of the various forms of safety-seeking behavior as different degrees to which the patient falls short of engaging the phobic cue in a nonfearful way. Table 2–3 lists different categories of avoidant coping.

The Methods of Coping Questionnaire facilitates the assessment of safety-seeking and other coping strategies used by patients. Since their degree of avoidance often corresponds to how fearful situations seems, asking patients how they have tried to deal with variously feared items, ranging from low to high fear, may reveal the extent of their avoidant coping strategies. For example, subtle avoidance such as distraction or

Table 2-3: Methods of Avoidant Coping (Phobic Safety-Seeking)

1. Avoidance: completely avoiding an encounter with the phobic cue.

2. Escape: approaching an encounter, but escaping in response to fear.

3. Evasion: approaching and enduring an encounter, but evasively (e.g., averting attention or keeping a safe distance from feared objects or situations).

4. Dependence on Safety Signal: approaching and enduring an encounter, but only with the aid of a safety signal or crutch (e.g., a safe individual, a medication, protective garments, or an object of superstitious belief).

5. Excessive Precaution: taking unnecessary precautionary measures (e.g., mapping out friends' houses, doctors' offices, and hospitals on a map before driving; going through superstitious rituals).

arranging convenient escape may be revealed through a discussion of situations that patients fear mildly but do not avoid routinely. Situations from which patients have escaped not only show their escape strategy, but may reveal the kinds of coping strategies, avoidant or non-avoidant, that patients are likely to use as their fear escalates. Of course, high-fear items often reveal complete avoidance.

Clinical Vignette

Bob shows that he has completely avoided some situations, escaped from others in response to escalating fear, and used many subtle avoidant coping strategies, such as averting his attention, using physical supports to steady himself (e.g., railings), and using a safety belt to tether himself to a sturdy object. He also demonstrates how the presence of another person, a common safety signal in other phobias, does not always make someone fearful of heights feel better.

Therapist: Bob, when anyone feels that a situation is potentially dangerous, it's natural for them to try to avoid that danger in one way or another. Sometimes we just stay away from it. Other times we do things in the situation that help make us feel safer. Let's talk about some of those, beginning with the ones you listed on your questionnaire [shows Bob the Methods of Coping Questionnaire]. What situations do you just not go into [assessing complete avoidance]?

Bob: Well, Lucy loves amusement park rides, but I won't go on any of them that go too high above the ground. It's the same with things like looking off an observation tower or out the window of a tall building. I just steer clear of those things.

Therapist: From your questionnaire and what you're saying, it sounds like things you don't have to do you avoid completely.

Bob: That's true. That's really why I'm here. If I didn't need this job, I wouldn't be climbing ladders and walking scaffoldings.

Therapist: You've escaped from some situations when you've gotten too anxious [assessing escape]?

Bob: Yeah, that's what got me into trouble. The other day, I got half-way up that ladder I was telling you about. I just couldn't move anymore. I had to come back down. That happens sometimes.

Therapist: Do you find yourself escaping from situations when you feel your fear is getting stronger [assessing possible emotional reasoning]?

Bob: Absolutely. If it looks like it's going to be bad, I try to get out of there.

Therapist: Some situations you've had to stay in. How have you tried to cope with those while you were feeling very nervous [assessing subtle avoidance and adaptive coping]?

Bob: Well, first of all, I try never to look down; You know—try to get my mind off the fact that I'm high in the air [subtle avoidance—distraction].

Therapist: Do you do other things in the situations that make you feel safer?

Bob: Like what?

Therapist: Well, when you're concerned that you could fall, how do you prevent it?

Bob: Oh, okay. Well, I'll hang on to things if they're there, like rails or hooks. But mostly I use a safety belt if I need it. It's my big crutch.

Therapist: What's a safety belt?

Bob: Did you ever see the leather belts that lineman used to use to climb telephone poles? They used to put it around themselves and the pole, in case they lost their footing?

Therapist: Yes, I know what you mean. Do you use it all the time?

Bob: No. If I know someone's going to see me, I won't bring it. I'll just hold on to ladders and railings and things like that if I need to.

Once I get there, if I can sit down and work, I do that. If I can't, I just deal with it.

Therapist: How?

Bob: I usually just try to get involved in what I'm doing, don't look around, get talking to whoever's there, or talk myself down, until it's better and I can leave.

Therapist: How do you talk yourself down?

Bob: You know, just tell myself, "Hang on, just take it easy, slow down." You know, stuff like that [adaptive coping].

Therapist: That helps, until you can get going again?

Bob: Yeah, that seems to help.

Therapist: Does it help to have someone with you?

Bob: Sometimes, like if someone I'm working with leads the way, then I'll kind of just do what they do [models adaptive behavior]. But if it could get bad, I don't want people watching, in case I freak out [avoidance].

Therapist: Would it help to have Lucy there?

Bob: I don't like to watch Lucy or the kids be in high places. I'm afraid they're going to fall. . . .

Although desirable, the assessment need not reveal all of the ways Bob avoids feared situations. Identifying enough avoidant coping methods to teach Bob in the next session how they serve to maintain his phobia is sufficient. Moreover, if other avoidant strategies went undetected today, they are likely to emerge when the therapist accompanies Bob during an exposure later in therapy. Figure 2–3 gives Bob's Methods of Coping Questionnaire (now revised by his therapist). Note that the presence of Lucy or the children is a phobic cue, not a safety cue, and has been incorporated into Bob's hierarchy (see Figure 2–2).

KEY CONCEPTS AND CLINICAL CONSIDERATIONS FOR ACCOMPLISHING SUBGOAL #1C—ASSESSING COGNITIVE BIASES

Patients unnecessarily seek safety from phobic objects and situations because they hold fearful beliefs about what could happen during an encounter. Identifying the cognitive biases that motivate patients' avoidance is the first step in eventually disconfirming them through exposure.

Figure 2–3: Bob's Methods of Coping Questionnaire

Type of Phobia: _Heights_____

Check   Method of coping

__✓__   Avoid it _(gets out of fearful jobs; makes excuses to work elsewhere)_

__✓__   Escape _(routinely plans escape)_

_____   Keep my distance from feared object(s) _(doesn't go near railing, balconies)_

_____   Avert my attention _(tries to never look down at ground)_

__✓__   Wear protective garments _lineman's belt_

_____   Have a safe person with me (who?)_____

_____   Have a safe object with me (what?)_____

__✓__   Talk to myself (what?) _just try to hang in there (mixed fearful/ nonfearful self talk.)_

_____   Pray_____

__✓__   Prepare for encounters (how?) _get belt if no one will be with me_

__✓__   Freeze or stand still _(very tense - holds on - holds still to prevent imbalance)_

_____   Take medicine/alcohol/drugs (specify) _____

_____   Try to be informed/read/learn about object or situation _____

__✓__   Fight off feelings _(tenses—may cause weakness/fatigue)_

_____   Try to relax _(deficit in this skill)_

_____   Others _(sits down to prevent falling)_
         (holds railings, etc.)

[Note: Therapist's notes are in parentheses.]

After completing this form, please complete the Fearful Thoughts Questionnaire.

Fearful Predictions

The array of cognitive contents and processes that can operate to perpetuate fear are numerous and unwieldy for most patients. The goal here is to organize them within a few constructs that can be easily recognized and managed by patients and that lend themselves to testing through exposure. The method described here involves reframing phobic thought processes into *fearful predictions* that patients make about what they fear could happen during phobic encounters.

Patients will then be taught how to test those predictions against alternative, unbiased predictions that they will later learn to generate and that will guide them during encounters.

For the present purpose of explanation, fearful cognitions can be thought of as primary and secondary predictions. Primary predictions refer to patients' beliefs that something personally significant to them is threatened. These are the terrible things patients fear could happen to them during phobic encounters. Most primary predictions overestimate the likelihood of the predicted event and are often catastrophic in nature (e.g., "There is a 10 percent chance that this plane will crash and I will die"). They usually represent some serious threat to the patient's life or physical or mental health. Some may not appear catastrophic on the surface (e.g., "We could hit turbulence," "The weather could be bad," "The pilot is young.") until their link to the catastrophic prediction is revealed (e.g., "We could hit turbulence, and then the plane will nose-dive," "The weather could be bad, so the plane will be struck by lightning and crash," "The pilot is young, so he or she won't know what to do and will crash"). Other primary predictions may be of more likely aversive consequences that engender fear only when combined with the secondary predictions discussed below (e.g., I will faint, I will embarrass myself). Table 2–4 presents examples of primary predictions in common phobias.

Table 2-4: Examples of Primary Predictions in Common Phobias

Flying	Animals
The plane will crash.	It will attack me.
The pilot is incompetent.	It will jump on me.
Parts are used and will break.	It will know I'm fearful.
Someone will shoot us out of the sky.	It will growl at me.
Driving	Claustrophobia
I will crash.	I will suffocate.
Others will crash into me.	I will be trapped.
Others will get mad at me.	I will be crushed.
My car will break down.	I will faint.

Table 2-4: Examples of Primary Predictions in
Common Phobias *(continued)*

Insects	All Phobias
It will sting or bite me.	I will die.
It will give me a disease.	I will suffer.
It will poison me.	I will be embarrassed.
It will hurt me.	I will lose control (physical; psychological).

Secondary predictions follow necessarily from primary predictions. They refer to patients' judgments about whether they can cope effectively with the challenge of phobic encounters. Secondary phobic predictions typically overestimate the demands necessary to cope with a phobic encounter and underestimate patients' abilities to deal with those demands. For example, without the secondary underestimation of coping ability (e.g., "I won't be able to catch my breath"), the claustrophobic patient's seemingly innocuous primary prediction that "I'll have to ride in the back seat" would not be so scary. Secondary predictions reflect a patient's low self-efficacy. They are often not as explicit in phobic thought as primary appraisals. Rather, thoughts about how patients plan to cope with the encounter may be notably absent. When apparent, secondary predictions picture patients as helpless victims of the consequences they fear (e.g., "I will be overwhelmed, lose control, or collapse," I will be embarrassed, and that will be devastating").

Identifying Fearful Predictions

Assessing fearful beliefs follows naturally from identifying phobic objects and situations and avoidant coping strategies. For example, high-fear situations that the patient consistently avoids usually reveal core predictions, where feared outcomes seem most likely and catastrophic. Conversely, low-fear and rarely avoided items often reflect situations where the patient feels threats are less likely, less catastrophic, or more manageable. Reviewing encounters from which patients have escaped often reveals moments when their fearful predictions and escalating anxiety have interacted to intensify fear and motivate escape.

Fearful beliefs can be assessed by direct questioning and by examining the patient's internal dialogues (self-talk) and images that occur in anticipation of and during phobic encounters. Table 2–5 presents examples of questions for eliciting fearful predictions.

Sometimes fearful beliefs are products of misinformation (e.g., animals are aggressive, air is insufficient in enclosed places). They may also involve misinterpretations of elements of the phobic object, situation, or the patient's own anxious feelings (e.g., "The dog is coming near me, so it's going to bite," "Did you hear that noise? The engine could be going out on the plane," "My legs feel weak. I'm going to collapse"). Therefore, while assessing patients' fearful predictions, it is also important to assess whether misinformation and misinterpretations of phobic cues contribute to them.

Common Obstacles

The strength of patients' belief in their fearful predictions varies, but is often greatest in and around the phobic encounter. Consequently, they may deny or minimize fearful beliefs during the assessment, because at that moment predictions may seem unconvincing or even embarrassing. For example, it may be hard for patients to admit that they thought they were going to die or go crazy during an encounter. Other factors, such as the patient or therapist's gender and race, may also affect how willing patients are to acknowledge their very personal fears. It may help to discuss how natural fearful thoughts are to phobic situations and provide some common, if not catastrophic, examples.

Table 2-5: Examples of Questions for Eliciting Fearful Predictions

1. What have you thought/felt/feared could happen in this situation?
2. While imagining the encounter, what frightening thoughts (or images) pop into your mind?
3. What have you feared others (or environment) might do in this situation?
4. What have you feared you might do in this situation?
5. Do any of the sensations (feelings) you get scare you?
6. What have been your "what if's" in this situation?
7. What have you pictured going wrong in this situation?
8. How is your confidence about managing this situation? Why?

Other patients may become hung up on the idea of identifying their thinking per se. They may say, "I don't know what I was thinking," or "I wasn't thinking, just reacting." Sometimes asking patients how they *felt* during certain moments will elicit what they *thought*.

Finally, as readers are probably well aware, many patients are not used to thinking about their thinking and its influence on how they feel or behave. Even with coaching, some patients may have difficulty identifying fearful predictions, particularly in retrospect. Before abandoning this effort, though, assessors may want to wait to see the results of this session's self-therapy exercise, which asks patients to approach a feared situation while recording, in part, their fearful predictions.

Clinical Vignette

Bob, like all patients who fear heights, overestimates the likelihood that he will fall. He misinterprets the physical sensations of fear he experiences, believing that they will cause him to collapse or be pulled off the edge of structures on which he stands. He also believes that, when intensely fearful, he could lose control of his judgment and jump intentionally. He holds misinformation about the sturdiness of structures such as balconies, staircases, and railings when they are in high places. He typically does not anticipate how he can cope in these situations, but rather sees himself as a helpless victim to all of these influences.

It is important to note that Bob's work situation does involve some element of danger; therefore, some of his concerns for safety may not be overestimates of danger. For example, it may not be advisable as well for him to work in certain high places outside while the wind is blowing strongly. Almost all phobic situations involve some degree of danger. Eventually, Bob will be encouraged to shift from focusing on the possibility of harm to the probability that he can safely manage phobic encounters. At this stage of therapy, though, he will have difficulty distinguishing proportionate from disproportionate threat. Although it is not unusual for patients to want to dive into these distinctions, seeking reassurance from the therapist, verbal reassurance is usually only temporarily effective, if effective at all. Helping Bob learn this distinction is an intervention better placed later in therapy.

Therapist: Bob, when you've faced climbing that 20-foot ladder and walking that catwalk, what have you feared could happen?

Bob: That I'm gonna fall somehow [primary prediction].

Therapist: When you've been really "locked on" that possibility, as you've said, how have you imagined it happening [eliciting specific predictions]?

Bob: Different ways, I guess. I've thought, "What if the scaffolding breaks?" or "What if I slip on a rung or lose my balance?" things like that.

Therapist: How might you lose your balance and fall?

Bob: I get weak when the phobia hits; I've done it before.

Therapist: You've lost your balance and fallen?

Bob: No, I haven't fallen [evidence that Bob overestimates falling]. But when I get in high places, my legs get weak. I feel like I can't support myself [fearful prediction based on misinterpretation].

Therapist: You get a weak feeling in your legs. Has it made you lose your balance?

Bob: No, not where I've fallen, usually that's when I sit down or hang on to something [avoidance may preclude disconfirmation of the fear].

Therapist: Have you ever not been able to sit down, hold onto something, or use your safety belt and saw what happened?

Bob: Yeah, sometimes I have to stand to work when I can't use my belt, because other people are around [fears embarrassment]. Nothing has happened. But most of the time I don't wait to find out. I'll sit down. If I can't, I'll hold on to something. It's pretty scary [overestimates falling, underestimates coping ability, seeks safety].

Therapist: I understand. It seems as if it's going to happen, so you don't chance it. Bob, do you get other feelings in high places that have scared you?

Bob: Sometimes I get the feeling like I'm being pulled off whatever it is I'm standing on [primary prediction based on misinterpretation].

Therapist: As if you're being pulled over the edge?

Bob: Yeah. You've probably never heard of that one? It hasn't happened either [evidence of overestimation], but it feels like it.

Therapist: Yes, I know what you're referring to. It's very common in a fear of heights, Bob. I also noticed another common one on your Fearful Thoughts Questionnaire. You indicated that you've thought you might jump [assessing for secondary prediction].

Bob: Yeah, I guess. It sounds crazy. But sometimes I feel like I can't control my mind when I'm nervous, like I'm gonna freak out or just give into it and jump [secondary prediction].

Therapist: Yeah, it's difficult when you don't feel that you have the control over your mind that you ordinarily do.

Bob: Yeah. My mind just seems to lock on that. I can't seem to convince myself that I'm going to be okay, even though I kind of know I am.

Therapist: Yes, when you're in the middle of it, it seems very convincing even though it doesn't happen. This is all part of what people experience with a phobia.

Bob: Yeah, but like now it seems stupid.

Therapist: That's another thing about a phobia, Bob. You can believe one thing in the situation, frightening stuff, and yet believe another thing, reassuring stuff, when you're not there. It doesn't mean you're stupid. This is what happens to everyone. It does mean, however, that both can't be true. Part of what therapy does is to help you find out which beliefs you can trust. But we can talk more about that next session, if that's okay.

Bob: Okay.

Therapist: Earlier, you said that sometimes you fear that the structures you have to walk on or the railings that you lean on may not be sturdy [assessing fearful predictions based on misinformation].

Bob: Yeah, I worry that they could come loose or break, or that I could fall over them.

Therapist: Have ladders and scaffoldings and different structures broken down at the plant [assessing actual likelihood]?

Bob: No, not that I know of [evidence of overestimation]. But you never know when it could happen [fearful hypervigilance].

Therapist: You said earlier that because you can see through most of the grates you walk on, it makes you feel uncomfortable.

Bob: Yeah, I never feel like I'm standing on safe ground [misinterpretation of stability].

Therapist: You get a sense that you're not walking on stable ground?

Bob: Exactly, like you could fall through or something. It's weird.

The assessment continues until Bob's primary fears are identified. Figure 2-4 depicts Bob's Fearful Thoughts Questionnaire (now revised by his therapist).

Figure 2–4: Bob's Fearful Thoughts Questionnaire

Type of Phobia _Heights_

Please use the following scale to rate *how often* the feared thought occurs:

0-------1-------2-------3-------4-------5-------6-------7-------8-------9-------10
Never   Seldom   Half the Time   Often   Always ·

Please use the following scale to rate *how believable* the thought has been:

0-------1-------2-------3-------4-------5-------6-------7-------8-------9-------10
No belief   Mildly   Moderately   Strongly   Completely

Fearful Thought	How Often (0–10)	Belief (0–10)
I could fall (can't maintain balance)	10	9
I could faint	6	5
I could jump (lose judgment)	4	5
I could be embarrassed (can't cope)	7	7
My legs could give out	9	9
(I will be pulled off edge)	(6)	(8)
(I will slip)	(4)	(6)
(I will flip over rail)	(4)	(6)
(Structures will break—rails)	(7)	(6)
(Others will fall—family)	(9)	(9)

[Note: Therapist's notes are in parentheses.]

After finishing this questionnaire, please complete the Phobic Sensations Questionnaire.

KEY CONCEPTS AND CLINICAL CONSIDERATIONS FOR ACCOMPLISHING SUBGOAL #1D—ASSESSING PHYSIOLOGICAL REACTIONS

Assessing the physical domain of patients' reactions to their phobic cues involves identifying the physical sensations they experience surrounding phobic encounters, as well as any fears of those based on misconceptions or misinterpretations. Since misinformation, misinterpretation, and fears of sensations were addressed under the cognitive assessment section, those will be omitted here. Examples of questions assessing common areas include:

1. What prominent sensations does the patient experience in anticipation of and during phobic encounters? These are typically those of the flight or fight response.

2. Are sensations predictable? Most phobic sensations occur reliably. That reliability can be pointed out to patients as they learn about the situationally bound nature of their phobic feelings and how to cope with them. This can be used to help patients develop a sense of predictability and controllability in phobic encounters.

3. Does the patient cope with sensations in ways that exacerbate or attenuate them? This information is useful when providing the rationale for coping strategies and teaching specific coping strategies.

4. Have the sensations actually interfered with patient's ability to perform a task, or rather do patients fear, without evidence of past interference, that this will happen? This information helps therapists decide whether somatic control will be emphasized over efforts to reduce fears of sensations or vice versa. For example, in situations where fainting interferes with patients' ability to have blood drawn, then somatic control such as applied tension would be used to counter fainting. If fainting is feared but never occurs, then cognitive restructuring of fears through exposure would be emphasized. In other situations, skills necessary for the exposure task may be deficient, indicating a skills assessment and training. Conversely, excessive fear may be interfering with adequate skills, again indicating a focus on fear reduction.

The assessment of physical reactions to the phobic situation can usually be done through direct questioning. Having patients complete the Phobic Sensations Form before the session can facilitate this assessment.

Clinical Vignette

Bob describes sensations typical of sympathetic nervous system arousal. They include shortness of breath, increased heart rate, muscle tension, and feelings of unsteadiness and weakness. Although he fears that the sensations of unsteadiness and weakness (probably results of breathing rapidly and sustained muscle tension) could cause him to faint, collapse, and fall, they never have. Bob does what he can to cope with his physical sensations. This usually involves some form of subtle avoidance, but has included deep breathing and coping self-talk—two techniques he will keep and later refine in treatment.

Therapist: Bob, you said that when you get anxious in high places, you feel weakness in your legs and a feeling that you're being pulled over the edge of whatever you're standing on. What other physical feelings do you have as you go into a high place?

Bob: Well, the first thing I notice is that my heart starts racing and pounding hard. I get this feeling of tightness in my chest like my heart is coming up my throat.

Therapist: Okay, do you get any other feelings?

After discussing other sensations, the session continues.

Therapist: Do you do anything to try to manage those sensations?

Bob: Like I said, sometimes I'll sit down if I start to feel too unsteady. When I've been stuck someplace, I just try to relax until it eases up a little bit.

Therapist: How?

Bob: It's not easy. I just try to take some deep breaths.

Therapist: Do they pass?

Bob: No, not usually. Not until I get down.

Therapist: Have you ever had to stay in a situation and see what happens to the feelings you have?

Bob: Well, they usually get better as time goes on, but sometimes they'll come on again.

Therapist: Do you know what makes them get stronger or weaker?

Bob: Sometimes when I get back up after sitting they get stronger [exposure to the phobic cue]. Or, if I sit down, they get weaker [subtle avoidance]. Sometimes just realizing where I'm at can make it come on again [exposure, after diverting attention].

Therapist: Bob, we talked about how you've worried that some of the things you feel could make you lose your balance or somehow result in your falling. When you've had to work while you were nervous, do those same feelings interfere with your ability to use your tools and do your electrical work [assessing interference]?

Bob: Well, that's a good question. I guess I can use my tools. I always do. I guess when I get into my work, I can do it.

Figure 2–5 depicts Bob's Phobic Sensations Questionnaire.

KEY CONCEPTS AND CLINICAL CONSIDERATIONS FOR ACCOMPLISHING GOAL #2—ORIENTING THE PATIENT TO THERAPY

Following the assessment, patients learn about the general style and structure of the therapy. Therapists briefly present a rationale for exposure emphasizing the notion of facing fears to overcome them. In the next session, patients will learn more about the details of how exposure targets the phobic cycle that maintains the phobia. The treatment is described in the three stages presented previously: education, preparation, and exposure. In anticipation that patients will be nervous discussing exposure, therapists may need to emphasize the therapeutic measures taken to support patients' efforts such as preparation, self-pacing, gradated tasks, and therapist and coach assistance.

Patients are also oriented to the goal-directed nature of the therapy. They learn that, unlike nondirective or exploratory approaches, exposure therapy aims to accomplish explicit treatment goals designed to reduce their distress and disability. Identifying those goals begins after the orientation.

The patient's likely course of recovery is discussed as well. Positive but realistic expectations are encouraged. For example, patients are told that change during treatment occurs as an incremental

Figure 2–5: Bob's Phobic Sensations Questionnaire

Type of Phobia _Heights_

Use this scale to rate the *intensity* (strength) and your *fear* of each sensation marked.

```
0-------1-------2-------3-------4-------5-------6-------7-------8-------9-------10
None           Mild              Moderate           Strong            Severe
```

Check	Feelings (Sensations)	Intensity (0–10)	Fear (0–10)
✓	Heart beats faster	8	2
✓	Heart pounds harder	8	2
✓	Breathing is faster	6	0
(✓)	Breathing is difficult *(shortness of breath)*	(7)	(2)
	Chest feels tight		
✓	Feel faint, dizzy, unsteady (Have you ever fainted? yes___ no ✓)	6	7
	Vision changes (how?_____)		
✓	Weakness (Have you ever collapsed? yes___ no ✓)	10	10
	Shaky or trembling		
	Numbness/tingling		
	Chills or hot flushes		
	Feeling detached from oneself		
✓	Other things seem unreal *(like things are moving)*	4	6
	Feeling of choking		
(✓)	Sweating	(3)	(0)
	Nauseous or other stomach distress (Have you ever vomited? yes___ no___)		
(✓)	Other (specify) _(muscle tension)_	(7)	(0)

[Note: Therapist's notes are in parentheses.]

learning process that will take some time, continue after formal therapy, and have its challenges. They are told about the success of exposure in facilitating long-term change, as well as the risks of setbacks and steps taken to reduce those risks. They learn that the goal of treatment is to get them well on their way toward recovery and able to pursue it independently.

Toward these ends, patients are asked to be active participants in their treatment, working collaboratively with therapists. As part of the patient's role, the importance of self-therapy exercises and record keeping are emphasized. The changing nature of the therapist's role, as the patient changes, is discussed. At this stage of therapy, patients often doubt their ability to be capable collaborators and may feel intimidated by the request to do so. Time spent reassuring them of the therapist's commitment to helping them overcome their phobia usually helps.

Clinical Vignette

Therapist: Bob, what have you thought this therapy will involve?
Bob: I'm not sure. I suppose I'll eventually need to go into high places.
Therapist: Eventually you want to be able to do that, don't you?
Bob: Yes. How soon though?
Therapist: Well, we'll decide that together. But before any of that, I'd like us to spend some sessions understanding the phobia, what it is, where it came from, why it's still here, and how we're going to approach overcoming it.
Bob: That sounds good. I want to learn all I can about it.
Therapist: We'll spend some time preparing for going back into high places. This usually involves learning some new ways of managing the feelings you have in these situations before going back into them. I'm glad Lucy has agreed to join us. We can spend some time learning how you two can work together to succeed. I know you have some hesitation, but also want to go through this as soon as possible. So we'll try to be sensitive to both while taking it at a pace you're comfortable with.
Bob: How long does it usually take?
Therapist: It depends on our pace, but I hope to see that you start feeling better as you learn about this thing and how to cope with it. We'll do that over the next few sessions. The changes you'll be most

pleased with, though, will come when we begin getting back into high places. You, Lucy, and I will start that together, gradually, if you like. Then you two will take over. And frankly, Bob, the speed of your progress depends on the efforts you make.

Bob: I know. I'm probably going to get out of this what I put in to it.

Therapist: Well, I know this seems like a lot when you're looking at it from the starting point. No one I've worked with starts this process certain that they'll succeed. Most feel like they'll be the exception. Like I said, though, if you want to do it, we'll work together a step at a time. And there's a very good chance that, if we stay with it, you're going to make some lasting changes.

Bob: Has this treatment worked for other people who have what I have?

Therapist: Yes, it has. Let me tell you about it.

The therapist discusses the evidence base for the therapy, finishes the orientation, then shifts into identifying treatment goals.

KEY CONCEPTS AND CLINICAL CONSIDERATIONS FOR ACCOMPLISHING GOAL #3—IDENTIFYING SPECIFIC AND REALISTIC TREATMENT GOALS

Results of the assessment should reveal the nature of patients' distress and disability, laying the groundwork for identifying treatment goals. The treatment goals target the types of changes the patient wants to achieve by the end of therapy and are related directly to reducing the distress and disability. They typically target symptom reduction and increased functioning, but may include corollary areas such as decreasing burden on the family, for example.

In working with specific phobias, symptom reduction usually involves decreasing the fear experienced by patients in anticipation and during encounters with their phobic cues. Patients with phobias often want to increase confidence in managing situations as well. Secondary distress, such as depressive features, may be targeted as well. Increasing function typically involves decreasing avoidance of phobic cues.

Treatment goals should be specific and realistic. For example, it is not unusual for patients who have experienced the intense distress of phobic fear to want to eliminate it from the phobic situation. A more realistic goal, however, involves reducing distress and increasing confidence in managing the encounter while reducing avoidance. Tying treatment goals to the fear and avoidance hierarchy helps accomplish these aims and is recommended. It not only helps target specific and realistic change, but allows both patients and providers to track treatment progress. Examples of specific outcome goals that target *distress* might include a pre- to post-treatment reduction in fear ratings of the most distressing and disabling items from the fear and avoidance hierarchy. An example of a realistic and specific treatment goal designed to *reduce disability* and *increase function* might be to decrease avoidance ratings of selected items. These goals are preferable to the general goal of "feeling better in phobic situations" or "not having this phobia" (see Outcomes Management in Chapter 10 for more on tracking treatment progress).

Clinical Vignette

Bob's therapist asks Bob about specific improvements he would like to achieve through therapy. Bob's primary concern is that he restores his ability to function in his job without undue anxiety. His goals also include participating in previously avoided recreational activities.

Therapist: Bob, what were you hoping to change as a result of coming to this treatment?

Bob: I need to be able to do my job. You know, go into some of these high places without freaking out.

Therapist: Why don't we identify some specific changes that you want to make. I suggest we use the fear and avoidance hierarchy for identifying them. Why don't we start with situations at work that you would like to be able to do?

Bob and his therapist selected six primary activities in which he would like to decrease his fear and avoidance, and increase his confidence. The targets address work and social activities, and are given in Figure 2–6.

Figure 2–6: Bob's Treatment Goals

1. Reduce fear and avoidance and increase confidence in managing high places *at work.* Targeted Changes on Fear and Avoidance Hierarchy: Item 1: Climbing to circuit box on the roof of power plant; Item 4: Catwalks at work; and Item 5: Freight elevator at work.
2. Reduce fear and avoidance and increase confidence in managing high places *outside of work.* Targeted Changes on Fear and Avoidance Hierarchy: Item 2: Ferris wheels or, if not available, observation tower at Heights Park; Item 3: Looking out windows of tall buildings; and Item 6: Climbing ladder to roof of house.

SELF-THERAPY EXERCISE

At the conclusion of this session, a self-therapy exercise is assigned. The exercise gives patients a recent, hands-on experience with the factors identified during the assessment. Its results can be used in the next session to help teach patients about the factors that maintain their phobia.

In this exercise, patients approach a feared object or situation while recording their cognitive, physical, and behavioral reactions. Patients should pick a phobic encounter that is the most difficult they can attempt at this stage of treatment. Although escape will be discouraged later in therapy, patients are given the explicit instruction to leave at any point during the exercise, as long as they record their reactions.

The Behavioral Assessment Form (Appendix 7) is an example of the type of form used for this exercise. The therapist demonstrates the use of the form to encourage the patient's compliance. After questions are answered, the next appointment is scheduled.

3

Treatment Session 2— Conveying the Therapeutic Model

SESSION OVERVIEW

This is an educational session, during which patients learn about the nature of their specific phobia, its maintenance, and development. Examples from last session's assessment, the self-therapy exercise, and patients' previous phobic encounters are used to convey key concepts. Communicating this wealth of information within a simple, understandable, and usable framework is the challenge of this session.

Before beginning, it is worth mentioning that the delivery of this educational material can set the tone of therapy—for better or worse. It is quick and easy to deliver much of this information as a monologue. Doing so, though, will probably ensure that much of it is forgotten and may inadvertently suggest to the patient that they should adopt a passive and dependent role. Before long, the therapist has assumed the role of lecturer. Of course, this is not only bad therapy, it is bad teaching. Being sensitive to this issue by using interactive methods of educating such as questioning, role reversal, and other "learn by doing" approaches facilitates better understanding of key concepts by patients and sets the course for encouraging their independence. Of course, no method is perfect, so it may help to audiotape or otherwise record this highly informational session for the patient's later reference.

SESSION GOALS

1. Overview the phobic cycle.
2. Discuss the onset and development of the phobia.

3. Overview the nature of a specific phobia.
4. Discuss the nature and role of cognitive biases in the maintenance of the phobia.
5. Discuss the nature and role of physiological reactions to the phobia.
6. Discuss the nature and role of avoidance in maintaining the phobia.

Goals 1 and 2 are the overriding objectives of the session. They overview and integrate key concepts given individual consideration under goals 3 through 6. As with the last session, the order and manner in which this session's goals are accomplished are at the therapist's discretion.

KEY CONCEPTS AND CLINICAL CONSIDERATIONS FOR ACCOMPLISHING GOAL #1—OVERVIEWING THE PHOBIC CYCLE

The session begins with an overview of the phobic cycle that can serve as the framework for explaining its cognitive, physiological, and behavioral features later in the session. At the minimum, it is conveyed that various forms of safety-seeking maintain the phobia by not allowing fears and doubts to be disconfirmed through corrective experiences (i.e., by escaping or avoiding, patients never learn that the phobic situation is in fact manageable). If patients come away with nothing more than that understanding, it provides them with a rationale for exposure. Of course, a more thorough understanding is desirable and involves introducing a handful of key concepts relating to what a specific phobia is and how it operates.

To begin, the phobia is defined as a predictable, situationally bound set of reactions to the phobic object or situation. Part of that reaction involves phobic beliefs. Patients learn that phobic beliefs differ from nonphobic thoughts because they overestimate the threat and unmanageability of a phobic encounter. They learn that phobic fears are always anticipatory in nature, and affect the way patients approach encounters. Examples are used to demonstrate that even though patients may learn to appreciate the biased nature of their phobic beliefs while apart from a phobic encounter, those beliefs are likely to reemerge automatically, very convincingly, and sometimes unbeknown to them during an encounter. In simple terms, phobic beliefs anticipate that something bad and unmanageable is likely to happen. This makes the phobic situation seem more threatening than it actually is, and sets off a chain of other reactions.

One set of those reactions involves the physical sensations patients feel. Patients learn that these sensations are a product of a sympathetic nervous system that is arousing the body to flee or fight. The flight or fight response is described as an ancient and adaptive alarm reaction to appraised threat. Although aversive, intense, or frightening, it is not dangerous and parts of it are manageable. Therapists also emphasize that the presence of the alarm does not mean that the anticipated threat is real; that is, the feeling of fear may not relate to the actual danger present in the situation. In phobia, the flight or fight response is a *false* alarm based on a misappraisal of threat.

Patients learn that as a result of misappraised threat and the false alarm, they naturally and understandably seek safety through avoidance of many forms including subtle evasion, reliance on safety signals, escape, or outright avoidance.

The persistence or maintenance of the phobia is explained through the concept of the repeating phobic cycle of fears, false alarms, and avoidance. With each encounter, safety-seeking precludes patients from learning that phobic objects and situations are actually less threatening and more manageable than they believe. Because encounters remain threatening, safety-seeking is likely to continue. Examples of how the cycle has played out in patients' past encounters with phobic objects or situations can convey these concepts. The self-therapy exercise completed prior to this session can serve as a recent example of the cycle in action. Figure 3–1 shows the results of Bob's exercise.

As suggested previously, instances where patients have escaped phobic encounters are particularly illustrative of the phobic cycle because they offer examples of how fearful beliefs and physiological reactions play off each other to escalate fear and prompt escape. During the discussion, therapists show patients how subtle avoidance such as reliance on crutches serves the same maintaining function as more obvious avoidance.

Another method of tying these concepts together, and the one used in the vignette below, is to use an analogy of the phobic cycle. Since the concept was based originally on Mowrer's two-factor theory (Mowrer 1947), it will be used as an example. Readers may recall that two-factor theory describes how fear can be acquired to a neutral (nondangerous) stimulus by pairing it with a naturally aversive one

Figure 3–1: Results of Bob's Behavioral Assessment

During this self-therapy exercise, you are asked to approach the feared object or situation that you and your therapist discussed. The purpose of this exercise is to learn more about your reactions to these encounters. Your goal is to approach the chosen object or situation and record your reactions to it using the attached form as your guide. You do not have to suffer through this exercise, and can stop it whenever you want.

INSTRUCTIONS:

Please describe the exposure: _Climb stairs to observation deck at Heights Park. Go as close to rail of deck as possible._

Immediately before the encounter, please complete these questions:

1. What are you fearing could happen during this encounter (list all fears)?
Could fall, tower might fall, might not make it up stairs, people might notice.

2. What physical sensations (feelings) are you experiencing?
Heart racing, little lightheaded.

3. Which (if any) of those sensations frighten you?
Lighthead — afraid my legs might give when I get there.

4. Do you have any urges to avoid? yes _✓_ no ___

5. How are you planning to cope when you start this encounter?
Take it slow — hold on to rails — only going to go until I feel bad.

Other comments? _Not looking forward to this!_

Now approach the object or situation. Monitor what is happening to you, your thoughts, feelings, how you find yourself behaving. End the encounter when you want. Then finish completing the rest of this form.

Figure 3–1: Results of Bob's Behavioral Assessment *(continued)*

Immediately after the encounter, complete these questions:

1. Did you have any other fears come up during the encounter?

Might collapse, might faint.

2. Did any of the things you feared happen?

No but I got real weak feeling and left.

3. What physical sensations did you actually experience during this encounter?

All of them. Weak, faint, heart.

4. Did any of those sensations frighten you?

Weak

5. How did you try to cope with the encounter (list all ways)?

Held on to rails — didn't go over to rail.

6. Why did you stop the exercise?

Too much — too weak.

Other comments?

I think I could have lost it if I would have pushed myself. This was the best I could do.

(factor one, classical conditioning). It is then maintained through subsequent avoidance of the neutral stimulus (factor two, operant conditioning—negative reinforcement). Although the model has been criticized for its limitations (e.g., it favors aversive conditioning as the means through which phobias are acquired), it provides another option for helping patients understand how fear of a phobic cue can be maintained indefinitely through avoidance of that cue. From there, different aspects of the phobic cycle can be shown, as can the concept of exposure as a means for breaking it. In practice, readers may want to use a story condensed from the expanded one presented here, or one of their own.

Clinical Vignette

After conveying key concepts through discussion of previous phobic encounters, Bob's therapist introduces him to the idea of avoidance learning through an example based on Mowrer's two-factor theory.

Therapist: Bob, bear with me a second while I take you through an example of how a situation that is actually not dangerous can come to be feared, then how that fear can either be overcome or continue depending on how we act in that situation. [The therapist draws the following scene while describing it to the patient, and routinely confirms that he or she understands the points being made.] Okay Bob, imagine this is a wooden box with a wooden divider in the middle separating the box into two rooms. Let's say in one room the walls are painted with clouds, a sky, the kinds of scenes you might see if you were up in the air. We'll call this the Heights Room because it shows those scenes. On the floor of that room is a metal grid that is connected by an electrical cord to a device outside the room. That device is capable of delivering an electrical shock through the grid floor. So if you push a button, a shock is delivered through the floor. Let's say the shock is uncomfortable, but not dangerous.

Now the other room—we'll call it the Ground Floor Room—is decorated differently. The floor is carpeted—let's say it's green like grass. The walls are painted with scenes of trees and bushes— the kind of things you would see if you were on the ground. There's a door in the divider between the two rooms that can be opened, allowing access between them. At this point, that door is closed.

Now let's say we place an animal, of your choice, in the Heights Room. Because this room isn't dangerous to this animal, the animal doesn't fear it. But it learns to fear it over the next few days because every time it is placed in that room, it receives brief electrical shocks delivered through the metal grid floor.

Now let's say that after those few days, during which the animal has received some shocks, the machine delivering the shocks is shut off. In fact, that machine is unplugged and will never be turned on again, so the animal will never again receive an electrical shock while it's in the Heights Room. But it doesn't necessarily know that.

After the shock machine is disconnected, the animal is put back in the Heights Room. Even though there is no chance of an electric shock, what do you think the animal will do when it is put back in there?

Bob: Well, it's probably going to be scared. It'll probably try to get off the metal grid.

Therapist: Exactly. Thinking about what you or I would feel if we were in that situation, what do you think the animal would be experiencing physically?

Bob: Fear. Its heart is probably racing, it's breathing fast, you know, that kind of stuff.

Therapist: Right. Remember the flight or fight reaction we were discussing? When this animal senses some danger, its body naturally reacts to that threat by preparing it to flee or fight. Its heart races. It breathes fast. It might jump. You've probably seen this in animals when they feel threatened or trapped.

Bob: Seen it?! I've felt it too! When I'm in a high place.

Therapist: That's right, the flight or fight reaction is what you or I experience and when we think something is potentially dangerous. It's our basic, natural instinct to flee or fight when we feel threatened. So we know what the animal feels. Again, putting ourselves in the animal's place, what do you think the animal believes is going to happen in this room that could threaten it?

Bob: The animal believes it's going to be shocked in there, like before.

Therapist: Yes, and because it believes that it's dangerous, does it make sense that its body is reacting this way?

Bob: Yeah, so it can get out of there, get away from the shock.

Therapist: Excellent. The animal's past experiences in that room, being shocked in there, make it think that it's in danger, and understandably so. But actually it will never again receive a shock. So the danger is not really there anymore, but the animal doesn't know that. So it believes that something dangerous could happen and its body reacts to that belief—even though no real danger is present. Make sense?

Bob: Yeah, because it's been shocked there, it believes it will now, even though it won't.

Therapist: Exactly. Now remember at this point, Bob, the door between the two rooms has been closed, not allowing the animal to leave the Heights Room and move into the Ground Floor Room. Let's say we open that door now, and put the animal in the Heights Room again. What do you think it's going to do?

Bob: Well, if the other side looks safe, it's going to run to it—to the ground side.

Therapist: Right. Just as we would. It flees what it thinks is dangerous for safer ground. So review with me. When we put the animal in the Heights Room, what was it believing was going to happen?

Bob: That it was going to be shocked. It was in danger.

Therapist: And because it sensed that danger, what did its body do?

Bob: The flight or fight thing.

Therapist: Good, you're getting all the terms down and everything. One way to think of the flight or fight reaction is as an alarm system. The switch for the alarm is the animal's sense that it's in danger. Once it senses that, the alarm comes on. So what then does the animal do when its alarm rings in the Heights Room?

Bob: It runs to the Ground Floor Room.

Therapist: Yes, it escapes what it thinks is dangerous. And how do you think it feels when it gets to the Ground Floor Room?

Bob: Ahhhh, relief, that was close. I can relate to that feeling.

Therapist: You've felt that when you've escaped from heights?

Bob: Yes, the nervousness leaves.

Therapist: Right, or we could say the alarm shuts down. So escape works. It relieves fear. Does that make sense to you?

Bob: Yes. That's true. If you get away from heights, the fear goes away.

Therapist: Consider this now, Bob. If the animal really is in danger and the alarm system goes off, then fleeing is good, because it keeps that animal out of that real danger. But, if the danger isn't really there but the animal mistakenly believes it is, then fleeing never allows the animal to learn that it's mistaken about the danger.

Bob: Hmm, I'm not sure I get that.

Therapist: Well, let's go on in the example. It will do a better job of explaining it than I am. Imagine that after we've allowed the animal to escape into the Ground Floor Room a few times, we then put it back in the Heights Room. What do you think it's going to do?

Bob: It's going to run into the Ground Room again, where it's safe.

Therapist: Right. Just as we've been talking about. But in reality, the Heights Room is safe—now. Is the animal actually going to receive a shock?

Bob: No.

Therapist: So it's running from a danger that's not really there.

Bob: All right, I see what you mean. It used to be, but it's not now.

Therapist: Right. Now how long will that animal remain fearful of the Heights Room, even though the Heights Room isn't dangerous any more, if it's allowed to escape every time it goes in that situation?

Bob: I gotcha. Forever. So even though leaving makes the thing feel safer, it's actually safe to begin with, but it can't see that because it ran.

Therapist: Exactly. Escape can make us feel safe in the short run, but in the long run it never lets us find out that the situation is safer than we think. So how is that animal going to learn that it can stay in the Heights Room and not be harmed?

Bob: Well, shut the door between the rooms and put the animal back in it.

Therapist: Well, let's say we do that. How do you think the animal is going to react?

Bob: It's going to flip out.

Therapist: No question. It will experience fear, phobic fear. Is the animal going to be shocked if it stays in the Heights Room?

Bob: No, but it'll be scared that it's going to be.

Therapist: So it's going to be fearful of being shocked at first. If the animal continues to enter the Heights Room, what do you think is going to happen to its fear of being shocked?

Bob: Well, I guess it would go away, wouldn't it?

Therapist: Yes. Being an electrician, it might help you to think of the alarm on a dimmer switch that slowly shuts off. As our sense of danger, harm, threat begins to dim, the alarm gradually gets less intense, less frequent, more manageable. And we get more confident and less fearful.

Bob: Okay, so if I go back into high situations and don't run, then eventually my fear of heights will come down.

Therapist: It's called exposure. Make sense?

Bob: Yeah, it makes sense. You're not going to drag me to the top of the Sears' Tower, are you?

Therapist: No, as we said, we're going to take this at a pace that you're comfortable with. And as I've also said, before we do any of that, we're going to prepare for it. But can you see how going back into situations can ultimately help you overcome your phobia?

Bob: Yes. It makes sense.

KEY CONCEPTS AND CLINICAL CONSIDERATIONS FOR ACCOMPLISHING GOAL #2— UNDERSTANDING ONSET AND DEVELOPMENT

Patients learn that there are many potential pathways to the onset and development of their phobias. As discussed in Chapter 1, these include aversive encounters as well as observation and informational learning. Where relevant, patients learn that vulnerabilities such as stress, physiological anomalies, and certain prior experiences with the phobic cue can make an individual more likely to develop a phobia. The question of how these factors may have influenced the onset and development of the patient's particular phobia is discussed.

Key concepts communicated to patients include the idea that to some degree these developmental factors reflect learning processes, some acute, some incremental, but all of which are modifiable. Thus, developmental factors do not necessarily establish a phobia permanently. The point that phobias are learned is also used to reassure concerned patients that having a phobia does not reflect immutable personal defects or weaknesses in the sense that they may fear. In addition, patients learn that insight into developmental influences will not necessarily change the phobia's present-day manifestations. This supports the rationale for targeting maintaining factors through exposure.

Clinical Vignette

Bob and his therapist explore how Bob's phobia may have developed.

Therapist: Bob, in the example we were just discussing, that animal came to see the Heights Room as potentially dangerous because it had received shocks there. In other words, it learned to associate that room with danger and threat. How do you think you have learned that high places should be feared and avoided?

Bob: Well, I'm not an expert and I'm not blaming anyone, but I've been thinking that maybe my dad had something to do with it. My dad was afraid of heights.

Therapist: Yes, I saw that in the report of your initial evaluation. How might have your dad's behavior mistakenly conveyed to you that heights were dangerous?

Bob: Oh, he wouldn't go on anything that was high. Like, he used to always have trouble working on the roof of our house.

Therapist: You remember, as a kid, seeing him that way?

Bob: Oh, yeah. It's kind of funny because I see a lot of him in me. Like when he used to go up and down the ladder to clear the leaves out of the gutters, he hugged it like it was a family member. I do the same thing.

Therapist: Do you ever remember him warning you about heights?

Bob: Oh, yeah. I remember that he never used to ride amusement park rides like ferris wheels or roller coasters. He wouldn't let us ride them either.

Therapist: He didn't let you ride them?

Bob: No, he always said that you could fall out, or they weren't safe, things like that. I remember once he said, "Human beings make those things, so they can always fall apart."

Therapist: It sounds as if your dad had a fear of falling, and in wanting to protect you guys from falling too, he inadvertently communicated through his actions and warnings that heights were dangerous.

Bob: Yeah, it's funny. I do that with Lucy and the kids.

Therapist: How's that?

Bob: Well, like when we're at the mall, on the second floor, it drives me crazy if the kids are over by the railing. So I'm always calling them back to me.

After discussion of other examples, the session continues.

Therapist: Well Bob, you seem to understand how you might have learned mistakenly that all high places are dangerous and should be avoided. Understanding that can help us see why high places that are actually safe also seem so dangerous to you. But you can probably also see that understanding that doesn't necessarily make the phobia go away.

Bob: No, it's still here. That's for sure.

Therapist: Do you think it's possible that these experiences have led you to believe that heights are more dangerous than they are?

Bob: Yeah. It makes sense to me that, instead of shocks, I had other ways to learn that heights are trouble.

Therapist: What does knowing that some of your fear of heights probably came from watching your dad struggle with those same situations make you feel like?

Bob: Well, kind of sad that my dad went through this same thing.

Therapist: Yeah, that's understandable. He may have learned it the same way.

Bob: I don't know.

Therapist: Do you think that because it's been in your family history that you're cursed to fear heights for the rest of your life?

Bob: Well, I hope not. It's not like it's genetic or something, is it?

Therapist: Well, actually, Bob, watching your dad and hearing warnings about height are two very common ways that we learn a lot of things, including fear. You've probably seen your own kids learn this way too—when they imitate you. [The evolutionary significance of height fear can be discussed as well.]

Bob: Oh, yeah. Sometimes you wish they wouldn't pick up on some things.

Therapist: Well, one very important thing to consider is that what is learned can be unlearned. Can you think of things that you've done earlier in life because others were doing them, but after learning more about them you don't do anymore? [Examples demonstrating the modifiability of learned behavior are discussed.]

Bob: Yeah, that's true. This thing has fear with it, though.

Therapist: Yeah, that can make it more challenging. Let's talk some about phobic fear.

KEY CONCEPTS AND CLINICAL CONSIDERATIONS FOR ACCOMPLISHING GOAL #3— UNDERSTANDING THE NATURE OF SPECIFIC PHOBIAS

While discussing the nature of the specific phobia, therapists highlight its situational specificity and any other features deemed helpful to patients such as epidemiology (e.g., who gets phobias, how common are they), how phobias differ from other mental disorders, or the evolutionary significance of phobias. For example, self-deprecating patients may be reassured to hear that their phobia is a set of specific reactions to a specific object or situation rather than a reflection of an immutable personality or character flaw. Learning about the widespread prevalence of phobias may help normalize the phobia from which an individual patient suffers. Patients may also benefit from learning that it is the disability caused by a phobia and not a personal defect that distinguishes the patient from the nonpatient.

Helping patients recognize the situational specificity of any or all aspects of their phobic reactions (i.e., cognitive, physiological, or behavioral) can be accomplished in many ways. One approach is to contrast patients' phobic behavior against the nonavoidant behavior they show in other areas of their life, some of which involve calculating risks (e.g., driving a car). Other times patients see the exaggerated nature of their own phobic actions through examples of phobias from which they do not suffer. It is sometimes easier first to recognize someone else's excesses before recognizing one's own.

Clinical Vignette

Bob: Do a lot of people fear heights?

Therapist: Yes. Actually, fear of heights is the most common fear in men above all other phobias.

Bob: Really. Do you see it a lot?

Therapist: Yes, but I also don't see a lot of people who will just avoid heights all their lives. It's usually when they need to tackle them that they come in.

Bob: Well, that's why I'm here; I need this job.

Therapist: Yes, Bob. Everybody has phobias. What makes them a problem most times is that they either bother people so much or interfere with their lives to such a degree that they recognize it's time to finally face and overcome them. This happens to millions of people. Does it make you feel better to know that your struggle is a common one for people?

Bob: Yeah, kind of. I wouldn't wish this on anyone. But you wonder if you're just nuts or something.

Therapist: Well, having fear is a natural part of being human.

Bob: Yeah, but having a fear like this. . . . I never thought of myself as being weak, but I guess I am.

Therapist: Bob, can you think of examples in your life where you've tackled something that you were initially nervous about, but you went ahead, tried it, and ended up accomplishing it?

Bob: [long pause] I guess I was nervous about working with high-voltage wires at first.

Therapist: I was wondering if you were going to mention that. I mean, you work every day in a situation where there's a high degree of risk and in a job that not everyone would attempt.

Bob: Actually, the risk isn't as high as you think, once you know what you're doing. Most times we work with wires while they're live.

Therapist: Well, Bob, there's an example that you're more than capable of approaching a potentially dangerous situation, getting to know it, and learning that its risks are manageable. What does that say about you being a "weak" person?

Bob: Yeah, I see what you mean. But with heights, it still makes you feel like a chicken.

Therapist: I can understand that. I mean, you're not doing this in other situations. It's understandable that you find it hard to accept in this one. In fact, that's what has brought you here to overcome it. I think that speaks to a strength, not a weakness.

Bob: I guess. Heights are a problem, though.

Therapist: Yes, heights specifically. It will help us focus our energies on making changes in that situation. As you do, I think you're going to find yourself drawing on the strengths you show in other areas of your life.

This excerpt is an example not only of the situational specificity of Bob's fear, but how his experience working with electricity demonstrates some of the principles of exposure. The latter can be revisited later in therapy, if needed.

KEY CONCEPTS AND CLINICAL CONSIDERATIONS FOR ACCOMPLISHING GOAL #4— UNDERSTANDING THE COGNITIVE FEATURES OF THE PHOBIC CYCLE

Phobic reactions are disproportionate to the threat actually posed by the phobic object or situation, but are quite understandable from the point of view of the patient. While helping patients understand the nature and role of fearful appraisals, therapists communicate several of the key concepts discussed previously. These include the idea that phobic thought overestimates threat, may catastrophize anticipated encounters, and often ignores or underestimates patients' ability to manage encounters. Those biases are reframed as fearful predictions.

Phobic beliefs are predictions in the sense that whether they occur well before an encounter or moment by moment during one, they are always anticipatory in nature. Patients learn that their fearful predictions can be accessed through their own self-talk, reflect reliable themes, and shape the way patients' anticipate phobic encounters, making those encounters seem more threatening and difficult to manage than they actually are.

The role of fearful predictions in triggering the flight or fight reactions and in motivating avoidance follows naturally from this discussion. Later in treatment, patients will be taught cognitive coping strategies to counter phobic trains of thought, as well as how to test fearful predictions through exposure. Learning their nature and how to access them now will facilitate that process later.

As discussed previously, the key concepts concerning cognitive biases can be detailed, complex, and confusing to patients. The therapeutic challenge is to communicate them in a simple and straightforward way that will facilitate prediction testing and the development of cognitive coping strategies. Therapists should use whatever methods they think will do this effectively.

The present example makes use of a classic analogy that likens fearful beliefs to an audiotape that plays inside patients' heads whenever they encounter the phobic object or situation and helps them take a more objective approach to working with their fears. It can be explained to patients, for example, that upon exposure to the phobic object or situation, their fearful tape begins running *automatically*, and as an *internal monologue*. It communicates *fearful predictions* that *overestimate danger, harm, or unmanageability* and *ignore or underestimate their ability to cope*. The analogy can be extended into later therapy when patients learn to develop a "second tape" on which less biased predictions about encounters, as well as cognitive coping statements that counter fearful thinking, are "recorded." In this sense, exposure serves, in part, as an arena to test Tape 1, the fearful tape, versus Tape 2, the less biased, experience-based alternative.

Clinical Vignette

Bob learns about the nature and role of his fearful beliefs.

Therapist: Bob, as part of preparing for exposure, we're going to practice some ways of managing the fearful feelings you have in high places—to help you to be able to overcome them. Part of that involves learning about what your mind is doing in those situations. We've already discussed that the fearful mind often sees the situation as more dangerous or harmful than it is and that this can make the alarm system ring. Do you recall that?

Bob: Yeah, when you see it as dangerous, then your body's going to react. But, you know, my mind seems to do that all by itself in those situations. It's not like I'm thinking about it. Sometimes I've gone into situations thinking "I'm going to do it this time" or "I'm not going to think about falling," but it just comes on anyway.

Therapist: Yes, that happens with phobias. The kind of thinking we're talking about isn't always like the kind of thinking we do, for example, about the weather or what we're going to eat. It can come on very quickly. Some people find it useful to think of it as a tape that plays fearful messages automatically. Does that make sense to you?

Bob: Yeah, it just starts playing.

Therapist: Well, if that makes sense, then let's talk about this as a tape that plays as soon as you get in a high situation. What I'd like to talk a little more about is what this tape is telling you and what effect that has on how you feel and what you do in high places. [introducing the idea of accessibility through self-talk] One way to get at what the tape is saying is to pay attention to your own internal self-talk that goes on pretty much all the time. For example, as I'm talking to you right now and you're listening, you may be aware that you're also talking to yourself, perhaps about what I'm saying or other things that you may be thinking. For example, you may be saying something like, "Okay, that makes sense" or "What is he talking about?" or "Boy, my back hurts."

Bob: I think I've thought all three of those things.

Therapist: [laughing] So you understand this idea of self-talk?

Bob: Yeah. It's like what you're really thinking inside your head. If you listen for it, you can hear it.

Therapist: Right. If you listen, you can often hear it. So, if you think about the tape that plays in your head whenever you're in a high place, what has it said to you?

Bob: I don't know. I just get locked on that I'm gonna fall, I guess.

Therapist: Okay, so the tape is telling you you're going to fall. What does that thought actually sound like in your head, in its uncensored, raw form?

Bob: Oh, probably something like, "Oh, God, I'm not going to make it," or "I gotta get down from here." I don't know. Probably something like that.

Therapist: Yes, that sounds very familiar. From what you've said before, it sounds as if the tape has said other things too, like about you jumping or the rails breaking.

Bob: I see. So it's almost like a tape of all my fears. "I'm gonna fall," or "The rail's gonna give way."

Therapist: Yes, that's a good way to think of it. You know, before you came in for your first appointment, you filled out this sheet [therapist pulls out Fearful Thoughts Questionnaire] that asks you to list some of the fearful thoughts you've had about heights [shows form to patient]. Are these some of the messages that have played on your tape?

Bob: Yes. I've thought that any of these things could happen at one time or another.

Therapist: [introducing the bias of the predictions by examining common themes] Bob, let's look at this list for a second and really examine the messages this tape is telling you. What are some things that these thoughts have in common?

Bob: Well, they're all bad things that could happen to me in this situation.

Therapist: Yes, some of them are downright catastrophic things, like your death. The other thing that you said about them is that they *could* happen. Do you see that in each case, these thoughts are anticipations or predictions of what *could* occur in high places?

Bob: Yeah, I guess they are, in a sense. Huh, I never thought about that.

Therapist: This is a very important thing about fearful thoughts. They're always anticipatory. We'll come back to that in a second. Let's go a little further with what the mind is doing in high places. When you encounter a high place, this tape starts running automatically. We've recognized that one of the messages that it conveys to you is that something bad, sometimes catastrophic, is going to happen to you.

Bob: Okay.

Therapist: Now besides that theme, there's another kind of hidden message it's giving you too—that you're not capable of dealing with this situation. Do you see how when the tape is running, the picture it paints of you is that you can't handle any of this? For example, in one you lose your balance and fall over the rail. In another one you faint and fall, and in one you get so anxious that you lose all control and jump off the high place.

Bob: I guess that's true. It sounds silly, but it feels that way when I'm caught up in it.

Therapist: Oh definitely, it seems anything but silly when you're there. It feels very convincing. But this is where the prediction part comes in. Does the fact that it's convincing mean that the tape is right about what it's predicting?

Bob: [pauses] Part of me says no, but another part thinks yes.

Therapist: Right. One side of you is this fearful tape that says you could lose your balance and fall or lose your mind and jump. Has that happened?

Bob: No, of course not.

Therapist: Of course. Then there's this other part of you that sees this, and says this is silly. That's the part of you that comes back when you're not in a high place. It's the part of you that we're going to strengthen, to bring back, and to start guiding you— instead of this fearful tape.

Bob: Why can't I see that in the high place?

Therapist: Well, let's talk about a few reasons. We know that this tape is capable of making our alarm systems come on. That alarm can make us feel as if our fears are very real, very possible, and ready to happen at any moment, even though they never have. Second, this alarm is so convincing that it makes us defensive, extremely cautious, and ready to run. When we get like that, we really never get a chance to relearn that we can manage and aren't in the danger we feel we're in. You can probably see that when that alarm isn't ringing like right now, it's a little easier to see that these fearful messages really aren't accurate about what happens in the situation.

Bob: That's true. It's easier when you're not caught up in it.

Therapist: Yes. Now let me ask you to consider this, Bob. When you're thinking about going into a high situation, this tape begins running. It tells you, "You could fall, you're going to lose your balance, you can't do this." It says that something bad is going to happen and you're not going to be able to do anything about it. At the same time, it gets your alarm system going. All of this is very convincing. Now let's imagine that you actually are entering the situation that you've been anticipating this way. Do you think, that with this tape running, it will be easier for you to stay and see that things are okay and manageable or will it make it more difficult?

Bob: More difficult, of course.

Therapist: Why do you think that is?

Bob: Well, you're just waiting for things to happen. You're ready to run.

Therapist: Exactly. So if something happens, for example, you feel that weakness in your legs or you feel unsteady, then it's easy to mistakenly believe that your fears are about to happen at any moment.

Bob: Yes, that's exactly what it feels like.

Therapist: So the alarm system can make the fearful thoughts more believable and lead you to think that you need to escape, or somehow get to safety.

Bob: That's right. It's just like that animal?

Therapist: Exactly.

As readers may see, the therapist can cover other aspects of the phobic cycle from a discussion of any of its single features. Although the chapter has separated components from explanatory purposes, this type of more integrated review is typical of what happens in the therapy session.

As discussed previously, misinformation fuels some fearful predictions. If possible, therapists correct that misinformation in session, and can supplement that intervention with other sources of information such as psychoeducational handouts, videotapes, or audiotapes.

In the end, there will be some patients who are unable to grasp the connection between their thoughts, physical feelings, and avoidant behaviors. Although preferred, it is not necessary for patients to acquire this skill. Clinical trials have shown that exposure without explicit cognitive techniques can be effective. Patients can learn to adapt to phobic situations without recognizing the processes involved. In our experience, most patients, given some guidance and practice, can understand the nature and role of the cognitive biases that maintain their phobia and benefit from that knowledge as they engage in the exposure exercises that will challenge and change them.

KEY CONCEPTS AND CLINICAL CONSIDERATIONS FOR ACCOMPLISHING GOAL #5— UNDERSTANDING THE PHYSICAL SENSATIONS WITHIN THE PHOBIC CYCLE

This therapeutic discussion aims at educating patients about their physical reactions to the phobic encounter. Information such as the nature and role of the flight or fight response and the distinction between false and true alarms is typically emphasized. Coping is introduced in the next session when patients learn concrete skills for managing these phobic sensations.

In addition to educating, therapists routinely address patients' misconceptions and misinterpretations of their physical sensations that serve to feed their fears. Common fears include the following:

1. The sensations could result in a catastrophic loss of control, incapacitation, or are generally unmanageable.
2. They are dangerous to my mental or physical health.
3. They are an indicator that a threat is actually present (emotional reasoning), or that one is weak and incapable.

In addressing the first fear, the extremely polarized nature of the belief should be revealed. Patients often fear that if they are not in *full* control, they are not in control at all. Often they are ignoring evidence that they are capable of functioning while anxious. Showing patients that they routinely carry out their decisions to escape or evade even though they are highly anxious can help demonstrate that, indeed, they are not incapacitated. For example, if the patient has experienced a previous encounter where he has been very anxious but unable to escape or avoid, then that incident may provide evidence that he can function despite considerable anxiety. But, again, convincing patients of these facts is not the goal of this intervention. Challenging these misconceptions leads to generating alternatives to these fearful predictions that exposure can test.

The second and third set of beliefs can be approached by demonstrating that the flight or fight reaction can be provoked by either an accurate appraisal of threat or its misappraisal, and therefore is not an indicator of either in and by itself. Although the alarm's presence is not dangerous by itself nor an indicator of danger, it does indicate that threat is being appraised, and suggests questioning the validity of that appraisal. This leads the therapist back to one of the purposes of exposure—testing the validity of phobic appraisals of threat. It also provides patients a rationale for coping skills training—to help patients manage the frightening sensations of their alarms in order to learn through exposure that, indeed, they are false.

Clinical Vignette

In this vignette, the therapist has discussed the flight or fight response and turns to addressing the notion that it is a false alarm of danger. In doing so, the therapist provides an example and simplified explanation of the connection between misappraising danger and the false alarm. Bob has also been a victim of emotional reasoning. He has believed that the danger he senses in high places must be real because it feels real. The therapist begins these interventions with a story showing Bob that his alarm is capable of being triggered falsely.

Bob: So what do you mean the alarm is false?

Therapist: Bob, it means that the alarm can come on mistakenly, when danger is not likely. It can be fooled to react as if danger were really present when it's not. Even though it's ringing and is very frightening and convincing, that doesn't mean that the danger we sense is really there and something that we need to avoid. Go with me for a second here, if you will. Let's imagine you're downtown at night. You've just finished eating dinner with friends at a restaurant. Now you're walking by yourself down an alley where you thought you had parked your car. As you proceed, you realize that your car is not in this alley. In fact, you realize that you're in the wrong alley, because this one is blocked off at the end and the one you parked in wasn't. So you turn around to go back, when suddenly you see three shadowy figures step into the entrance to the alley and begin walking toward you. At this moment, how is your body going to react to this situation?

Bob: Well, I'm going to get the alarm.

Therapist: Exactly. It gets you ready to flee or fight. For example, the heart and lungs speed up, sending oxygen carrying blood to large muscles where it's needed in case you decide to run—as we discussed. Why would the alarm be ringing at that moment?

Bob: Well, because I'm in danger.

Therapist: Okay. Could we say, instead of "I'm in danger," that you're anticipating or predicting danger?

Bob: Right, I'm thinking that my life could be in danger, but I'm not absolutely sure.

Therapist: Exactly. So the moment you sense that threat, your alarm system comes on to help you flee. Make sense?

Bob: Yes. But I can't flee because you said the alley was blocked off.

Therapist: Right, I did that on purpose. Does that make the situation seem more dangerous?

Bob: Oh, yeah. I see. If I can't escape, I get worse.

Therapist: So what do you think the alarm system is going to do then?

Bob: It's probably going to get stronger.

Therapist: Why do you think?

Bob: Because now I feel really trapped.

Therapist: Right, the danger seems even more likely now. The more likely it seems, the stronger the alarm. Am I making sense?

Bob: Yes, I get it.

Therapist: When you feel falling is very possible and you can't escape right away, do you sometimes feel strong fear?

Bob: Oh yes, I almost feel like I can't move. That's when I've felt like I could lose it, maybe even jump.

Therapist: Exactly, the alarm is on, ringing strongly. So do you see that sensing threat, like the three shadowy figures, the blocked alley, or even falling can make your alarm ring and surge?

Bob: Oh, yeah.

Therapist: When you feel this way, does it seem more real, more believable that things could get bad?

Bob: Yes, it's always very real.

Therapist: All right, now let's say that the three individuals step underneath a street lamp that's in the alley and you recognize them as the people with whom you ate dinner. They're coming down to tell you that they saw you walk down this wrong alley, and that your car is parked in another one. What's your body going to do at that moment?

Bob: Whew! Relief!

Therapist: The alarm system is going to . . . ?

Bob: Shut down.

Therapist: What changed at that moment, Bob, that shut down the alarm system?

Bob: I don't know. Maybe because I saw that they were my friends and not people who were going to harm me.

Therapist: Exactly. And when you suddenly realized that you were no longer in danger, the alarm shut down. The threat wasn't as likely as it seemed seconds ago.

Bob: Yeah, I thought they were going to hurt me, then I didn't. The danger went away.

Therapist: Right. If you think of this in terms of tapes running, when the tape says danger, the alarm rings; when the tape says no danger, the alarm shuts down. Does this connection seem believable to you, based on your experiences?

Bob: Definitely. I know when I'm caught up in it, it gets real intense.

Therapist: Does it make sense to you that the alarm is there to help you?

Bob: Yeah, it doesn't feel like that, but I can see that it's just trying to help me escape.

Therapist: And this is important—can you see that just because the alarm system is on, that it doesn't mean that the danger is actually there?

Bob: But the danger was there.

Therapist: Well, the anticipation of danger was there—the prediction. Go with me again. When you thought those three people were dangerous, the alarm system came on, but in reality were they dangerous?

Bob: No, but I didn't know that they were my friends at first. So I thought it was dangerous. I mean I should have. Wouldn't you?

Therapist: Yes, I would have too. It's perfectly understandable to believe they were dangerous, because you didn't have all the information, so to speak. But does that mean that the danger was really there?

Bob: No, I see what you mean.

Therapist: This is why the feelings we have in phobic situations are called false alarms, because they're triggered by a mistaken belief that danger is likely.

Bob: All right. But how can you know that ahead of time?

Therapist: You can't always, can you? And if you heard that heights were dangerous as you were growing up, your inclination would be to perceive them as dangerous. In fact, it would be natural and automatic to do that, don't you think?

Bob: Yeah, that makes sense.

Therapist: So when your alarm goes off in a high place, you feel fear, but don't know differently . . .

Bob: Then I believe that I could fall.

Therapist: But just because the alarm comes on, does that mean that falling is actually likely?

Bob: No, but it sure seems that way when I'm up there.

Therapist: I know. And it will for a while. Understanding this is usually helpful, but doesn't usually change it next time you're there.

Bob: You got to go there and prove it, don't you—like the animal had to do?

Therapist: That's what works best—repeated exposure.

Bob: Yeah, it makes sense. It's like facing the fears to disprove them. If you just go with the alarm you'll run, and never get over it. But I don't always leave the situation and I still have the fear.

Therapist: Well, for exposure to be effective we have to do it in certain ways. We'll talk more about them next session. One thing we'll have to do is to see if you have been coping with these situations by avoiding in subtle ways. I mean, we can "escape" in lots of subtle ways, even while we're in the situation. When we do that, it works the same as if we actually had escaped. And exposures are less effective.

Patients typically voice an understanding of the flight or fight process, but may still have concerns about specific physical sensations and their potential for harming or incapacitating them. Therapists address that misinformation and, if necessary, supplement that intervention, again, with appropriate educational material, although it usually takes repeated exposure to finally quiet those concerns.

KEY CONCEPTS AND CLINICAL CONSIDERATIONS FOR ACCOMPLISHING GOAL #6— UNDERSTANDING SAFETY-SEEKING IN THE PHOBIC CYCLE

To this point in therapy, patients' experiences with their phobias have taught them that it is a frightening feeling relieved through escape. This discussion introduces patients to the various forms of avoidance and their role in maintaining fears.

Examples drawn from the initial assessment, self-therapy exercise, or Methods of Coping Questionnaire can introduce patients to the range of subtle and obvious avoidance strategies they have used to cope. Contrasting patients' behavior during phobic encounters to how they would act if guaranteed that no harm would come to them can reveal avoidance. Likewise, as suggested previously, contrasting patients' phobic behavior to their own nonavoidant behavior in other risky situations may help as well. As always, specific strategies are at the therapist's discretion. Whatever the strategy used, patients should learn that their avoidance is motivated by fears that overestimate threat and vulnerability. From there, the role of avoidance in maintaining those fears follows naturally.

Clinical Vignette

Through the following example, Bob learns that he often copes by using subtle avoidance, precluding him from overcoming fearful beliefs.

Bob: Yeah, I've thought that I could faint or lose my balance. And even though it hasn't happened, I'm still concerned it could.

Therapist: What have you done to cope with the feeling that you're going to lose your balance?

Bob: I've had to sit down sometimes, because I got weak.

Therapist: Let me see if I understand that, then. Please correct me if I'm wrong. You're in a high place, and feeling fear—your alarm is going off. As part of that alarm, you feel a sense of weakness. Feeling that sensation leads you to believe what?

Bob: That I could lose my legs and fall. It feels like they're going out on me.

Therapist: Okay, so because you believe that your legs are going out and you're about to fall, you sit down—to prevent you from falling?

Bob: Yeah.

Therapist: So, Bob, by sitting down, you feel you're protecting yourself from losing your balance?

Bob: Right.

Therapist: But by sitting down you also don't really know if you would have actually lost your balance.

Bob: True. I guess I can't be totally sure. But it feels like I will, so I'll sit if I can. Better safe than sorry.

Therapist: I understand. If I thought I was falling, I'd try to do the same thing. And if you really are going to fall, then sitting helps prevent that. But let's say, just for example, that you will not fall. It only feels that way. But because you feel strongly that you're about to, you sit. Can you see that by sitting, you'll never find out that although your legs feel weak, they can support you? And although you feel as if you'll fall, you won't.

Bob: So sitting is like that animal leaving the room? When I sit, it's like running?

Therapist: If weakness and falling are a fear but are actually not likely, then yes, sitting prevents you from learning that you really won't fall. It's a subtle form of avoiding what you fear, namely that your legs will collapse and you'll fall. Have you ever not been able to sit when you've felt weak?

Bob: Yeah.

Therapist: What's happened?

Bob: Nothing, I guess. I mean I haven't fallen or anything. I just hang in there. I see what you mean. But how come I still fear it?

Therapist: Bob, I'm not sure you've actually challenged your fear of falling, really proven it to yourself that you can manage without sitting or avoiding in other subtle ways. Like everyone who starts treatment, your approach thus far has been to try to prevent falling—"steer clear of it," as you've said—rather than test it, gradually challenge it, and overcome it. And that's perfectly natural because up until now you haven't really had to overcome it. So it's gone unchallenged, untested.

Bob: I think you're right. That's been the way I deal with it.

Therapist: Does it make sense to you that sitting can be a subtle way of avoiding, and doesn't let you see that you actually can keep your balance?

Bob: Yeah, I'd never thought about it that way, but it does. It's like I'm always on the lookout and protecting myself.

SELF-THERAPY EXERCISE

Between sessions, patients are asked to update their Methods of Coping and Fearful Thoughts Questionnaires, identifying subtle and obvious avoidance and specific fearful predictions revealed during this session. Supplemental readings are assigned if necessary. After questions are answered, the next appointment is scheduled.

4

Treatment Session 3— Understanding Exposure

SESSION OUTLINE

This session begins with a review of the patient's self-therapy exercise and key concepts from last session. Next, the major guidelines for exposure are introduced, followed by a discussion of the role of the therapeutic coach, if one is assisting. During the remainder of the session, patients prepare for exposure. This involves learning how to do prediction testing, set goals for an exposure, and use somatic and cognitive coping strategies. As usual, the session concludes with the assignment of a self-therapy exercise.

SESSION GOALS

1. To review patients' self-therapy exercises, their understanding of the phobic cycle in maintaining their phobias, and the role of exposure in breaking that cycle.
2. To introduce general guidelines for exposure.
3. To develop the role of the therapeutic coach (if applicable).
4. To prepare patients for exposure, including training specific coping skills.

KEY CONCEPTS AND CLINICAL CONSIDERATIONS FOR ACCOMPLISHING GOAL #1—REVIEWING KEY CONCEPTS

During the last few sessions, patients have heard about the factors that maintain their phobias. During this session, those are reviewed to check for understanding, if deemed necessary. At the minimum, patients should know that avoidance perpetuates fears. Ideally, they will understand how the phobic cycle of fearful predictions, false alarms, and the various forms of safety-seeking operate to maintain a phobia.

Reviewing last session's self-therapy exercise, which asked patients to update their original Fearful Thoughts and Coping Methods Questionnaires based on what they had learned to date, can help therapists assess the extent to which patients are grasping key concepts. Patients typically show the ability to identify primary predictions (e.g., falling, suffocating) and obvious safety-seeking actions (e.g., escape and avoidance), but struggle to recognize subtler fears and avoidant tendencies (e.g., secondary appraisals, reliance on others, distraction). To assess patients' understanding of these areas, it may help to select items from the fear and avoidance hierarchy and see if patients can identify the types of fearful thoughts, physical sensations, and avoidant coping tendencies they have been prone to have and are likely to have during future encounters. Educational interventions can then be made accordingly.

Role reversal is another useful therapeutic technique for assessing and increasing a patient's understanding of key concepts. In role reversal, the patient takes the role of the therapist or advisor answering questions posed by the actual therapist, who acts as a hypothetical patient or advisee. When using role reversal for assessment purposes, it is preferable to start with general, open-ended questions, such as "How did I get my phobia?" and "Why doesn't it go away?" and then move to more specific ones, such as "How is it possible that I'm avoiding while I'm in the situation?" and "Is symptom X dangerous to me?"

Clinical Vignette

Role reversal demonstrates that Bob has a good grasp of the factors that maintain his phobia.

Therapist: Bob, we've talked about a lot of information over the past few sessions regarding how your phobia probably developed and some of the reasons why it persists. If you don't mind, I'd like to review some of those ideas before we move on to some new things. Maybe we can do this in a way that might make it a little more interesting [describes the role reversal exercise].

Bob: Okay, this sounds all right, but you may be in trouble. I don't know if I can answer all your questions.

Therapist: Well, some you may and some you may not. Let's just see where it goes. Why do I have a fear of high places?

Bob: Well, you've learned that high places are dangerous when you were younger.

Therapist: Okay, then if they are really dangerous, shouldn't I fear them?

Bob: Oh, this is going to be tough. Okay . . . what I mean is that you've learned that heights are more dangerous than they actually are.

Therapist: How have I learned that?

Bob: Lots of ways. For one, you watched your dad. When you're a young kid and you see that, it's like that's what you learn about them.

Therapist: But my dad never fell from a high place. Neither have I.

Bob: Well, you don't need to fall to learn that. You know, you can just get the message by watching someone act scared.

Therapist: But heights are dangerous. Don't a lot of people fall from high places?

Bob: That's true. People do fall, but it doesn't happen very often.

Therapist: Okay, but all that stuff was in the past and I can understand it. How come I still have a phobia now?

Bob: I'm not really sure how to answer that one.

Therapist: Bob, what do I do now in those situations that might keep that fear alive?

Bob: Okay, you avoid them.

Therapist: Why?

Bob: Because you're expecting the bad things that can happen to you. That makes them seem dangerous. So you avoid.

Therapist: I don't feel as if I'm expecting anything. I feel as if it just happens to me.

Bob: Well, it feels like that, but you can hear your fear if you listen for it.

Therapist: Then why do I feel all the physical stuff if nothing is really wrong?

Bob: Well, that's just your body telling you that something's wrong. I mean, that you're expecting something bad. So it prepares you to escape.

Therapist: Well, if my body's telling me that something's wrong, shouldn't I flee?

Bob: No, that's not what I mean. This is hard. I don't know how to explain it. It's a false alarm.

Therapist: Why is it a false alarm and not a true alarm?

Bob: I'm not sure how to put it in words.

Therapist: Use your own words, Bob.

Bob: Okay. Think of it like a switched circuit. When you're expecting the bad things that could happen, that switches the alarm system. It comes on. But the bad stuff isn't, um . . . what is probably going to happen. So the alarm is sounding when there's actually no fire. So it's a false alarm.

Therapist: Yeah, but it feels likely to me. So when the alarm comes on, it feels bad, as if things are going to get bad.

Bob: Yeah, but just because you feel that way doesn't mean that the bad stuff is really going to happen. That's what the false alarm means.

After discussing the role of avoidance in maintaining the phobia, Bob's therapist helps him see how he will put this knowledge to use through exposure.

Therapist: Bob, that's really good, you seem to be developing a fine understanding of the phobia.

Bob: Yeah, but it's easier to give this advice than to take it.

Therapist: Well, let's go back into the roles for a second and find out how we might deal with that. . . . Well, I can understand these ideas, but I don't really believe them deep down. What do I need to do to start believing this, so I can practice what I preach?

Bob: Well, you gotta go see for yourself. Like the animal going back into the shock room. It'll take some time, but you'll see. Then you'll believe it.

Therapist: So I have to practice what I preach to learn to believe it?

Bob: Yeah, I guess that's right. You've got to do it, then it will sink in. How's that?

Therapist: Great. What do you think?

Bob: Not bad. It actually feels good just saying it. But doing it? I hope that's as easy.

The therapist and patient continue this process until the desired key concepts are covered.

KEY CONCEPTS AND CLINICAL CONSIDERATIONS FOR ACCOMPLISHING GOAL #2—INTRODUCING THE GUIDELINES FOR EXPOSURE

Patients may assert that they have been doing exposure of sorts with no effect on their fears. Usually, though, when they describe specifically what they have done, it fails to meet the guidelines for effective exposure. To address that issue or prevent it from arising later in therapy, patients and therapists need to be in agreement regarding how to do exposure.

In this section, guidelines and other considerations for exposure are reviewed. This review is directed to therapists as an overview of major issues. From it, guidelines can be drawn and presented to the patient, for example, as an exposure instruction sheet (see Table 4–1 for one such example). Guidelines can also be built into the form on which patients record their exposure experiences (see the Exposure Record Form, Appendix 8).

Planning for Initial Exposures

Patients' reactions to phobic objects and situations are usually well entrenched, automatic, and seemingly beyond their control. Even the most highly motivated patients can become discouraged when their old thoughts and feelings come flooding back during an exposure session. Patients entering initial exposures with a prepared plan and specific goals to guide their actions stand a better chance of not being overpowered by their old fearful habits than do unprepared patients. Specific procedures for planning an exposure are presented later in this chapter in Accomplishing Goal #4—Developing a Plan for Coping.

The Duration of an Exposure

Generally speaking, exposures where patients stay in the presence of feared objects and situations for long periods of time have proven more therapeutic than brief exposures (see Marks 1975, 1978 for reviews). Brief exposures lend themselves to evasive coping or escape. They may not allow patients to habituate to the initial anxiety pro-

Table 4-1: Exposure Instructions

General Guidelines
1. Give yourself plenty of time.
2. Repeat the same exposure until it becomes very familiar.
3. Do exposure as frequently as possible, given your schedule and time needed for breaks.
4. Challenge yourself by tackling progressively more difficult exposures.
Prior to Exposures
1. Identify fearful predictions, then an alternative one that predicts the most likely challenges and how you intend to cope.
2. Lay out a plan for conducting the exposure. Break it down into small, manageable steps if necessary.
During Exposure
1. Focus on accomplishing your plan.
2. Go at your own pace.
3. Focus on the present, staying off of "what if's."
4. Use any feelings of anxiety as a signal to cope, not to run or fight the feelings.
5. Face and challenge fears, showing yourself that you can succeed.
6. Although you have the option of using subtle avoidance or escape, try not using them first. Try your coping strategies; give them some time to work.
7. Leave the exposure when you feel you have accomplished your plan.
After Exposure
Review the exposure as soon after it as possible using the Exposure Record Form.

voked by the phobic object or situation. Prolonged exposures give patients the opportunity to identify and abandon avoidant ways of coping, develop more adaptive coping strategies, gather experiential evidence that disconfirms their fears, and develop a sense of mastery in managing the encounter.

When to Leave an Exposure

The time-honored rule of exposure is to stay in the presence of the phobic object or situation until anxiety wanes. Leaving before that time is synonymous with escape, which can reinforce patients' fears and doubts. So should therapists ban escape? Empirical evidence suggests the answer is no. University of British Columbia psychologist Stanley Rachman and colleagues have reported that patients given the option to escape during exposure benefited as much as those instructed not to escape (deSilva and Rachman 1984, Rachman et al. 1986). These researchers suggested that patients allowed to escape may have been more willing to take the chance of challenging their fears. Interestingly, most patients given the safety net of escape did not opt to use it. Knowing it was there was sufficient comfort.

In general, patients should set the goal of staying within the exposure for a long duration, often a few hours or more, depending on the nature of the task. They should not, however, be forced to stay in feared situations. Escape remains a choice, but moves further down the list of options. For example, it may help to encourage patients to attempt to delay escape for manageable periods of time to see what happens. Often, if they delay escape for 15 minutes or so, their apprehension and desire to escape will wane. However, patients who do opt to escape should be helped to learn from the encounter by identifying the fears that motivated the escape, developing a plan for overcoming them, and trying the exposure again.

How to Schedule Exposures

An early study of exposure schedules found that it was advantageous to do them in *massed* versus *spaced* fashion (Foa et al. 1980). Massed practice refers to doing exposures frequently, grouping them together as opposed to spreading them out over time. Some authors have noted, however, that massed practice can be impractical or too stressful for some patients (Barlow 1988, Jansson and Ost 1982). A more recent empirical investigation showed no significant advantage for a massed regimen in dropout or improvement rates; although, many of those who did drop out of the massed condition cited stress and scheduling problems (Chambless 1990). Thus, although it seems advantageous to schedule exposures as frequently as possible, it is not necessary and may be impractical or too stressful. Scheduling should encourage frequent and repeated practice, but with sensitivity to patients' schedules and their readiness to face fear frequently.

Optimizing Exposure

Experts have differed regarding how anxious a patient should become
during exposure to obtain its optimal benefit. For example, in systematic desensitization, patients' distress is minimized by using relaxation or another competing response whenever anxiety emerges. At
the other end of the continuum lies flooding, during which intense
anxiety is an expected part of the process. To date, no particular level
of anxiety has been shown to produce a consistently superior outcome. Nor does it seem necessary to generate extremely high levels of
anxiety during exposure to achieve an optimal result (Foa and Kozak
1985, Rachman 1985).

Of course, recommendations about optimizing exposure cannot be
separated from how its mechanisms of action have been conceptualized. For example, when exposure has been viewed as an arena for
counterconditioning, as in systematic desensitization, then minimizing
anxiety in the presence of the phobic cue has been deemed important.
When habituation has been emphasized, then prolonged exposure to
fear cues, as in flooding, has been favored. When exposure has been
viewed as an arena to acquire new ways of managing the phobic
encounter and build a sense personal efficacy in doing so (as in participant modeling), then arranging exposures to maximize successful and
unassisted completion of the task has taken precedence over provoking or preventing anxiety per se. Until any one method produces a consistently superior outcome or any one mechanism is confirmed,
measures taken to optimize exposures will vary between therapists.

It is becoming increasingly accepted that it may be a bit artificial to
focus exclusively on a patient's anxiety, as a general construct, in
judging whether an exposure will be optimal. Prominent theorists
(e.g., Barlow 1988, Foa and Kozak 1985, 1986, Lang 1968, 1977,
Rachman 1985) have suggested that fear and anxiety are multidimen-
sional constructs involving thoughts, feelings, and urges to escape,
which may be involved in the phobic reaction at different levels
depending on several factors related to the patient and the phobic
object or situation.

Recent research is also supporting the advantages of a more comprehensive approach to exposure. For example, recent work with an exposure technique called *guided mastery* (see Williams and Zane 1997 for a
brief review) suggests that the effectiveness of exposures is enhanced
when patients are helped to go beyond merely entering and staying in
feared situations. In guided mastery, therapists guide patients to iden-

tify and gradually remove subtle avoidant actions while developing alternative, nonavoidant behaviors designed to increase patients' sense of mastery. Modeling, feedback, and gradated tasks are combined to decrease fear and enhance confidence. A recent study of agoraphobic avoidance reported that patients who underwent this type of exposure showed greater reductions in subjective phobic anxiety during treatment than those who underwent exposure aimed exclusively at keeping them in the presence of the phobic cues (Williams and Zane 1989). Guided mastery patients also continued to show improvement after treatment, while the comparison group maintained but did not improve upon gains made during therapy. It remains unclear whether patients can learn to do this without therapist assistance or whether some initial guidance is sufficient (Zane and Williams 1993).

How does the practicing clinician approach the task of trying to optimize exposure? One practical suggestion is to first ask themselves whether the exposure task is likely to provide a valid test of the patient's fears. In some cases, this may not require patients to experience high levels of arousal (e.g., "I'm afraid railings will break and I will fall"). In others, generating high anxiety may be a specific goal of the exposure (e.g., "If my anxiety gets too high, I will go crazy").

In addition to their primary fears, most patients fear that they will not be able to cope with the demands of the situation. This speaks to structuring initial exposures to increase patients' chances of coping successfully by including, for example, procedures such as planning, coping skills training, and therapist modeling. In addition, optimizing exposure involves eliminating factors (safety signal, other avoidance) to which patients may mistakenly attribute their success at the expense of building personal efficacy.

In practice, getting the most from exposures is a developmental process that becomes more refined as patients and their therapists discover successful means to challenge and conquer fears and overcome obstacles to those goals.

KEY CONCEPTS AND CLINICAL CONSIDERATIONS FOR ACCOMPLISHING GOAL #3—THE ROLE OF THE THERAPEUTIC COACH

Empirical evidence supporting the benefit of including a therapeutic coach in exposure has come primarily from studies of patients using spouse-assisted exposure to overcome agoraphobic avoidance. Although not necessary for successful treatment (Cobb et al. 1984), coach-assisted exposure has produced significant and sustained improvement in independent studies at 2 years (Cerny et al. 1987) and 4 to 9 years (Munby and Johnston 1980) after treatment.

The question of why coach assistance helps remains uncertain, but several hypotheses have been advanced. Patients often report that a coach's support helps them meet the challenges of exposure. Coaches can also help patients prepare for exposures, as well as model non-avoidant behavior and adaptive coping strategies. Practically speaking, a coach's presence may enhance a patient's compliance. In a broader sense, therapeutic change in patients can disrupt their social systems in ways that may discourage sustained improvement. To the degree that the coach is part of that system, change may be more easily accommodated.

Of course, few things can disrupt therapeutic progress like a bad coach. Less than helpful coaching styles are probably well known to readers. For example, the unempathic "just snap out of it," or the omniscient "here's what you need to do" approaches usually fail. "Sergeant Coach" is rarely effective. A patient being told to "do it, do it, do it" is very likely not to do it.

So, what qualities are desirable in a therapeutic coach? A few considerations are practical. For example, coaches should not fear the same object or situation as the patient. They should be available for treatment and exposure sessions too. Beyond that, a good coach is someone who is willing to be supportive, demonstrate difficult tasks, reassure, and encourage. Specific coaching techniques are discussed in Chapter 6.

KEY CONCEPTS AND CLINICAL CONSIDERATIONS FOR ACCOMPLISHING GOAL #4—PREPARING FOR EXPOSURE

Exposure therapy asks patients to stay in the presence of phobic objects and situations—a request that goes against all they feel in that circumstance. Most patients begin this endeavor with little confidence. The possibility that patients' well-established phobic reactions will unseat what little hope they have is not remote. Clearly, exposures are challenging, a challenge for which patients want to be prepared.

Part of the preparation involves being equipped with coping strategies for managing fearful reactions, identifying fearful and nonfearful predictions to test during exposure, and setting specific goals for how to proceed.

Somatic Control Strategies

To help patients manage the physiological aspects of fear, they learn an exercise that combines paced diaphragmatic breathing with muscular relaxation. The exercise is described in Appendix 10, which can be used as a patient handout. During the session, the therapist demonstrates the exercise and uses corrective feedback to ensure that the patient can do it correctly. The patient is then asked to practice the exercise at least once a day, preferably more, between sessions. During the next session, the exercise will be simplified into a coping strategy for use on demand during exposures. The last section of the exercise handout describes the on-demand coping technique.

Patients who have a history of fainting upon exposure to a phobic cue (e.g., blood, injection, and injury phobias) learn an applied tension technique (see Ost and Sterner 1987 for a description of applied tension as a therapeutic program). This technique is used at the first signs of fainting following the initiation of exposure. At that point, the muscles of their neck, torso, and lower body are contracted until warmth suffuses the face. Patients can do this in a way that allows unrestricted diaphragmatic breathing, but may need to experiment with the procedure to accomplish that. As indicated previously, fainting results from stimulation of the vagal nerve, which causes a sudden drop in blood pressure. Applied tension mitigates fainting by curtailing the flow of blood away from the brain. Used correctly, it has been shown to decrease the prevalence of fainting during exposure (Ost et al. 1984). The applied tension exercise is described in Appendix 11, which also can be used as a patient handout. As with the other somatic control strategies, patients learn to do applied tension early in therapy, practice it as a daily exercise between sessions, then practice it as an on-demand coping strategy in preparation for exposure.

There is always a chance that patients using applied tension will faint anyway. Although fainting is often not the most likely outcome of the exposure, patients may fear the consequences of doing so. Therefore, patients should be reassured that fainting is not dangerous, usually brief, and that precautions will be taken to help them regain consciousness quickly if it should occur. If fainting is a risk, it is most likely to occur during initial or otherwise challenging exposures. Those types of exposures in particular should be done in the presence of a therapist or coach trained to help patients regain consciousness. Initial exposures should be conducted in a safe area, such as on a couch or in a reclining chair. If fainting occurs, recovery involves reclining the patient so that their head is lower than the rest of their body, facilitating blood flow back into the brain. While unconscious, patients are turned on their side to prevent choking in the rare case that they vomit. Applied tension should be gradually weaned as exposures are repeated and patients' fears wane.

A common problem presents when patients attempt to use their new coping strategies to *stop* anxiety. Having experienced strong fear during past encounters, their desire to try to eliminate it is entirely understandable. Unfortunately, it is unrealistic to remove fear during phobic encounters, and usually patients are even more alarmed when they discover this. Misusing coping strategies in this way usually represents another form of subtle avoidance—avoidance of the fear that the sensations could bring upon catastrophic consequences.

As with removing other forms of avoidance, abandoning this one may need to be done gradually. First, patients should understand this desire, that it is ultimately counterproductive, and that their goal is to use the strategies to help them accomplish their behavioral goals of exposure, not simply fight to prevent fearful feelings. The therapeutic plan may need to allow patients initially to overfocus on managing sensations initially until their confidence builds. Then patients can be gently urged to try tolerating sensations and gradually shift their focus from managing sensations to managing the exposure task. In short, coping strategies are a tool to help patients ride out the false alarm, not eliminate it. In doing so, patients learn that its sensations are not dangerous, not an indicator of danger, and will not prevent them from learning to master encounters.

Coping Self-Talk

Patients' fearful reactions to phobic objects, situations, or to their own sensations are influenced by their appraisal of those cues. Coping self-statements are an effective means to countering phobic thoughts with more adaptive, less fear-engendering alternatives that encourage perseverance (Denny et al. 1977, Meichenbaum 1971, 1977).

The specifics of coping self-statements will differ from patient to patient. Generally, they should reflect themes of safety and personal efficacy, themes counter to those of fearful self-talk. Examples include, "Okay, relax," "I'm not in danger," "Give it time, it will pass," or "I can do this."

However, self-statements do not have to counter directly the themes of fearful thoughts to be useful. For example, they can be motivational in nature (e.g., "Just do it," "It's now or never," or "I have to do this"). Some patients prefer these, feeling that they provide a supportive push to challenge fears. For others, however, those types of thoughts may be inappropriately demanding. Patients should choose favored coping self-statements, test them during exposure, and modify them as desired. A spirit of experimentation, flexibility, and adaptability is encouraged.

It is necessary at times for patients to stop an anxious train of thought before initiating their new ways of coping. Thought stopping, a technique used successfully in managing obsessive ruminations, can be used for these purposes. Thought stopping is like snapping a rubber band on one's wrist, but much less painful. It involves having patients silently and to themselves yell, "Stop" or "Wait," like someone trying (rudely) to silence a noisy crowd. Its disruptive effect is brief, though, so it should be followed immediately by use of the other coping strategies described. Patients may find it useful to record their coping strategies on a note card or audiotape. That recording may also be helpful to the therapeutic coach.

Identifying Predictions

The pertinent section of the Exposure Record Form (Appendix 8) takes patients through the process of identifying fearful and alternative predictions. If possible, therapists should use that form to teach patients this task and then encourage its routine use.

By now, patients are familiar with the kinds of fearful predictions they are likely to make in anticipation of a phobic encounter. Before an encounter, those are listed on the form in specific but brief phrases that communicate the theme of the prediction (e.g., "I will suffocate,"

"I will run screaming"). Although predictions that are common to all exposures can be placed permanently on the form, if desired, it is therapeutic to have patients also learn the skill of identifying (and eventually managing) fearful predictions at the moment they are occurring. That skill will help patients handle new or unexpected fears that may arise during future exposures.

One method for generating fearful predictions asks patients to run through the exposure imaginally and chronologically. While doing this, patients allow their fears to surface unchallenged and identify how they imagine the exposure going awry. Those fears are then listed on the form as specific predictions. Another, possibly easier, method is to ask patients to record whatever fears pop into their minds when asked to think about conducting the exposure, in a sort of free association of fears. After identifying each fearful prediction, patients rate its believability. This allows therapists and patients to track changes in the strength of fears across exposures.

Clinical Vignette

Bob and his therapist imagine an exposure involving looking over a railing and identify fearful predictions.

Bob: [describing aloud the imagined scenario] And then I'd step up to the railing on the balcony and that's when I'd start to get that bad feeling.

Therapist: What bad feeling?

Bob: That weak feeling, like I'm gonna fall or get pulled over.

Therapist: Can you see yourself falling?

Bob: Yeah, that's what scares me.

Therapist: Describe how you see yourself falling, Bob.

Bob: Well, I'd get weak and lose my balance. My knees would buckle. I'd fall towards the rail and flip right over it, or fall through it. It might break. But it doesn't sound very believable when I say it like that.

Therapist: Well, that's the part of you that's always been able to keep perspective and question these fears. What we're interested in now is simply generating these fears and letting them run unchallenged. So for the purpose of identifying fearful predictions, let's not challenge these yet. Just let the fearful tape run and record what fears come to mind.

Bob: Okay.

Therapist: So the prediction "I'll fall through the rail," how believable did it feel at the moment you pictured it?

Bob: Moderate.

Therapist: So zero to ten, what would you give it?

Bob: A 5.

Therapist: So let's put that prediction on the form and give it a 5 rating under believability.

Bob: Okay [Bob records the prediction].

Bob and his therapist then repeat the procedure, recording and rating each fear that comes to mind.

Patients are also asked to note on the form some reminder that their primary fears assume that they will be unable to cope with the challenges of the exposure (secondary predictions). Like some primary predictions, secondary predictions can, and often do, become a permanent feature of the form.

Therapist: Bob, at that moment, how do you see yourself trying to cope with the feeling of weakness and imbalance?

Bob: Well, I don't see really coping at all.

Therapist: Exactly. Remember that that's always a part of your fearful prediction—that you won't be able to manage these difficult moments. So let's put that down as a prediction, too.

Bob: That's true, isn't it? I kind of saw myself trying to grab the rail. But I either flipped over it or it broke and I fell.

After identifying fearful predictions, patients generate an alternative scenario. To do so, they are asked to imagine doing the exposure again, but this time identifying likely challenges and how they plan to manage them. Alternative predictions should counter the overestimations of threat and implicit underestimations of patients' capabilities to manage encounters that characterize their fearful predictions.

In developing alternative predictions, patients are encouraged to take an objective stance. Preferably, patients base these predictions on their prior experience in similar situations and on what they are learning about their phobia (i.e., what is the most likely event to occur and how they are most likely to cope with it). Some patients see this process as an appeal to their logic. If so, it may help to ask,

"What does your logical mind predict is likely to occur here even though your fear may doubt it?"). Having patients assume the role of advisor or therapist, as in the role reversal exercise, may also help them generate alternative outcomes (e.g., "What would you tell another person faced with this situation are the most likely things they will face?" and "How would you advise them to cope with those?"). Alternative scenarios should be realistic and specific, not unrealistically optimistic and general (e.g., "Everything will be fine"). They should include depictions of patients facing anxiety, possibly moments of high anxiety and doubt, and times during which they will not cope perfectly, if those are the most likely outcomes. If the outcome is uncertain, it may help to err on the side of anticipating difficulty and plan coping strategies for managing it. An experience that disconfirms expected difficulty will be more therapeutic than one that disconfirms the unrealistic expectation that "everything will be fine."

To generate alternatives, Bob's therapist asks him to identify what is likely to happen and how he intends to cope with it. Special attention is paid to the challenges Bob identified in the fearful scenario.

Therapist: Now, in this prediction, Bob, as you approach the balcony, the first thing you said is that you're going to feel weak. Considering your past experience and knowing that fearful predictions often overestimate the actual likelihood of a feared event, your first question is, "Is that actually the most likely thing to happen to you when you get to that point?"

Bob: Yes, I think it's likely.

Therapist: Okay, ask yourself, "In similar situations in the past, what percentage of the time do you think you have experienced this feeling?"

Bob: I don't know, a lot, maybe 80 to 90 percent.

Therapist: All right, so the actual probability is high that you'll feel this feeling because in the past it has happened often.

Bob: Yes.

Therapist: Good. So in our alternative prediction, then, let's expect that you're going to feel that feeling. Now, in the fearful scenario, Bob, that feeling causes you to collapse and fall. How often has that happened in the past?

Bob: Never.

Therapist: It's never happened. So the probability is what?

Bob: Zero?

Therapist: Exactly. So if falling isn't likely, what is?

Bob: I'll probably hang on to something or sit down.

Therapist: Right, that will be your inclination. But as we've said, even though you have the option of using those avoidant ways of coping, what might you try as your first choice?

Bob: Oh, right, I see. So I'll try to stand.

Therapist: Okay. Let's go further. In generating alternative predictions, Bob, let's do this: when you get to those points where you're likely to face a challenge, let's review how you intend to try to cope and how that will most likely turn out. So how do you see yourself trying to cope with that feeling, so that you can stay in that situation and carry on with what you're doing?

Bob: Well, I guess I would just try to talk myself through it.

Therapist: And how specifically would you like to try to do that?

Bob: Well, remind myself that just because I'm feeling this doesn't mean I'm in trouble.

Therapist: Good. Can you think of one or two brief coping statements, as we discussed, that you would like to be able to say to yourself to help you cope?

Bob: Yeah, I was thinking that I'll probably say something like, "You're okay, just let it pass."

Therapist: Would it help you to put that on your coping card?

Bob: Yeah, that might be a good idea.

Therapist: Do you want to plan to use any of your other coping strategies?

Bob: Yeah, I'll do the breathing and try to relax.

Therapist: So in your alternative prediction, when you approach the balcony, you're most likely to feel that weak feeling, but you're going to use your coping strategies to help you try to remain standing.

Bob: Yeah, that's a good plan.

Therapist: Yes, it is. Now, let's put that down and rate its believability. Can you see that by laying out these two scenarios, one based on Tape 1 and one on Tape 2, the exposure is going to show which is more accurate?

Bob: Yeah, one or the other is going to happen.

Therapist: Okay, let's go through the remainder of the exposure and do this. We'll practice this some more next session, too. With practice, this will become more natural.

Bob and his therapist proceed through the imagined scenario anticipating likely challenges and developing a plan for coping with them.

As depicted in the last vignette, patients learn to anticipate which avoidant coping strategies they are likely to use and replace them with their new nonavoidant methods. Sometimes, to get patients started, the alternative prediction may allow them to cope initially by using avoidant strategies then later shifting to nonavoidant strategies.

Patients are not expected to be good at generating alternative predictions initially. They have not had much practice at this. They also are not expected to believe in them strongly. Indeed, at this stage of therapy most patients believe more in the fearful scenarios than the alternatives. Bob may recognize that "one or the other is going to happen," as he stated, but his fears when provoked will be more convincing than his alternative plan. The ability to generate alternative predictions and believe them comes through repeated exposures that confirm their validity. In the meantime, patients are reminded that the goal of this effort is simply to generate a more objective scenario. It will serve as the map for guiding their actions, and will be the primary focus of their efforts. Not feeling fully confident about whether it will be accurate and successful is an expected part of the change process.

Sometimes not all fears can be predicted prior to exposure, nor should an inordinate amount of time be spent trying to do so. If patients cannot master this skill and are not likely to with practice, the goal shifts to helping them identify only major fearful themes (e.g., "I could suffocate") and develop a routine plan for coping (e.g., "When I feel fearful, I'm going to try to do . . . ").

In whatever form it takes, the process of identifying predictions serves several useful purposes. It reminds patients prior to an exposure that one of its purposes is to challenge and test fears. The procedure of generating alternative predictions itself is therapeutic because it forces patients to counter the biased, sometimes catastrophic nature of their fears—a skill that has been underused. Prediction testing also surfaces patients' often implicit assumption that they cannot cope, and asks them to lay out specific plans for doing so.

Setting Goals for the Exposure

After identifying predictions, patients develop a plan to guide their actions during exposure that follows from the alternative predictions, rather than allowing their fears to guide them. Plans will vary from patient to patient and depend on the nature of the exposures. The following are general procedures, written to the patient, for developing an exposure plan. They can be recorded on a card or audiotape, if desired.

1. Lay out the exposure chronologically (e.g., "I will start by doing this, then go to that . . . ").
2. Identify and focus on performing simple, manageable tasks toward the goal of completing the exposure (moving within 10 feet of a feared object, stopping, regrouping, then move within 5 feet, etc.).
3. Mentally, stay in the present, focusing on accomplishing each goal and using your coping strategies rather than concerning yourself with what might happen (e.g., "What if . . . ").
4. If a moment of fear, doubt, or something unexpected happens, do not fight it. Wait, use your coping strategies, and give it time to pass. Then carry on with the next step of your plan.
5. Reassure and encourage yourself throughout the exposure. Try to talk to yourself as you would someone else who was trying to manage the same situation.

After-Exposure Review

One of the most potentially therapeutic moments of exposure occurs after it, when patients have an opportunity to review and consolidate what has occurred. As with the prediction testing procedure, the Exposure Record Form takes patients through a review of their exposure. Its use is recommended for teaching patients this procedure. Some review questions ask patients to evaluate which predictions were supported during the exposure. Others help patients learn from successes and failures, and apply this knowledge to future exposures. The importance of reviewing exposures may need reiteration. It is easy for patients to forget to do it. Therapists ask patients to bring the completed forms to the next treatment session, where they are reviewed and discussed. For the most part, exposures go as planned in alternative scenarios. The review process helps patients see that.

SELF-THERAPY EXERCISE

Between sessions, patients are asked (1) to practice their somatic control strategies; (2) to use the Exposure Record Form to generate fearful and alternative predictions for two or three selected exposure tasks from their hierarchy; and (3) to begin converting their Fear and Avoidance Hierarchy into specific exposure tasks that fall within the guidelines for exposure discussed during this session. After these exercises are explained and questions addressed, the next appointment is scheduled.

5

Treatment Session 4—
Bringing It All Together

SESSION OVERVIEW

In this session, the educational information and preparatory skills introduced in previous sessions are put to practice in an exposure exercise of one form or another. The session can be organized several ways. Within the format described here, therapists first have the option of reviewing pertinent information presented during past sessions. Next, the paced diaphragmatic breathing and relaxation exercise practiced between sessions is combined with selected self-statements to form a somatic and cognitive coping strategy that patients can use on demand. Then, the Fear and Avoidance Hierarchy, revised between sessions, is reviewed and refined. Following these preliminaries, patients begin their first exposure exercise.

Therapists have the option of starting with any modality of exposure they feel is most appropriate given considerations such as the type of phobia and the patient's readiness. Since some patients will begin with imaginal or interoceptive exposure or an imaginal rehearsal, those procedures are described in this chapter. Of course, therapists may decide to begin with exposure in vivo. For practical purposes, however, it is described in the next chapter. Consequently, the approach presented in the vignette should be considered a conservative, slow-paced one, and one of several optional approaches to beginning exposure. In general, a gradual approach is recommended because it allows patients to practice and develop their coping skills in relatively low-anxiety situations, building confidence before entering more challenging encounters.

SESSION GOALS

1. To review key concepts presented previously (if necessary);
2. To develop the on-demand coping strategy;
3. To review and refine the Fear and Avoidance Hierarchy;
4. To conduct an imaginal rehearsal with or without an initial exposure of choice.

KEY CONCEPTS AND CLINICAL CONSIDERATIONS FOR ACCOMPLISHING GOAL #1—REVIEWING KEY CONCEPTS

To ensure patients are grasping key concepts, therapists can briefly review them. The following is a brief summary of the primary concepts presented thus far.

1. Through any of several developmental pathways, patients develop fear of the phobic object or situation that is maintained by a phobic cycle of fearful beliefs, false alarms, and safety-seeking actions.
2. Fearful beliefs are biased toward overestimating the likelihood of threats. They may catastrophize the outcome of phobic encounters and often ignore or underestimate the patients' abilities to manage the demands of those encounters.
3. The physical reactions to the phobic cue are a natural response to appraising threat in phobic situations. Since the reaction occurs in the context of a misappraisal of threat, it is a false alarm of that threat. Although the sensations of the alarm may occur rapidly, intensely, and aversively, they are not dangerous or harmful to patients, nor do they indicate that danger or harm are actually present.
4. The strong urge to seek safety from the phobic object or situation also is a natural and expected consequence of experiencing phobic fear. Safety-seeking can be obvious, as in escape or avoidance, or subtle, as with evasive actions or the use of safety signals. Because safety-seeking occurs in response to misappraisals of threat and of the patients' efficacy, it is actually unnecessary, but prevents patients from learning that, and thus maintains the phobia.

5. By repeatedly approaching and learning to manage feared objects and situations (exposure), patients' urges to escape and avoid, their physical sensations of flight or fight, and appraisals of threat, all of which have become an interwoven response to the phobic cues, weaken, while their confidence in managing phobic encounters strengthens.

The primary guidelines for exposure were depicted in Table 4–1 and have also been incorporated into the Exposure Record Form, either of which can be reviewed with the patient or patient and coach.

Clinical Vignette

Bob demonstrates his grasp of key concepts and guidelines for exposure introduced in previous sessions.

Therapist: [reviewing guidelines for exposure] Bob, imagine you're advising someone how to conduct exposure. From what we've discussed, what would you tell them to do?

Bob: Plan it out. Think about how you're going to deal with the hard parts.

Therapist: What about during the exposure?

Bob: Try to hang in there. Try not to leave.

Therapist: That's good. Maybe you should take my place the rest of the day. What about how long should you do exposure?

Bob: The longer, the better from what you said. I took from it that I need to stay until I feel like I've done the thing. You know, don't quit because you're scared. Quit because you've done it.

Therapist: Good. What does "done it" mean to you, Bob?

Bob: Faced it. To me, it means to prove to myself that I can handle it.

Therapist: Yes, I think that's a good way to think about it. You also said you should try to hang in there. How would you do that if you found yourself getting more and more nervous and feeling the urge to escape or start avoiding subtly?

Bob: My plan is to try to stop, regroup, and then go ahead when I feel ready. Give it some time to see if it will pass.

Therapist: "Stop, regroup, and go ahead." It sounds as if that would make a useful coping statement for you.

Bob: Yeah, I kind of got that in my head now to use during exposure.

KEY CONCEPTS AND CLINICAL CONSIDERATIONS FOR ACCOMPLISHING GOAL #2—DEVELOPING AN ON-DEMAND COPING STRATEGY

Last session, patients learned an exercise that combines paced diaphragmatic breathing and relaxation to help manage physical sensations. They also learned about coping self-statements, which help focus their attention adaptively during exposure. Those techniques are combined into a coping strategy that can be used on demand. Again, a description of the on-demand coping strategy can be found at the end of the section Developing Your Coping Strategies (Appendix 10). As discussed previously, therapists may need to reemphasize that the coping strategy is to be used to manage fearful reactions while patients focus on achieving their behavioral goals of the exposure.

Clinical Vignette

After practicing the on-demand coping strategy, Bob is asked to demonstrate how and when he will use it.

Therapist: So let's imagine you're walking on a catwalk at work and suddenly you feel that familiar surge of adrenaline—your false alarm. Instead of escaping, will you show me how you're going to use your new coping strategies to ride this out?

Bob: Well, like we've practiced, first, I'll yell inside my head, "Stop," if I need to. Then I'll tell myself to "regroup, calm down." I'll start my breathing [demonstrates paced diaphragmatic breathing] and stretching [demonstrates stretching and relaxing], and then give it some time to calm down.

Therapist: Do you plan to use any coping statements that you think would be helpful for those moments, in addition to "regroup" and "calm down"?

Bob: Yeah, I like the "stop, regroup, and move on," maybe "give it some time to calm down," and "you're not in danger"—things like that.

Therapist: Good. Use what you feel will help focus you on coping. We can see afterwards which are most helpful. Will you show me how you'll do this?

After the demonstration and feedback, if necessary, the session continues.

Therapist: [reviewing anticipated challenges] Let's imagine a more challenging experience. Let's say you're in a higher place and your anxiety remains very high even though you're using the coping strategies. You're becoming very anxious and fearing that you could lose control.

Bob: Whoa, I guess I'm just going to have to give it some time and wait it out. I'd probably just slow down and take it a step at a time. I can't think of anything else to do.

Therapist: I like that, Bob. No need to rush it or stop it immediately. The idea is to ride it out using your strategies, whether the feelings are strong, weak, or changing. It may help you to remember to stay focused in the present, coping, and staying with the exposure task at hand, trying to stay off all the "what if's," all the catastrophic possibilities.

Bob: Right, try not to get off on all the things that could happen. I like thinking of this as tapes, the way we talked. If Tape 1 starts rolling, I try to get Tape 2 going. Then, I try to stay with Tape 2.

Therapist: I think that's a good goal. How will you know when Tape 1 starts rolling [helping Bob recognize a cue for coping]?

Bob: I'll hear it, I guess. You know, "You're gonna fall, you can't do this, you need to get out of here." It happens every time.

Therapist: Okay. You might hear it. Let me be picky here though, Bob. Sometimes we know what our self-talk is. Other times, we're so engrossed that we are unaware of it. Besides hearing it, another way you can tell Tape 1 is running is by feeling it.

Bob: Feeling it?

Therapist: Yes, when Tape 1 is rolling, you feel the alarm.

Bob: So it might be better to just use that feeling to know when to start the coping?

Therapist: Yes, it might be easier to know "I'm feeling nervous" than "I'm thinking about this or that."

Bob: That's probably true.

Therapist: Well, we can try it and see. If it's not helpful, we can find something else that is. But what we're talking about here, Bob, is changing the way you react to your feelings of fear. The alarm is now a signal to wait and cope, not a signal that you're in danger and need to leave.

Bob: I understand.

KEY CONCEPTS AND CLINICAL CONSIDERATIONS FOR ACCOMPLISHING GOAL #3—REVIEWING AND REFINING THE FEAR AND AVOIDANCE HIERARCHY

Prior to this session, patients were asked to convert the items from their Fear and Avoidance Hierarchy into specific exposure exercises. At some point in this session, the therapist and patient review and refine that list with the following considerations in mind:

1. Are the exercises doable within the guidelines for exposure and considering the patient's personal and practical resources? For example, does the exercise allow sufficient time, and can it be done frequently enough to provide a benefit?
2. Does the list contain a workable number of steps to establish a new nonavoidant approach to the phobic object or situation (generally 5–15, depending on the nature of the task)?
3. Will patients begin with situations that increase the likelihood of a successful start?
4. Does the list include exposures that will address the patient's social or occupational disability?

Clinical Vignette

Bob does well choosing exposure exercises, but misses a practical consideration that could make his initial exposure less than optimal. The therapist detects this and suggests appropriate changes.

Therapist: Bob, one of your initial exposures involves looking over the balcony next to your work station. Can you describe that scene to me?

Bob: Yeah, at the processing plant my desk is in an office area that's subdivided by those movable partitions, you know, that form cubicles. Anyway, the offices are up on this long, second-floor platform that overlooks other work stations on the ground floor. At the edge of the platform is a walkway with a railing that overlooks the ground floor. You have to walk along it to get to our offices. I was thinking I could just walk up next to that rail and kind of look over it.

Therapist: It sounds as if you probably walk by that railing a lot to get in and out of your work station.

Bob: Yeah, I do. But I usually don't go near the rail. That's why I thought it would be a good one. I'm kind of used to it. It's not too high off the ground, so it's not too scary. But all the floors are concrete, so it is a little scary. It's a 2 or 3 on the scale.

Therapist: Well, it sounds like a good exposure to start with. Is it one that allows you to stay there until you feel more comfortable and confident?

Bob: Yeah, I guess. I'll just stay as long as I need to, like we've said.

Therapist: What about interruptions? Is it busy there?

Bob: Yeah, it can be. Sometimes people walk by it. Maybe I could try to do it when it's not too busy.

Therapist: Could you do that and be certain that you won't be interrupted?

Bob: Hmm . . . I couldn't guarantee it.

Therapist: Well, it sounds as if it would be a good initial exposure. But I'm concerned that you might be interrupted, and won't be able to stay long enough to practice your new coping skills and get comfortable. What would you think about starting with another balcony exposure, but one where you won't be interrupted?

Bob: Well, I don't know where that would be.

Therapist: What about the balcony on the second floor of this building?

Bob: Well, I guess that would work. I'm not as familiar with your balcony, though. It may not be a 2 or 3.

Therapist: Let's go take a look and see.

After inspecting the balcony, the session continues.

Therapist: Well, what about doing that as a starting point while you take whatever opportunities you can to do exposure to the railing at work?

Bob: Okay.

Therapist: Do you understand why I'm suggesting this?

Bob: Yeah. So I won't be interrupted.

Therapist: Yes. So you can stay as long as you need to feel more comfortable with the exposure—as the guidelines suggest.

Figure 5–1 shows Bob's revised Fear and Avoidance Hierarchy.

**Figure 5-1: Bob's Revised Fear and Avoidance Hierarchy
(with confidence rating)**

Rank	Object, Situation, or Activity	Fear (0–10)	Avoidance (0–10)	Confidence (0–10)
1	Climbing to circuit box on the roof of power plant	10	10	1
2	Ferris wheels at Six Flags	10	10	1
3	Observation tower at Heights Park Next to rail Away from rail	 10 8	 10 10	 1 2
4	Catwalks at work (outside) (inside)	 8 6	 7 3	 3 3
5	Freight elevators at work (>2–4 stories) (<2 stories)	 6 4	 10 10	 4 6
6	Driving across McCluggage Bridge Inside land Next to guard rail	 3 5	 4 7	 6 4
7	Climbing ladder to roof of house (sitting on roof)	3	3	6
8	Looking over balcony at mall (watching family do this) at mall (doing it by himself) at work at therapist's office	 3 2 2 2	 5 6 3 3	 6 7 8 8

KEY CONCEPTS AND CLINICAL CONSIDERATIONS FOR ACCOMPLISHING GOAL #4—BEGINNING EXPOSURE

Patients begin some form of exposure this session. In this section, interoceptive exposure, imaginal exposure, and imaginal rehearsal are described. The clinical vignette below depicts the first and the last. Any or all of these techniques are available to therapists as adjuncts to exposure in vivo. If necessary, though, imaginal exposure can replace live exposure when the latter is unavailable.

Interoceptive Exposure

Interoceptive exposure, like other forms of exposure, involves having patients encounter the object of their fear in a systematic and repeated way in an effort to make it less threatening and more predictable, and to build their confidence in managing it. It differs from object or situation exposure though, in that it targets patients' own feared sensations. This technique is used commonly for treating panic disorder, where fear of sensations can predominate the clinical picture. As discussed in Chapter 1, patients with specific phobias may fear the sensations of their phobic reaction as well, but often for different reasons than do sufferers of panic disorder. For example, a person fearful of snakes may fear shaking, not because they fear it may represent some underlying neurological problem (a common misinterpretation in panic disorder), but because it could provoke the snake to attack them. A patient phobic of heights may fear feelings of weakness, not because they fear a stroke, for example (another common misinterpretation in panic disorder), but because it makes falling seem more likely. Most patients whose phobic reactions involve intense sensations fear that if those feelings get too intense, they could make patients lose control and do something dangerous, embarrassing, or worse. Thus, fears of sensations can be an integral part of a patient's primary fear of a phobic object or situation, warranting attention in the treatment plan.

Most often, therapists can address a patient's fears of sensations through exposure to the phobic object or situation, without formal interoceptive exposure. Situational exposure is often sufficient to reduce fears of sensations as well. In some cases though, fears of sensations are so salient that they can interfere with situational exposure. Preliminary interoceptive exposure may help attenuate those fears prior to facing a situational exposure. Interoceptive exercises can also be used simply to allow patients an opportunity to practice their coping strategies in response to self-induced physical sensations, regardless of whether they fear those sensations.

The Sensation Exposure Record (Appendix 9) details the formal interoceptive exposure procedure. In brief, it involves having the patient voluntarily induce potentially feared physical sensations by doing some form of exercise, then recovering from those feelings using coping strategies. To begin, a specific exercise designed to induce feared sensations is selected. The patient then starts the exercise until sensations are felt. At that point, the patient continues the exercise for a predetermined duration (e.g., 5, 10, 15 seconds). This ensures that the phobic cues (the sensations) are fully present, and discourages the patient from stopping the exercise (escaping) at the first sign of feared feelings. After stopping the exercise, the patient uses coping strategies to recover. While recovering or shortly thereafter, the patient indicates on the Sensation Exposure Record what sensations were felt during or immediately after stopping the exercise. The intensity of each sensation is recorded on a 0–10 Likert-type scale. Then, the patient indicates whether anxiety was sensed during the experience by rating its intensity using the same 0–10 scale. After recovering and returning to baseline, the patient repeats the exercise/recover cycle as follows: if no anxiety emerged in response to the induced sensations, then the cycle is repeated a few more times, testing for anxiety, before moving on to the next exercise. If anxiety did emerge, the cycle is repeated until anxiety ratings wane sufficiently.

Although it is usually not necessary for patients with specific phobias, interoceptive exposure can be gradated for those who are wary about producing intense sensations initially. This can be done by varying the duration that patients extend the exercise after sensations are first felt. For example, during the first cycle, a patient producing lightheadedness by breathing rapidly might extend initial sets of this exercise one to two seconds after feeling sensations. After mastering that level, the following sets would be extended for 5, 10, or up to 30 seconds after sensations were felt.

It is also not unusual for patients to avoid provoking what they fear will be overwhelming sensations by not doing exercises vigorously enough to produce strong sensations. Therefore, whether using a gradated approach or not, patients are asked to try to produce strong sensations during at least one of the trials (preferably most of them) before moving to another exercise. Although patients may fear only one or two sensations, therapists should urge patients to err on the side of testing a broad range of exercises and sensations. The Sensation Exposure Record describes a number of exercises for that purpose.

Sometimes interoceptive exposure exercises do not engender anxiety despite producing strong sensations. The fact that sensations are being induced voluntarily, often in a safe environment, or in the presence of a safe individual may mitigate patients' fear of them. It may be only in the phobic situation that the sensations are feared. If the exercises fail to produce anxiety, they have not been a waste of time, though. The procedure is useful in allowing patients to practice their coping skills in response to strong sensations. In addition, practicing the induction exercises now may help patients later in therapy when they may be asked to induce sensations during situational exposure.

The goal of interoceptive exposure is to have patients experience feared sensations without inappropriate anxiety and develop confidence in their ability to cope with those sensations. Of course, as with any patient undergoing exposure therapy, and particularly those with preexisting medical conditions, medical clearance for interoceptive exposure should be obtained.

Clinical Vignette

The strong fear of the unsteadiness Bob feels in high situations is targeted for interoceptive exposure prior to exposure in vivo. The therapist begins with a rapid breathing exercise designed to induce lightheadedness, a sensation Bob has feared could result in his loss of balance. As part of his self-therapy exercise between sessions, Bob will be asked to try other exercises that produce similar sensations of unsteadiness or weakness (e.g., spinning in place and sustained muscle tension). After discussing the rationale for this type of exposure, Bob's therapist demonstrates a gradated interoceptive exposure procedure.

Therapist: Okay, Bob, this rapid breathing exercise may help us produce the feelings of unsteadiness and lightheadedness that you've worried could make you lose your balance. To produce those feelings, we need to do this breathing exercise in a way opposite of the way you breathe to cope. It involves chest breathing, deeply and quickly, and exhaling with force. You repeat this rapidly so that you inhale and exhale about once every second. Let me demonstrate what it looks like [demonstrates rapid breathing]. As you continue breathing like this, you'll begin to feel some lightheadedness or unsteadiness. When you do, I want you to raise your left hand to let me know that you're feeling those. At that point, I want you to continue doing the breathing exercise for 5 more seconds and then stop. I'll count those seconds out loud after you raise your hand. After you stop, use your coping strategies to recover from any feelings of unsteadiness you may have. I'll remind and help you do that when the time comes—until you get it down. Let me demonstrate that [demonstrates the symptom induction exercise and the use of coping strategies involving paced diaphragmatic breathing and coping self-talk]. As you recover, you use this Sensation Exposure Record to indicate which feelings you felt during the exercise and how strongly you felt them using this 0–10 scale. So, for example, during the exercise I just did, here's what I felt [completes form]. After rating what feelings you had, I'd like you then to indicate whether you felt anxiety at any time during or after the procedure and at what level, 0–10 [demonstrates use of the form].

Now, this next part is a little detailed. After you recover, if you didn't feel anxiety of at least a 5 level, then let's repeat the exercise, lengthening it to 10 seconds after you first feel the sensations and raise your hand. This will make the sensations a little stronger. If you still don't feel anxiety at 10 seconds, then we'll lengthen the exercise to 15, 20, or up to 30 seconds. If you still don't experience anxiety at 30 seconds, try it once more, doing it vigorously, before you move to the next exercise. Let me demonstrate this [demonstrates procedure]. We can practice this a little more too, until you get it down.

You may not experience any anxiety even though you feel the sensations, and that's okay. It's a good opportunity for you to practice using your coping strategies the way you will when you go to a high place. If you feel anxiety, though, I'd like you to repeat the exercise over and over until the anxiety bottoms out, that is, you would exercise to get the feelings, recover, record, then repeat those until your anxiety ratings bottom out and level off. Let me give you an example of what the form would look like if that occurred [demonstrates how the form is used when anxiety is produced]. Okay, why don't we have you try it now.

After therapists demonstrate the interoceptive exposure procedure using one exercise as an example, they should demonstrate each of the exercises listed on the form. The list of exercises is not exhaustive. Other creative ways of inducing symptoms are encouraged, as long as patients can do them safely. After the demonstration, patients practice interoceptive exposure between sessions. Figure 5–2 shows a completed Sensation Exposure Record for a rapid breathing exercise.

Figure 5–2: Bob's Completed Sensation Exposure Record

Name *Bob*   Date *3-22-96*

After each exercise, record which sensations you experienced and how frightening they were using the scale below:

0-------1-------2-------3-------4-------5-------6-------7-------8-------9-------10
Not at all   Mild   Moderate   Strong   Severe

Exercise (see attached list): *breathing rapidly (20 seconds extended)*

Sensations:	Sample	1st cycle	2nd	3rd	4th	5th	6th	7th	8th
Dizziness, unsteady feelings, or faintness	3	5	6	5	5	5	6	5	5
Palpitations or accelerated heart rate	4	1	2	1	0	1	1	1	1
Shortness of breath or smothering sensations									
Hot flashes or chills	1		2						
Weakness									
Trembling or shaking									
Sweating	1	1	2	1	1	1	2	1	1
Nausea or abdominal distress									
Numbness or tingling sensations		3	3	0	1	0	0	0	0
Self or surroundings seem strange or unreal									
Chest pain or discomfort									
Choking									
Lump in throat									
How frightening were the feelings	3	7	8	5	3	3	1	1	1

Imaginal Exposure

Therapists considering the use of imaginal exposure can choose from systematic desensitization, imaginal flooding, or some modification of these two classic approaches, depending on the needs and readiness of the patient.

As discussed, systematic desensitization uses a gradated approach to exposure wherein anxiety is minimized. The procedure begins with the selection of a low-fear item from the fear and avoidance hierarchy. Next, the patient induces relaxation. When relaxed, the patient imagines a neutral (nonanxiety-provoking) scene, invoking as many senses as possible (e.g., imagining smells, sights, sounds, etc.) in order to enhance the strength of the image. Once that image is clear, the patient switches to imagining the feared scene in the same vivid manner. When the feared image is clear, the patient indicates that, if desired, by giving a predetermined signal (e.g., saying "okay" or raising the left index finger). If no anxiety is experienced, the patient continues to visualize the scene for a designated period of time (usually less than 30 seconds for low-fear items, a minute or two for high-fear items). If anxiety is felt while visualizing the feared scene, however, the patient gives a predetermined signal indicating that (e.g., raising their right hand). At that point, the therapist instructs the patient to stop visualizing and begin relaxing again. The patient's level of anxiety is assessed using a verbal, 0–10 subjective units of discomfort (SUDs) rating (0 = no anxiety, 10 = as anxious as I can imagine). The SUDs ratings are elicited periodically until they show that anxiety has waned. When anxiety has returned to a baseline, the patient revisualizes the feared scene. This procedure is repeated until the selected scene can be visualized without excessive anxiety. After another brief relaxation period, the patient proceeds to the next scene on the hierarchy. The desensitization procedure continues in the same fashion until all feared scenes have been imaged without inappropriate anxiety.

As discussed, traditional imaginal flooding involved prolonged imaginal exposure to patients' most feared scenes. The use of responses that compete with anxiety, such as relaxation, were not encouraged. Rather, patients stayed in the imagined presence of the feared scene for as long as it took for their anxiety to habituate.

The procedure begins with the therapist getting a detailed description of the patient's most feared scenes. Next, the patient visualizes a chosen scene, again invoking as many senses as possible and indicating when clarity is achieved. Therapists encourage patients to attend to detail and resist what is usually a strong urge to stop visualizing the feared scenes. The details of scenes should be realistic. They need not, however, include grisly features to be effective (Foa et al. 1977). For fears related to drowning in deep water, for example, it is sufficient to depict a swimmer struggling to swim while highly anxious, rather than picturing them drowning and sinking to the bottom of a lake. Zero to 10 SUDs ratings are taken periodically throughout the description of the scene. The exposure ends after SUDs ratings wane.

Imaginal exposure can be enhanced by the use of props that simulate elements of the actual feared situation. For example, the use of alcohol swabs, toothpaste, and sounds of dental instruments can enhance imaginal exposure to dental procedures. Exposures to animals can involve the use of taxidermic props. Fake insects or other items can be used to simulate the tactile sensations of an insect crawling on the patient while the patient imagines the real bug crawling on them. Audiotapes can provide phobic cues that are hard to present in imagination or are not routinely accessible in vivo (e.g., sound of thunderstorms, a growling dog, airplane noises). Because these props can be very convincing and provocative, the patient should be fully informed and agree to their use.

There is evidence that gains made through imaginal exposure do not transfer completely to live situations (e.g., Barlow et al. 1969). This is one reason why imaginal exposure is not considered a replacement for exposure in vivo unless the latter is unavailable or too frightening. When imaginal exposure is a precursor to live exposure, patients should be prepared to face more demanding challenges during the initial live exposures.

Imaginal Rehearsal

In contrast to imaginal exposure, imaginal rehearsal deemphasizes anxiety reduction in favor of simply providing patients an opportunity to rehearse how they will conduct a subsequent exposure in vivo. Readers will recognize that elements of imaginal rehearsal have been incorporated into the procedure for identifying alternative predictions that patients go through before exposure (described in Chapter 4).

After selecting an exposure task, patients begin by visualizing and describing how they will proceed through it chronologically. If desired, therapists can have patients describe pre-exposure activities like completing the Exposure Record Form or talking over plans with the therapeutic coach. If anxiety reduction is of interest, periodic SUDs ratings can be taken before and during this imaginal rehearsal. As patients describe the unfolding scene, they are asked to anticipate likely challenges and how they intend to manage them, that is, patients imagine successfully accomplishing the challenges that the exposure task is likely to present. During the rehearsal, patients can be asked to demonstrate coping strategies, if desired. After the rehearsal is completed, patients can go over the exposure review section of the Exposure Record Form, if desired.

Clinical Vignette

In this vignette, Bob rehearses preparing, conducting, and reviewing the exposure that he will do in vivo next session. In addition, Bob has some fears about whether he can do the imaginal rehearsal itself. Therefore, Bob's therapist shows him how to identify fearful predictions and generate alternatives in response to those fears. After that, Bob proceeds with the rehearsal. In this sense, Bob is conducting an imaginal rehearsal of an upcoming exposure while doing an exposure in vivo to the rehearsal itself. His therapist makes use of both opportunities.

Therapist: Bob, before we begin, are you a little nervous?

Bob: Yeah, I'm not quite sure what to expect.

Therapist: How nervous are you? What's your SUDs rating right now?

Bob: Oh, a 2.

Therapist: Okay. Well, first we're going to use the Exposure Record Form to identify any Tape 1 fearful predictions and your alternative Tape 2 plan as you would if this was live. Before we practice that for the upcoming balcony exposure, let's do it for the anxiety you have about today's session. The fact that you're a little nervous about doing this rehearsal means that Tape 1 is running. If we listen to it, we can identify some fearful predictions that you might be having about today's session. This is the same thing that you want to do before an exposure—use your anticipatory anxiety to identify and record what the fearful tape says is going to happen.

Bob: Okay. Where do we start?

Therapist: Can you identify any fearful predictions you're having now about what could happen today?

Bob: Well, my biggest concern is that I might just get too nervous and make a fool out of myself.

Therapist: How do you see that happening?

Bob: I'm not sure, maybe get too nervous and lose control—do something stupid like get up and run out of here.

After identifying other fears, the session continues.

Therapist: Okay, after we've put those on the form and rated their believability, do you recall what we do next?

Bob: Make Tape 2.

Therapist: Yes. Do you remember the general procedure for making Tape 2?

Bob: Well, I've got to think about how I'm going to cope instead of just letting things happen.

Therapist: Right, that's one thing. But rather than do that for every single fear, it will help to consider, first, that Tape 1 often overestimates how likely the feared prediction is. So try to ask yourself whether a fear you have is most likely or if something else is, then make a plan for how you're going to cope with what is most likely. Does that make sense?

Bob: Yeah, I'm following it.

Therapist: So the first question is, "Is the feared prediction most likely?" In this instance, Bob, is getting extremely anxious and running out of here the most likely event to occur?

Bob: Well, I don't know. I've gotten that way before.

Therapist: That's good that you're thinking about your past experience to try to answer this question. You want to try to be objective. Has it been your experience that you get highly anxious and run when you *imagine* going into a high situation? Because that's what you're going to be asked to do in just a little while.

Bob: Well, it happens sometimes, sometimes not. I've been nervous thinking about doing something and then decided to skip it.

Therapist: So based on your experience, it sounds like there's about a 50/50 chance that you're going to get highly anxious and run.

Bob: Well, no, when you put it like that . . . it probably won't be that bad. I probably won't run, because you're here [identifying a safety signal]. Maybe I'll just get a little nervous.

Therapist: Zero to 10, then?

Bob: I don't know, maybe a 2 or 3.

Therapist: Okay. So there's a 50/50 chance of being nervous at a 2 or 3.

Bob: Yeah.

Therapist: So let's make that part of your other, Tape 2 prediction. Now let's move onto the second part of this, how you intend to cope with it if you start feeling that 2-to-3 level of anxiety.

Bob: Well, like we've said, I'm going to stop, regroup, do my breathing, talk to myself until the anxiety comes down.

Therapist: Good, that's the way you do this. You'll find it helpful if you imagine that scene—getting anxious and coping with it—in some detail. It looks as if you're getting this down. Before your actual balcony exposure, you'll do the same thing. So to identify your Tape 2 scenario you ask yourself if what you fear is most likely, and if not, then what is. Then, you ask yourself, "How will I cope with it?" Bob, if you think that the fearful Tape 1 scenario is most likely or if it just keeps intruding into your mind, then try reviewing how you would try to cope if something like it started to occur, as we've discussed. But when you plan how to proceed with the exposure, plan for what is most likely. As you do exposures, you'll get better and better at anticipating what actually happens during the exposure. Let's imagine for a second, though, that your fearful prediction about getting frightened and leaving is most likely or bothering you, and go through the process of coping with that. So if you actually did get extremely anxious and ran, how would you try to handle it?

Bob: That would be bad.

Therapist: You probably would feel bad. But force yourself to see the consequences and how you would try to cope with them. Ask yourself this, Bob, "If that really happened, what would I do to try to cope with it?"

Bob: Probably call you up and apologize, first.

Therapist: Okay, and I'd accept your apology, and probably say, "There's no need to apologize to me. What you did was understandable." Then I'd ask you what you want to do next?

Bob: I guess I'd try it again.

Therapist: And I'd suggest some ways we might try to overcome your urge to flee.

Bob: I guess it wouldn't be horrible, would it?

Therapist: Difficult? Probably. Horrible? Probably not. When we're thinking fearfully, though, we often don't think about how we are going to cope, or we imagine ourselves not coping at all. When we force ourselves to think about it, it helps us see that no matter what the situation, we would probably try to do something. Even if that something is difficult, embarrassing, or painful.

Bob: Yeah, I guess I just hate thinking about it.

Therapist: I know. Who doesn't? These are the unlikely, frightening things—sometimes worst-case scenarios. But our goal is not to run from them anymore. It's to try to face them, even when its difficult.

Bob: So it's like avoidance—to not want to think about it?

Therapist: At this stage of the game, let's try to treat it like that, and err on the side of thinking about it and how we're going to cope. With time we won't need to do this so intentionally because they won't seem as frightening anymore.

After rehearsing the use of the Exposure Record Form for the imaginal scene, Bob begins his imaginal rehearsal of the balcony exposure.

Bob: [describing an imaginal scenario] Okay, I'm walking across the floor towards the balcony railing and that's where I'm probably going to start feeling a little nervous.

Therapist: Okay, Bob, hold that scene. As you walk toward the railing, what are you likely to feel [guiding the patient to rehearse successfully coping with likely events]?

Bob: Well, when I start getting close and I see how high I am, that's usually when I feel the first signs of it, the weakness in my legs. My heart will probably take off.

Therapist: Okay, imagine that feeling, holding that scene [pauses]. Now, Bob, as you're imagining that scene, imagine and describe to me how you're going to cope. [Therapist could have patient induce sensations through exercise then recover, if desired.]

Bob: I'm stopping and doing my stomach breathing. I'm talking to myself.

Therapist: What are you saying?

Bob: "You're okay." "Give it time." "It will pass."

Therapist: Bob, what's your actual SUDs rating right now [optional question]?

Bob: Oh, a 1 maybe.

Therapist: While you're imagining yourself in that scene, why don't you actually practice the paced diaphragmatic breathing and relaxation.

Therapist: [after some time] What's your actual SUDs level now, Bob?

Bob: Oh, a zero. This isn't as scary as I'd thought.

Therapist: Right, the anticipation is often worse, as we've said. Okay, let's go ahead with the scenario—moving closer to the rail.

Bob: All right. As I step up close to the rail, I will feel my anxiety getting stronger.

Therapist: Imagine that—how it feels [pauses]. How strong is it?

Bob: Maybe a 2 or 3. I thought just now that this is where I could get that feeling of being pulled over.

Therapist: Okay, imagine feeling that. Try to feel the unsteadiness, the weakness, and the fear about losing your balance [pauses]. What's your actual SUDs level now?

Bob: Oh, just a 2 or so.

Therapist: Okay, do you have the image clearly in mind now?

Bob: Yes.

Therapist: [after allowing Bob to imagine the scene] Now then, just as we did before and as you'll do when you're there, ask yourself how will you cope with that feeling?

Bob: Well, I'll want to hang on to the rail, but I'm going to try not to do that. Wait, I just had that thought about "What if the rail's not sturdy?" I guess I'm afraid of supporting myself against it.

Therapist: Okay, that's Tape 1. That's a fear you've had before, and it's likely to come up during exposures. So again, how do you want to cope if this fear pops up during the live situation?

Bob: Well, I could try to stand there. Maybe not touch it.

Therapist: Okay, maybe you won't touch it initially while you stop and regroup. But if you don't touch it at all, how will you know if your fear that the rail is unsturdy is true or just another fearful message from Tape 1?

Bob: That's true. I'd want to calm down a little first, though.

Therapist: All right. How would you do that?

Bob: Same way, I guess. Just do my breathing, and talk to myself—until the feeling passes.

Therapist: Good. Bob, how many times have you fallen because you've gotten weak in your legs?

Bob: None.

Therapist: Think about that for a second. Try hard to be objective, even if it's not that convincing. What's more likely than falling?

Bob: That I'll be nervous, but okay. I'll have to let it pass.

Therapist: Good. Is that believable to you now?

Bob: A little. It's probably going to be harder when I'm there.

Therapist: That's true. Do you think that you'll also be doubtful of your ability to cope during the actual situation?

Bob: Probably.

Therapist: Okay then, let's imagine that you will. How will you deal with that?

Bob: Just stick to my plan, I guess. Hang in there. Try not to get hung up on it too much.

Therapist: Good, Bob. It probably will not be super-convincing, but you want to try to stick to coping?

Bob: I know, focus on doing it, even if I'm feeling bad. That'll be hard.

Therapist: I know it sounds difficult but, as you've found, anticipating is usually worse than what happens.

Bob: Yeah. I'm going to try.

Therapist: All right. Bob, you said that you also fear that the railing might not support you. As we said, one of the things we want to do during exposures is to test fears.

Bob: All right, but how?

Therapist: Well, what about as you're standing there, after you've regrouped, you grab the rail and shake it to see how sturdy it is?

Bob: Whoa! I don't know if that's a good idea.

Therapist: That's just it, Bob. Tape 1 is going to say it's not a good idea. What about Tape 2?

Bob: I'm not so sure Tape 2's convinced about it either [nervous laughter].

Therapist: I understand. It's hard to believe that it can be safe. And the railing may not be sturdy. It also might be very solid.

Bob: It's probably sturdy.

Therapist: Well, let's try safely testing the rail in your imagination. If you want, imagine yourself balanced so that if it is loose, you don't have all your weight against it.

Bob: Okay, it's funny because as I imagine it, it's probably solid as a rock.

Therapist: Well, that's the part of you that can see that that's the most likely outcome. But let's also go over the scenario that you shake it and it is actually loose. How would you want to try to cope with that situation?

Bob: Whoa, that might be a little too much.

Therapist: How would you cope?

Bob: Well, if it was loose, I'd back away from it.

Therapist: Exactly. That would be the appropriate and safe thing to do if a railing really was broken. What if you find out, though, that the railing is sturdy? How would you proceed?

Bob: Well, maybe to stand by it for a while until I get used to it.

Therapist: Good. What if Tape 1 kept coming back saying, "The rail could give way"?

Bob: Should I shake it again?

Therapist: Would that help?

Bob: I think it would.

Therapist: I think so, too. You'd be testing the fear, showing yourself over and over again that Tape 1 isn't telling the truth about this being an unsafe place.

Later in the session, the therapist continues.

Therapist: [after discussing the use of the Exposure Record Form to do the after-exposure review] Okay, Bob, now that you see how to finish the Exposure Record Form, let's go back over the fearful predictions the phobia made before today's session.

Bob: Well, it looks like Tape 2 came out ahead again.

Therapist: Yes, you're right. Let's go through each of the fearful predictions. What about getting so anxious that you'd get up and run?

Bob: Well, I did get a little anxious, but I didn't embarrass myself; I did fine.

Therapist: That was the alternative prediction, wasn't it?

Bob: Yeah.

Therapist: [after reviewing other predictions] As you said, Bob, your alternative predictions, the ones where you try to guess the most likely outcome, the ones that picture you as capable, were more like what actually happened than were your very convincing fears. It's important to go back over the exposure to see what really happened versus what the phobia said would happen.

Bob: Yeah, but part of me realizes that this wasn't as hard as the real thing.

Therapist: True. This will mean a lot more when we're doing it in the actual situation. But let's not count it out. Look at what happened today, for example. Before we began, Bob, did you have a moment when you thought this could go bad, when you could get too anxious and maybe embarrass yourself?

Bob: Yeah, right before I got here, and right before we began.

Therapist: At those moments, were your fears believable?

Bob: Oh, yeah. I wasn't sure about whether I really wanted to do this.

Therapist: Well, I'm glad you decided to. Because now you can see that despite the fact that it felt like all that could happen, did it?

Bob: No.

Therapist: It's important to see that, to really think about that, when you review your future exposures: at the time that you were feeling that fear, and it felt real, and it felt as if it could happen, and it was highly believable, despite all that, it still wasn't true.

Bob: Yeah, I guess that's the point of this—to see that, isn't it? It sure does feel true at the time, though.

Therapist: Yeah. And it will for a while. But you got another example today that just because it feels real and believable . . .

Bob: Doesn't mean that it is. I'm getting it.

Therapist: I know you are. And every time that you do exposure and you see a fearful prediction not upheld by what happened, it's another example that you can draw upon when you're facing these fears in the future.

Bob: Sometimes I think it helps me to think of Tape 1 as a liar, a person who tells you all these bad things are going to happen.

Therapist: Yeah, I think that's a helpful way of thinking about it. It can be a pretty convincing liar when it has that alarm working with it. But once you start really challenging it, it's not so believable any more. Our first goal is to be able to imagine the situation differently. This will make it more likely that you will be able to apply what you've learned to the actual situation. You've made a good start today. Let's talk about how you can practice some more before next session. Then we can schedule that appointment.

SELF-THERAPY EXERCISE

Between sessions, patients repeat whatever version of exposure or rehearsal they underwent this session. Arrangements are made for conducting a therapist- and coach-assisted in vivo exposure exercise next session.

6

Treatment Session 5— Facing Fears

SESSION OUTLINE

This chapter describes a therapist- and coach-assisted exposure in vivo. The session can take place in or outside the office setting depending on the target of exposure, and may be longer than the conventional one hour session.

The session can be broken down procedurally into three broad phases: preparation, exposure, and review. As discussed, the Exposure Record Form follows the same format, and is recommended for use to guide patients and record their experiences. The session concludes with the assignment of self-therapy exposure exercises from the Fear and Avoidance Hierarchy.

SESSION GOALS

1. To prepare for exposure, including identifying fearful and alternative predictions, as well as laying out a plan of action for completing the exposure.
2. To assist the patient in conducting an exposure in vivo, including instruction and modeling by the therapist for the patient and therapeutic coach and a review of managing high-fear moments.
3. To review the exposure with the patient in an effort to consolidate learning and identify future directions.

KEY CONCEPTS AND CLINICAL CONSIDERATIONS FOR ACCOMPLISHING GOAL #1—PREPARING FOR EXPOSURE

In previous sessions, patients have been encouraged and taught how to prepare for exposure, especially initial ones. Preparation provides patients a sense of direction and purpose. It channels their anticipatory fears into a constructive activity. It encourages the use of adaptive, nonavoidant actions and lays the groundwork for building a sense of predictability and controllability during phobic encounters. Preparation involves identifying fearful and alternative predictions and laying out a plan of action for conducting the exposure. Since those procedures were described previously, only a few considerations for preparing for live exposures follow.

Identifying Predictions

During initial exposures in vivo, anticipatory anxiety is likely to be strong and disconcerting. Patients may need extra guidance and support in translating that anxiety into fearful predictions, and often struggle particularly with the task of identifying alternatives to their fearful predictions. They find it difficult to be objective in the face of fear. Alternative scenarios will usually seem unconvincing. Reversing roles with the therapist, as discussed previously, may help them with this task. Patients should be reassured that it is not unusual to find their alternative scenario unconvincing at this stage of treatment. Accordingly, patients' ratings of their belief in that scenario should reflect their honest, "gut-level" belief rather than what they think they *should* believe, even if the strength of the honest belief is low.

Identifying a Plan of Action

As presented previously, one method of developing a plan for exposure is to identify behavioral subgoals. This involves breaking down the exposure task into discrete, manageable, and, if desired, graduated subtasks that culminate in the completion of the feared activity. Strategies for breaking down the exposure depend on the nature of the task. Most can be subdivided into successive approximations of the final goal by identifying the chain of behaviors that are necessary to complete the exposure. For example, exposures involving proximity to an object can be broken down by the distance from the feared object (e.g., 10 feet, 5 feet, 1 foot, encounter). Table 6–1 shows an example of how an exposure culminating in having blood drawn can be arranged into subtasks. Each subtask represents a mini-exposure that patients master before moving to the next one.

Other exposures may need to be broken down by allowing patients knowingly to use avoidant or escape strategies initially (e.g., distraction, brief escape, wearing protective clothing, or allowing the presence of safety cues), and then gradually remove those aids. This procedure may be necessary for all-or-nothing exposures where patients have to confront the object or situation fully. For example, a patient faced with driving over a feared bridge may begin by driving over quickly, in a "safe" lane, and without looking below. Each of these safety measures would be removed during successive exposures. In cases where patients have to handle the phobic object or situation (e.g., insect or animal phobias), they may begin by wearing protective clothing such as gloves and then eventually abandon them. Patients are usually the best source for identifying what "crutch" will be most helpful. The goal is to get patients started successfully, then gradually exchange avoidant for more proactive coping as they gain familiarity and confidence.

Table 6-1: An Example of Exposure Subtasks
Example: having blood drawn

Step 1: Sitting in a chair with a needle and other equipment on an adjacent table.
Step 2: Inspecting the needle.
Step 3: Having the needle lay on the patient's arm.
Step 4: Having the needle point rest against the patient's arm.
Step 5: Having the needle penetrate the patient's skin.
Step 6: Having the blood drawn.

KEY CONCEPTS AND CLINICAL CONSIDERATIONS FOR ACCOMPLISHING GOAL #2—CONDUCTING AN EXPOSURE IN VIVO

After identifying fearful and alternative predictions and a plan of action, patients begin the exposure proper.

Therapist Modeling

The therapist models each or all of the steps of the exposure prior to having the patient do them. Adaptive coping actions are demonstrated in detailed fashion. During modeling, therapists are advised to "think aloud," voicing patients' most likely anxious concerns, then demonstrate managing them. It helps patients immensely when therapists recognize and model managing vulnerable moments, where patients are likely to be challenged by fears and revert to avoidant methods of coping.

Clinical Vignette

During today's exposure, Bob tackles the task rehearsed last session involving standing next to the railing of a balcony located on the second floor of the therapist's office. Bob's exposure has been broken down into the following behavioral subtasks:

1. Walk within three feet of the balcony rail.
2. Stand next to the balcony without holding onto the rail.
3. Test the sturdiness of the rail by shaking it.
4. If the railing proves sturdy, look over it to the parking lot below.
5. Bob has also indicated that looking toward the sky, giving him no frame of reference for judging how high he is, sometimes provokes his fears. His 5th subtask is to do that and cope with the feelings it produces.

Bob's therapist demonstrates all of these subgoals before Bob tries them. They could also be taken one at a time, if desired.

Therapist: [thinking aloud while modeling the behavioral subtasks] Okay, Bob, before I start, I want to get my mind on accomplishing my first goal. I'm talking to myself in an encouraging and positive way. I'm saying things such as, "I can do this." I recognize that I might have some strong anxiety while I do this. If I do, I have a plan for coping with it. If it comes, I'm going to stop, regroup, and then go on at my pace.

Now, as I walk towards the railing, I'm going to stop 2 to 3 feet from it as we planned. I'm using this opportunity to practice coping. As I expected, I can feel my legs starting to get weak as I see that I'm above the ground, but I can deal with this. I'm going to relax and control my breathing. I'm saying to myself, "I'm doing fine." My nervous feelings aren't gone, but I'm okay enough to go on.

Now watch this, Bob. To test my fear and prove to myself that my legs aren't so weak and that I can't keep my balance, I'm going to lean one way and then the other [demonstrates being able to maintain balance]. It makes me feel better when I show myself this. In this way, I'm challenging my fears, and proving again to myself that my fearful feelings are not to be trusted. I can do this.

Okay, now I'm ready to approach the railing. As I approach, I can feel the false alarm getting stronger. I can still feel it in my legs. It seems to get stronger when I look down and I realize how high I am. My Tape 1 is saying "Oh no, what am I doing? I can't do this." That makes me frightened. But I'm going to stop and regroup, hang in there, and continue to look down while I talk to myself, relax, and do my paced breathing. Bob, what is it you wanted to say to yourself when you're in this situation?

Bob: "You're okay, you can do this."

Therapist: Good. When I'm feeling the false alarm this strongly, sometimes those thoughts aren't so believable. But they don't need to be. I'm just sticking to my plan and coping, even through I'm not completely confident. I'll just wait until I feel more comfortable. As I do so, I'm going to say to myself, "Stay here and ride this wave out. Don't fight it. Let it pass." You see?

Bob: Yes.

Therapist: As I stay here I'm feeling more confident that it's okay. Again, just to show myself that even though I'm feeling unsteady I can still maintain my balance, I'm going to shift my weight back and forth a little bit. I might even bend my knees some [demonstrates maintaining balance].

Okay, now it's time to test this railing. As you can see, I'm going to get my balance set just in case the railing isn't sturdy. Thinking about that makes me nervous, but I'm simply taking a reasonable precaution. Okay, as I shake it cautiously, it seems solid. So now I want to get in a position where I can shake this railing more vigorously and give it a good test [demonstrates shaking the railing]. It feels very solid. I was a little nervous doing that, but I feel better seeing how solid that railing really is. Again I'm proving to myself that my fears aren't happening.

My next goal now is to put my hands on top of the railing, lean my head over, and look down at the parking lot. As I get ready to do this, I realize that my false alarm is likely to get stronger, because this is a challenge for me. So I stop and regroup—do my breathing and tell myself, "I can do this." I want to get myself ready, so I can stay focused on remaining in that position, and give any anxiety I feel time to pass [demonstrates looking over railing]. Okay, right when I started, I felt a wave of flight or fight feelings. Again, I felt the feeling in my legs. My heart is beating very rapidly, too. I'm starting to get scared. Tape 1 is running. I want to quit. So I thought-stop, by yelling inside my head, "Wait!" Now I begin talking to myself, saying "You're okay. Just stay here. Give it time to pass. You're doing fine." Now, Bob, I'm going to stay here as long as it takes for my anxiety to settle and for me to feel like I'm ready to go on. For the sake of demonstration, though, I'm going to go on now. But if that takes 5 minutes or 30, you want to try to stay there until you're ready to move to the next goal. Although, if you feel you need to take a break, that's all right.

Bob: Okay.

Therapist: Now, the last thing that we've planned is to look up into the sky. I'm going to put my hand up to block my vision of the foreground, to see if that makes my alarm ring. If it does, I'm going to stay in that position and continue to look that way [demonstrates that action]. Okay, it did trigger the alarm, not as bad as I thought, but I can feel my heart racing. I felt a little wave of unsteadiness, too. So I'm going to stand here, breathe through my stomach, relax, and talk to myself. In fact, as you'll notice, while I'm standing here I'm going to stretch a little, tighten some tense muscles and then loosen them, breathe through my stomach and relax. I'm thinking that even though I've been anxious, I've been able to manage this situation so far. In fact, I'm doing well.

Now, after my anxiety comes down and before leaving, I'm going to repeat some of the things I've done previously. For example, I might shake the rail again. I may lean over and look straight down again. Or I may look up into the sky again [demonstrates each of those actions]. If any of those things make my alarm ring again, I'm going to stay with them until I've ridden out my anxiety and feel more confident that I'm safe and can do them. That's what I'd like you to do too, Bob, before leaving any exposure. Give yourself enough time to go back and do things repeatedly until you're comfortable with them.

Bob: All right.

Therapist: Now let's have you give it a try.

After the modeling demonstration, the patient conducts the exposure with the assistance of the therapist. Patients are reassured that they can take the exposure at their own pace and that they have the final say regarding what is done, including stopping the exposure if they desire. As the therapist did previously, patients think aloud while proceeding through the exposure. Periodically, SUDs ratings are elicited by the therapist to track the patients anxiety level. Although SUDs ratings help therapists monitor patients' anxiety, they should be used to provide the patient feedback. That feedback can demonstrate, for example, that anxiety wanes during sessions, that the patient can indeed function at high levels of anxiety, and that exposure becomes more manageable and less distressing as it is repeated. In this sense, SUDs ratings can take on a therapeutic function.

Initially, the therapist's style is reassuring and supportive, as well as directive and instructional, if necessary. If modeling needs to be repeated, it is. Therapists wean direct assistance as patients progress through exposures allowing patients to attribute successes to themselves. Therapists also remain keen to those factors that increase patients' anxiety during the exposure (as reflected in their verbal or nonverbal behavior). Those factors are likely phobic cues that should become a target of this or a subsequent exposure. Conversely, an unexpected absence of anxiety may signal some form of subtle avoidance. Throughout the exposure, therapists teach patients to identify these factors, face fears, and cope. Social reinforcement in the form of sincere praise and encouragement is given as patients try new ways of managing feared situations. Again, the overriding goal is to make this first exposure a success upon which patients can build.

The therapist accompanies Bob throughout this first exposure providing assistance, support, and reassurance.[1]

Therapist: Before we begin, Bob, what's your SUDs level?

Bob: Four. Higher than I thought it would be.

Therapist: Are you ready to begin or do you want to relax some?

Bob: No, let's do it.

Therapist: Good, let's start.

Bob: [beginning the first subgoal] So I should talk during this thing?

Therapist: Yes, let me know what's going on with you as we do this.

Bob: [walks to within a few feet of the railing] Okay, I'm doing alright. I'm going to stop here.

Therapist: What's your SUDs, Bob?

Bob: Four still.

Therapist: Tell me how you're doing.

Bob: Breathing. Tape 1 is going, though.

Therapist: Okay. What do you want to try to do?

Bob: Wait. [after some time] Okay. I'm ready.

Therapist: Your SUDs?

Bob: Three.

Therapist: Okay, Bob, before we move from here to the rail, I've noticed that you haven't looked out into the parking lot. That's probably a subtle way you're avoiding feeling anxious. Since we want to challenge and overcome this thing at each step, why don't you try that and manage any feelings it brings. You go when you're ready.

Bob: Okay. [looks at the parking lot] That makes me a little nervous. I'm starting to feel a little weak. I don't think I'm ready to go up to the railing yet.

Therapist: That's okay. What's your SUDs?

Bob: Four again, maybe 5. It's not really going down. It's getting a little stronger.

---

1. Bob finds that although he thought this task would be a low-fear exposure, it is not. This scenario has been created primarily for demonstration purposes. When exposure tasks are gradated in the manner described previously, initial exposures are often uneventful. Instead of depicting that, we have chosen to depict an unexpectedly fearful encounter, which is more challenging for the patient and therapist alike.

Therapist: Okay, that's normal, Bob, let's focus. What's your plan for coping with these feelings?

Bob: Um, I forget. Um, I'm starting to get pretty nervous.

Therapist: Okay, Bob, listen to me. You can do this. Are you on Tape 1?

Bob: Yeah.

Therapist: How do we want to try to stop Tape 1?

Bob: Yelling, "Shut up." But maybe I should do that silently so those people in the parking lot won't be offended.

The humor helps break some of Bob's anxiety. The therapist recognizes that it may be a helpful coping tool for him. In this situation, it serves to stop his fearful train of thought.

Therapist: That was great, Bob. You used your sense of humor to help you stop Tape 1. Now, after you've stopped it, what do you do?

Bob: [taking a deep breath, then beginning his diaphragmatic breathing skill] I'm going to be all right.

Therapist: Good. I noticed you took a deep breath. Are you doing your stomach breathing and relaxation, too?

Bob: I am. I'm starting to feel a little bit better. It was just that first wave, you know.

Therapist: Yes, I know. You're doing fine. You've already done Goal 1 and you did a good job of coping with that initial rush of feelings. Those initial rushes are common and difficult. You'll get better and better with them as you practice. It seems you're standing very still right now.

Bob: Yeah, I kind of feel unsteady. I guess stiffening up is a habit.

Therapist: Do you want to move a little bit to show yourself that this feeling doesn't mean you're actually weak and will lose your balance?

Bob: Yeah. When I saw you doing that, I thought that might be a good thing for me to do too [shifts his weight demonstrating that he can maintain his balance] Yeah, that helps. It does make me feel a little bit stronger. I'm feeling a little more confident.

Therapist: Good. It seems that doing the thought stopping, regrouping, and then showing yourself that you're not unsteady helps you.

Bob: Yeah, it does.

Therapist: Well, why don't we do that as we proceed to this second goal?

Bob: Okay.

Therapist: What's your SUDs level now Bob?

Bob: One or 2.

Therapist: Notice how your anxiety always comes down eventually when you stay and cope?

Bob: Yep.

Therapist: Most times fear and doubt are strongest at the start of the exposure and become better as you continue to face them. Are you about ready to go to the railing?

Bob: Yeah, let's do it.

As Bob nears the railing, he begins averting his attention away from the parking lot again. This seems to be an habitual way Bob subtly avoids. The therapist allows this so that Bob can position himself next to the railing. After Bob is set, though, the therapist will point it out and help Bob to manage his reaction to reengaging his attention on the phobic cue.

Bob: Okay, I'm here.

Therapist: How are you feeling?

Bob: Not as nervous as I thought [probably due to the subtle avoidance].

Therapist: Well, you're doing fine. You're right up here next to the railing. Are you feeling relaxed?

Bob: Mostly. The stomach breathing helps, so does shifting my weight. It helps me feel steadier.

Therapist: Good. Now I'd like you to try another thing at each step: ask yourself if you're avoiding subtly. Are you?

Bob: Hmm . . . no, I don't think so. I'm here next to the rail. I'm not holding on to it.

Therapist: You're right about not avoiding in those ways. I noticed that you're not looking down. Is that avoidance?

Bob: Hmm, that's true, isn't it. I guess it's a habit—you know, "Don't look down!" But it's avoidance, isn't it?

Therapist: Unfortunately, I think it is.

Bob: I don't know if I can just stop it.

Therapist: Well, it may take some time. Let's just try to pick up on it, change it when you're ready, and then cope—to show yourself that you can. You want to try it now?

Bob: All right.

Therapist: Okay, in just a second I'd like you to move your attention toward the parking lot again. Now, as you do that, what do you think is going to happen [facilitating predictability and planning]?

Bob: Well, I think I'm probably going to get nervous [making darting eye movements toward the parking lot].

Therapist: Right, so what's the plan?

Bob: Stop. Regroup. Give it time to pass.

Therapist: Good, I know you can do this, Bob. Let's try it.

Bob: [looking at the parking lot] Well, I can feel it, but it's not as bad as I thought.

Therapist: What's your SUDs?

Bob: Three.

Therapist: All right. How do you think you're doing?

Bob: I'm doing pretty well—relaxing—talking to myself.

Therapist: What are you finding out?

Bob: I'm steadier than I thought I would be. Even though I still feel a little weird, moving around kind of helps.

Therapist: You want to move around some more?

Bob: Yeah [shifts weight, demonstrating his steadiness].

After some time, the therapist continues.

Therapist: What's your SUDs rating now, Bob?

Bob: It's down to a 1 or 2, pretty quickly too.

Therapist: Are you ready to try the next step?

Bob: Yeah, this isn't as bad as I thought it would be since I already saw you shake the rail.

Therapist: Okay.

Bob: [positions himself, grabs hold of the rail, and shakes it cautiously].

Therapist: What are you finding out?

Bob: It seems sturdy.

Therapist: You don't sound too convinced. What's your SUDs?

Bob: Well, maybe a 4.

Therapist: All right. How can you give this a good test, Bob—to prove that it's either sturdy or it's not?

Bob: Get myself set and give it a good shake [shaking the rail more strongly]. Yeah, it's solid.

Therapist: What's your SUDs rating now, Bob?

Bob: It's coming down, a 3 or 2.

Therapist: Great. That's exactly what you want to do to challenge your fears. It's difficult, I know. But, you're doing it. . . . Okay, Bob, are you ready to go on to the next step?

Bob: I'm a little scared about doing this one. I'm still getting a flash like, "What if that railing breaks while I'm looking over it?"

Therapist: All right. It sounds like Tape 1 is going again.

Bob: Yeah, it is. But what if it does break?

Therapist: Bob, as you just did, can you test this fear?

Bob: Yeah, I did. I shook the rail.

Therapist: Is it sturdy?

Bob: Yeah.

Therapist: Are you sure?

Bob: Let me do it some more.

Therapist: Yes. Do it as many times as you need to.

Bob: [shaking the railing vigorously] It's not moving at all [shakes railing again]. That does help. I shook the hell out of that thing, and it didn't budge.

Therapist: Good. How are you feeling about it breaking now?

Bob: Better, but I'm still a little nervous about this next one. What if I flip over it?

Therapist: Okay. Do you see how you're fearful predictions are coming up like you thought they would?

Bob: Yeah.

Therapist: Remember what we know: "Just because they're here doesn't mean they're true." How can you prove this to yourself in a safe way?

Bob: Just take it easy, I guess. Look slowly, until I'm used to it.

Therapist: Good. And how are you going to cope with the feelings you get when you look over it?

Bob: I'm going to stop and regroup and give it time to pass.

Therapist: And that's what you've been able to do so far. Remember that you always have the option to stop and pull back if you want to. But how about trying to cope with this one the way you coped with the other ones?

Bob: Okay, I'm ready. [steadies himself, places his hands on the rail, and looks over the side] Whoa, I can feel it.

Therapist: What's your SUDs Bob?

Bob: [very tense] Five or 6. It's bad.

Therapist: All right, hang in there. How do you want to cope, Bob?

Bob: [does not answer]

Therapist: Bob, do you need to thought stop?

Bob: Yeah, I'm not thinking straight. I can't . . . um . . . I don't want to look [looks away from the ground, but remains motionless in fear, breathing rapidly].

Therapist: Okay, Bob, listen to me. Let's cope. You want to take that deep breath that helped you earlier?

Bob: [breathes deeply, exhales slowly, and begins paced breathing]

Therapist: Good, you're doing it.

Bob: I am, aren't I?

Therapist: Yes, you are. Let's focus on doing your breathing, on coping.

Bob: [stays in this position, breathing diaphragmatically, while his therapist waits for signs that he is calming] Boy, that was tough.

Therapist: Are you feeling calmer?

Bob: Yeah. It was that initial wave again.

Therapist: Yeah, that was a big one, but you hung in there and rode it out. Good job.

Bob: Thanks.

Therapist: What helped you ride it out?

Bob: Just focusing on coping, and not giving in to it.

Therapist: As you're finding out, sometimes when the wave is strong it's best to just focus intently on coping, stay in the moment, and wait for it to pass.

Bob: Yeah, I felt kind of frozen until I started focusing on coping.

Therapist: What's your SUDs rating now?

Bob: I'm at about a 2 now. I'm reverberating [laughs].

Therapist: Well, you don't look any worse for the wear. Was this too much too soon?

Bob: No, I guess not. It was hard, but I actually feel better, like I've done something.

Therapist: You want to try it some more, until it's easier?

Bob: Yeah.

Bob completes this and the final subgoal of the exposure. Over the remainder of the session, he repeats the entire sequence with less therapist assistance once more, does one exposure coach-assisted, then completes one unassisted.

The Therapeutic Coach

After patients demonstrate some comfort in managing an initial exposure, attention can be turned to helping coaches understand their role in the process.

To facilitate communication between patients and their coaches, it is helpful to establish a few guidelines. First, the exposure should be taken at the patient's pace. In other words, patients do exposure to accomplish their goals at their pace, while coaches support and assist them. This guideline is designed not to discourage coaches from offering unsolicited support and assistance, but to afford patients a sense of controllability. Stylistically, coaches are urged to use questions as their primary means for assisting patients when assistance is unsolicited (e.g., "How would you like me to help you here?" or "Do you want to take a deep breath?"). In addition, since coaches are partially dependent on patients' directions, patients are asked to communicate their wants honestly, directly, and politely. Patients should not expect their coaches to know when and how to assist. That can cause miscommunication and make situations more difficult. Finally, patients and coaches are urged to review their plans for accomplishing an exposure together, anticipating where they may need to help each other.

A formidable challenge therapeutic coaches often face is dealing with the patient's distress. Patients undergoing exposure may cry, panic, or even get angry at times. It will usually be a coach's impulse to want to reduce that distress immediately, often by inadvertently facilitating some form of escape. While discussing the guidelines for coaches' behavior, therapists may therefore want to pay particular attention to helping coaches develop a plan for managing these moments therapeutically (also see Managing Moments of Strong Fear in this chapter).

Paradoxically, it can be distressing for some patients to watch coaches model a feared activity. To patients, it may seem just as likely for feared consequences to happen to coaches as to themselves. In this sense, patients simultaneously undergo an exposure of their own while watching coaches model a feared activity. If distress seems likely, patients are helped to expect some anxiety during coach modeling, resist the urge to ask coaches to stop, cope with those fears as they would any other fears, and focus on learning the modeled behavior. Likewise, coaches are asked to demonstrate adaptive, nonavoidant behavior while remaining sensitive to the patients' fears.

Therapists can help coaches develop these and other specific skills by using modeling and instruction during these initial therapist-assisted exposures. Eventually, as with the therapist, the coach's assistance should be weaned as patients gain more confidence handling the feared object or situation themselves.

Clinical Vignette

Bob's spouse and coach, Lucy, models the exposure, while the therapist facilitates.

Therapist: Okay, Lucy, why don't you demonstrate the exposure to Bob. I'm going to jump in and out as you two proceed.

Lucy: Okay, Bob, I'm going to walk up here within a few feet of the railing.

Therapist: Bob, let us know what you're feeling as Lucy does this.

Bob: Okay, I'm a little nervous, watching.

Therapist: All right, do you feel you're managing those concerns okay?

Bob: Yeah.

Therapist: Good.

Lucy: Okay, Bob, I'm going to walk up over here by the railing. I'm not feeling nervous or anything. Actually, the view is kind of nice from up here.

Bob: Lucy, just be careful, will ya?

Lucy: I'm all right, Bob. Now I'm going to shake the rail and make sure it's sturdy like you did.

Therapist: Good. You two just did some very helpful things that I'd like to point out. Lucy, as you're seeing, Bob's likely to feel concerned as you demonstrate exposures. He may say things like he just did. And Bob, even though you may want Lucy to quit and can stop the exposure if you want, our goal is to have her continue while you focus on watching and manage your own concerns. You were doing that when you expressed your concern, but didn't ask her to stop. It was also helpful, Lucy, when you showed Bob that you were steady, feeling okay, and that the situation wasn't as dangerous as it might appear to him.

Lucy: Should I reassure Bob as I do things?

Therapist: Good question. It probably has helped Bob this first session to hear that you're confident and capable.

Bob: It has.

Therapist: Eventually, Bob, we want to get to the place where you don't feel a need to be reassured as often as you may now—where your fears aren't so strong. We've also talked about practicing your coping skills. When reassurance eases your concerns, you don't get to practice reassuring yourself. So, what about setting it up as we do with avoidance or escape? Lucy can demonstrate the activity, without reassuring you. If you feel you need reassurance, Bob, you can always seek it. But let's set the goal of not seeking it right away, and rather trying to ease those concerns by reassuring yourself—managing it the way you always manage Tape 1.

Bob: So should I just quit asking her to be careful and stuff?

Therapist: What do you think would help you most to develop your coping skills in managing Tape 1, to stop cold turkey or ease away from seeking reassurance?

Bob: I think I should just try to stop.

Therapist: Okay, let's try it. If you find yourself doing it a lot, let's just bring it back to your next session, and we can work it out.

Bob: Good.

Therapist: Lucy, are you ready to go on?

Lucy: Yeah. Bob, look. I'm going to see if the railing is sturdy [shakes the railing vigorously to show that it's sturdy]. And now I'm going to put my hands on the railing and look over the side. I can see how this would make someone nervous, if you thought this wasn't sturdy. But it is.

Therapist: Yes. Lucy, you're doing wonderfully. I like the way you're telling Bob what you're doing and feeling. Bob, how are you with this?

Bob: Okay, a little nervous, but it kind of helps to hear what Lucy thinks when she's doing these things. I can feel my fear jump around a little, but I can handle it.

After Lucy demonstrates the exposure, she and Bob do it together. The therapist continues to encourage a simple, straightforward, and direct style of communication between the two.

Therapist: When you two do exposures together, another option you have is for Lucy to do the first step followed by you, Bob. Take it step by step. Let's talk about how you two can communicate with each other during exposures to help them go smoothly and avoid misunderstandings.

Bob: Well, one of the things that helped me during the last exposure was to do thought stopping and take a big deep breath to get focused. Maybe Lucy could help remind me to do that like you did if I get too caught up in it.

Therapist: Sure, that's fine. So how are you going to let Lucy know when to do that?

Bob: She'll know. She can read me well.

Therapist: Well, she probably can, Bob, but this can be confusing. We don't want to set this up where either of you has to read the other's mind. Do you see how that could cause a lot of miscommunication?

Lucy: I can, because it's not always easy for me to tell what Bob's thinking or feeling, when he's nervous. It doesn't always show.

Bob: That's probably true.

Therapist: So can we agree that if you need Lucy's assistance Bob, that you try to let her know that?

Bob: Okay.

Therapist: It will help if you two can do that in the simplest, most direct, and polite way, which isn't always easy when you're anxious, even though you're a polite guy, Bob. For example, you might simply say, "Lucy, would you stand next to me when we do this or that?" or, if you can anticipate it, "Lucy, this may be a difficult one. Can you be ready to do this or that when we start?"

Bob: We just need to keep talking, let each other know what's going on.

Therapist: Yes. And Lucy, if you think Bob needs some assistance or if you're not sure, you should just ask him directly. For example, you might ask, "Bob, do you need to thought stop?" Or you could ask, "Bob, do you need to take a deep breath?"

Lucy: Okay, like you did when he didn't answer you?

Therapist: Yes, that's an example.

Lucy: You said it might be helpful if Bob and I discuss beforehand what kind of help he's probably going to want. That way we can be prepared.

Therapist: Yes, I think you'll find that helps a lot. As you've seen today, Bob, you're a pretty good judge of what's likely to happen, when Tape 1 isn't talking.

Bob: Yeah, I'd like to erase that damn Tape 1.

Therapist: You're on your way to it. I know this all seems a bit awkward and stilted at this point. But as you two practice exposures, it will become easier and more comfortable. If problems arise, let's bring them back here next session and work them out. Are you ready to practice again?

Bob & Lucy: Sure.

Managing Moments of Strong Fear

Some of the most therapeutic exposures are those in which patients feel they have truly challenged their fears; however, these are often the ones that involve moments of strong fear. Coping with these moments can be particularly challenging to patients and coaches. Therefore, they should receive some special attention before exposure is attempted without a therapist's assistance.

Sometimes moments of high fear can be predicted. For example, they are most common at the start of an encounter or during one if a particularly feared cue arises. Accordingly, patient and coach are asked to review the plan for each exposure together, discussing where these particular challenges are likely and how they plan to cope. But they can also come unexpectedly, requiring some preplanning for those moments as well.

When patients truly engage a phobic cue, they can show it in ways ranging from stunned silence to an emotional outburst. Physical sensations usually surge strongly. The patient's self-talk often reflects intense fearful ruminations (e.g., "Oh my, oh my," "I can't do it," or "I gotta get out of here"). It is often intensely frightening. To avoid confusion, the coping plan for these moments is the same as that used for any challenge. It involves thought stopping, coping self-statements, diaphragmatic breathing, relaxation, or other coping strategies (e.g., applied tension in blood, injection, and injury phobia). As with other fearful moments, patients are encouraged to focus on the present, here-and-now demands of managing their own fear. During very intense fear, patients should be prepared to use their coping strategies in a repetitive, almost ritualistic, way initially until the experience becomes more manageable. If coaches are assisting, they may have to reassure and remind patients how to cope in simple, straightforward language, sometimes modeling coping techniques until patients have regained control.

Patients should expect to have a strong initial urge to escape. They will be inclined to avert their attention or otherwise evade the fearful elements of the situation. Although they may have to do this initially, their goal is to try eventually to attend to what frightens them while coping simultaneously. As the encounter unfolds, they should try to look for evidence that, although they are very fearful at that time, they are not in danger and are managing the challenge.

As discussed previously, it is not necessary to create high-fear moments throughout therapy for patients to benefit from exposure. A gradual approach is preferred and just as effective. But be prepared to manage strong surges of fear. As patients progress through therapy, these moments become inevitable. Curiously, some patients will express a desire to create them, often later in therapy, to prove to themselves that they can manage. Others may not wish them, but find them occurring anyway. The outcome of these encounters can be pivotal to therapeutic progress. Preparation improves the likelihood that they will facilitate progress. Those triumphs are some of the most therapeutic that patients will experience.

KEY CONCEPTS AND CLINICAL CONSIDERATIONS FOR ACCOMPLISHING GOAL #3—REVIEWING THE EXPOSURE

After each exposure, patients return to the Exposure Record Form to record the experience while it is still fresh. One line of review questions asks patients to indicate whether fearful or alternative predictions were supported by the experiential evidence gathered. Completion of the prediction testing process is important because it forces patients to consider the evidence that disconfirms their fearful predictions, discouraging them from the common inclination to dismiss or qualify those data. They get to see that many of their fearful predictions, regardless of their apparent veracity, either did not occur as feared or were more manageable than imagined.

During the review, patients also are asked to indicate which coping techniques they found helpful. That information can help refine those strategies for future use. If patients use a coping card or similar resource, it can be revised accordingly. Patients also are asked to indicate whether they used any avoidant coping strategies, where and why the strategies were used, and how they would like to meet those challenges differently next time.

Having patients complete the Exposure Record Form facilitates next session's review, and is a first step toward helping patients develop the skill of reviewing and learning from exposure experiences themselves.

Clinical Vignette

Bob is shown the value of the review in helping him to learn from exposure and plan future ones.

Therapist: [using the Exposure Record Form] Okay, Bob, when you're done with an exposure, it's very important to finish completing this Exposure Record Form. I'd like you to bring these completed forms to the session so we can go over them. Let's go through the form as we did last time and fill it out for the exposures you did today. Bob, here's a prediction that the railing was going to be unsturdy. What did you find out during the exposure?

Bob: It definitely was not.

Therapist: Okay, then let's just indicate that here on the form [Bob does so]. Here's another prediction that you were going to get unsteady and flip over or collapse and fall through the railing.

Bob: Obviously, that didn't happen either. In fact, none of these things happened.

Therapist: True, but as we discussed, it will really help to go through each one as we're doing now. One reason for that is what you're experiencing now: it helps us to get this message over and over—that the fears either don't happen or are more manageable than Tape 1 would have you believe.

Bob: That's true; it does give me a better feeling. But I also feel kind of stupid now, just for thinking these things.

Therapist: I understand. But that may be part of letting go of these fears. Maybe you have to feel stupid to start questioning these things.

Bob: Yeah, it kind of makes me mad that they can get to me so much.

Therapist: Can you use that frustration to help you challenge your fears, to give you strength to resist being persuaded by them as you continue with exposure?

Bob: I've done that before. Got so mad that I just did it.

Therapist: That's a source of strength that you can channel. Of course, we're not talking about getting so mad that you do foolish things. We try to use it to help us face and challenge fears.

Bob: You think that will ever sink in to where I don't have to work so hard at it?

Therapist: I know it's frustrating that it doesn't change right away. How do you think you can help it to become more believable?

Bob: I guess keep doing this.

Therapist: Yes. It'll come. You've gotten a good start today. Going through this review and thinking about what you're learning from the exposure helps, too. Let's go ahead and go through the rest of these questions and see how that works. . . . Here's a question: "What coping strategies were most helpful?" What did you find helpful?

Bob: Well, I was kind of surprised. I thought a lot of the self-talk would help and it does. But when I was really nervous, just taking a deep breath and trying to stop everything for a second was best. Almost not try to think—just wait, then cope.

Therapist: Good, then let's make some changes to your coping strategy so that it works better that way. How would you do it differently?

Bob and his therapist modify his coping strategy.

Therapist: Let's see, what about, "What were your biggest challenges during the exposure?" What do you think?

Bob: Well, when I looked over the railing or started stuff.

Therapist: Yes, those definitely made your alarm ring.

Bob: Yeah, it seemed to go off right when I started to do whatever it was that I had to do, whether it was step up to the rail, look over it, or whatever.

Therapist: You've found that when you begin whatever it is you have to do, that's the most challenging point. After you cleared that hurdle, your feelings were more manageable?

Bob: Yeah, that's what happened. The worst was getting started, then it was easier.

Therapist: Bob, that's like a law of exposure—the anticipation and the beginning of the exposure are often its biggest challenges. It's something that you can expect and be ready for each time. Why do you think it would be worse right before the exposure than later in it?

Bob: I don't know, except that maybe I'm expecting the worst. Once I'm actually there, I just do it.

Therapist: Yeah, it ends up not being as bad as the anticipation. Alfred Hitchcock once said, "There's no terror in a bang, it's the anticipation of it." Does that make sense to you?

Bob: Definitely. It's easy to expect the worst, but once you get there it's different. And you just deal with it.

Therapist: I think you're starting some positive changes, Bob.

Bob: I hope so.

Therapist: Bob, this question on the form asks whether you found yourself avoiding subtly. Do you remember using subtle avoidance as a way of coping during the exposure?

Bob: Well, you pointed out that I was looking away sometimes. I can see that I do that a lot.

Therapist: That's true. It is a subtle form of avoidance that you have a habit of using. I thought you did a good job of trying that this session, then coping using your strategies. Do you think you can work at catching that habit yourself when you do exposures in the future?

Bob: Yeah. This could be something Lucy and I can kind of work on, couldn't it?

Therapist: Yes, definitely. Let's discuss how you two can do that with this habit and some others you might find yourself doing.

SELF-THERAPY EXERCISE

At the conclusion of this session, patients are asked to repeat this particular exposure between sessions until they feel comfortable with it. They also select like-rated and more challenging exposures to complete between sessions.

Considerations to help increase compliance with those exposures are:

1. If possible, have patients schedule the exposures ahead of time. For example, while the patient is in session, identify dates and times that they can complete exposure exercises and then write them down for the patient to take home.
2. Ask patients to describe briefly which exposures they have selected and, in general, how they intend to conduct them. This allows the therapist to identify any likely obstacles to compliance.
3. If the exposures are coach-assisted, involve the coach in the scheduling process. Making a social commitment like this to the coach can help increase compliance with the exercises.
4. Ask the patient to leave a message on your answering machine after the exercise, letting you know how it went.
5. Supply and encourage the use of the Exposure Record Forms.

The next session should be scheduled to allow patients enough time to complete their scheduled exposures.

7

Treatment Session 6—
Encouraging Change

SESSION OUTLINE

During this session, patients' self-therapy exposure exercises are reviewed with the aim of encouraging therapeutic progress while identifying and overcoming obstacles to it. From this review, specific self-therapy exposure exercises are created and scheduled.

SESSION GOALS

While reviewing recent exposures, therapists work toward the following goals:

1. Facilitating compliance with specific guidelines for exposure;
2. Identifying and encouraging adaptive versus avoidant coping;
3. Continuing patient education;
4. Problem-solving potential obstacles to therapeutic progress;
5. Creating self-therapy exercises that address identified problems and encourage advancement through the Fear and Avoidance Hierarchy.

Patients are much more likely to meet these goals when they use the Exposure Record Form to guide them through exposure exercises. Unless patients cannot use the form, completed forms are reviewed during this session. If completed forms are unavailable, therapists get this same information through discussion with the patient and coach.

KEY CONCEPTS AND CLINICAL CONSIDERATIONS FOR ACCOMPLISHING GOAL #1—FACILITATING COMPLIANCE WITH EXPOSURE GUIDELINES

While reviewing recent exposures, therapists work to maximize the benefits gained from them. Much of that effort involves helping patients to conduct exposures within guidelines discussed previously. Key considerations include whether patients are testing predictions, preparing appropriately for exposures, coping adaptively, and conducting exposures in ways that encourage fear reduction and an increasing sense of mastery. Reducing avoidance behavior, another key guideline, is discussed separately in the next section.

Are exposures serving to test fearful predictions?

The ideal outcomes here are that patients are laying out fearful and alternative predictions prior to exposure, conducting exposures in ways that test predictions, and showing signs that their fears are being disconfirmed. Common obstacles to these outcomes include the incorrect use of the prediction testing procedure and failure of the procedure to disconfirm fears due to several potential obstacles.

When problems with prediction testing are due to patients' misunderstanding of how to identify predictions, sensitive and corrective feedback and practice often solve this problem. When noncompliance is the issue, therapists reemphasize the importance of prediction testing, but then follow up with measures that facilitate adherence to the prediction testing procedure. Examples include using memory prompts such as an instruction card, enlisting the help of the therapeutic coach, or other methods that simplify the recording process, such as using a dictating machine, small cassette recorder, or making common predictions a permanent part of the form, as discussed previously.

If patients demonstrate noncompliance with the formal prediction testing procedure, but seem to be improving anyway, then there may be no need to push the formal recording procedure. However, if patients are suffering from their noncompliance, efforts designed to facilitate compliance should be tested (for more on facilitating compliance see Problem 7 under Overcoming Potential Obstacles in this chapter and Facilitating Treatment Compliance in Chapter 10).

Sometimes the prediction testing procedure is being done correctly, but fails to weaken fears. In addressing this problem it is important to note, first, that at one level prediction testing attempts to change inductive processes. Whether fully cognizant of the process or not, patients gather experiential evidence about the actual likelihood of feared events and their own ability to managing feared encounters. Each exposure that disconfirms fearful predictions is an instance from which patients can draw the generalization that future encounters are also likely to be less threatening and patients themselves more capable than the patients' fears would have them believe. Looking for obstacles to this process helps focus the therapist's intervention.

Several obstacles can emerge. One is the presence of safety signals and other avoidant coping strategies to which patients may attribute the successful outcome of exposures at the expense of developing self-efficacy. Reducing avoidant safety-seeking is discussed further in the next section. Another obstacle occurs when exposures do not test predictions adequately. For example, the patient fearful of collapsing may not collapse during an exposure, but may not have experienced fear at an intensity sufficient to test their fear convincingly. If the untested fearful prediction can be identified, then a more convincing test of it is created. When the specific fearful predictions cannot be identified or a specific convincing test created, therapists must rely on a more broad-based approach to exposure with the hope that operative fears will be reduced (i.e., a shotgun approach). Other patients cannot overcome what might be considered a pessimistic version of "lottery logic." This is the notion that the more I play (do exposure), the better my chance of winning (experiencing the feared outcome). Of course, this ignores probability theory, but that point alone may mean nothing to the fearful patient. Repeated exposure may eventually dispute the validity of this belief. Finally, some patients are not easily persuaded by experiences that disconfirm the biases in their inductive reasoning. As some have said, "Just because it [the feared outcome] hasn't happened, doesn't mean it won't." Many patients will voice this belief early in exposure therapy, but shift positions or become less concerned by this fact through repeated successful exposures. When repeated exposure fails to dispel fearful thoughts, though, therapists have few options but to help patients tolerate the probabilistic nature of catastrophic outcomes, as they do in other areas of their lives where those types of outcomes can occur. Absolute certainty of complete safety from the improbable catastrophes of life is unattainable. Helping patients gain comfort with that uncertainty becomes the goal. Attaining that acceptance is made more likely when patients develop stronger personal efficacy in managing challenges. And thus, even with this most challenging of obstacles, encouraging repeated exposure is a fundamental part of the continuing treatment plan.

Clinical Vignette

Bob knows his fearful predictions well, but expresses difficulty generating alternative, nonfear-based predictions prior to new exposures. The therapist intervenes by reviewing its rationale and then providing a simplified version of the procedure.

Therapist: On your form, Bob, you noted that you're having trouble developing alternative predictions for your exposures.

Bob: Yeah, I've found that I'm not exactly sure what I'm doing there.

Therapist: Well, let me go over the general idea and then we can talk about a straightforward way to do it. The idea here, Bob, is that fearful Tape 1 predictions often overestimate the likelihood of the bad stuff. For example, before your exposure to the balcony some of your fearful predictions were that you could fall over the railing, fall through it, or somehow lose your balance and suffer a bad consequence. These are overestimates, because when you compare them to what has actually happened in your own experience, they haven't occurred. Even though they're frightening and at times very believable, they are remote and unlikely. So one of the steps in identifying an alternative prediction is to take those overestimations out and replace them with more objective guesses. So ask yourself, "Are these the most likely things to happen, and if not, what is?" To help you answer that, look at what has happened in similar situations before or, if you haven't had a previous experience, what typically happens to others in this situation. When you ask it that way, you can see that falling isn't the most likely thing to happen. "What does usually happen" should be the alternative prediction. Sometimes it's difficult to come up with this alternative because it doesn't seem convincing. It doesn't have to be. Go for accuracy. Be objective. Like if you were telling someone else what the most likely thing is to happen. Confidence in your alternative will come with repeated exposure. So Step One is to ask, "What is the most likely outcome of this exposure?"

The other part of alternative predictions is to include how you plan to cope. This is different from Tape 1 predictions that paint us as helpless victims, incapable of dealing with the catastrophic event we fear. You want to rehearse how you're actually going to try to manage the challenges of the exposure. And usually this means thinking about how you want to use your coping strategies. So, Step Two is to rehearse how you intend to cope.

Bob: Well, I think I'm doing this, but don't really understand exactly how to go about it. This seems more straightforward. So I ask, "What are the most likely things and how am I going to cope?"

Therapist: That's it in a nutshell, Bob. The idea is that if the worst isn't going to happen and I'm not completely helpless, then what is likely to happen and how am I going to manage it?

Bob: What happens if my fear is the most likely thing to happen?

Therapist: Good question. Like what, for example?

Bob: Well, like being embarrassed if I'm with other people.

Therapist: Okay, Bob, in that situation if we use the formula we've talked about, the first step is to ask objectively, "Is this the most likely thing to occur?" Sometimes we think that we're going to be embarrassed and, in actuality, that's not the most likely event. But if it is likely, and sometimes embarrassment can happen, then we still go to the second step and talk about how we're going to cope with that. When we're fearful, we often believe that feeling embarrassed is something that we couldn't bear. So treat that fearful question, "What if I get embarrassed," as a serious question. Let's practice. How actually would you try to handle it if someone made fun of you because you were showing your anxiety?

Bob: Well, my first thought is that I'd probably be mad.

Therapist: Why?

Bob: Well, I wouldn't treat somebody else like that if they were nervous.

Therapist: Yes, that's what seems very likely to me, too. So how would you try specifically to handle that person?

Bob: Well, I guess I'd probably try to ignore them or maybe say something like, "Why don't you go make fun of someone else?"

Therapist: You know, it may not be pleasant, but that's probably the way it would come down—not catastrophic, not pleasant, but manageable. So when the fearful prediction is the most likely outcome, then you still think about how you're actually going to cope with it.

You can do this even if a fearful prediction isn't likely, Bob—like when it's just bothering you or won't go away. Just treat it like a serious question, and review how you would try to cope if something like the worst case was beginning to happen. Some people end up feeling like, "Well, that's all I could do" or "So what, I'll just deal with it" after reviewing it like this. It helps put it in perspective. But then your alternative prediction should concern itself with what is most likely; and your plan for conducting the exposure should too.

Bob: All right, I think I got it now.

Therapist: Good. We can practice in a second. But let me say one more thing about fear of embarrassment, Bob, because it may come up again. When you fear embarrassment, it's important to go through the process of asking yourself whether it really is the most likely thing to happen. A lot of times people can't tell others are anxious. Even if you get anxious, no one may notice. Plus, when people see us frightened, they're often more likely to be sympathetic than negatively judgmental. Those that do make fun of us usually arouse our anger, not our fears. But if you think that it's likely that you'll be embarrassed, then see if it helps to treat it as we've discussed—as a serious question and ask yourself how you want to cope if something like that begins to happen. Let's go through a few examples of the exposures that you did until you feel comfortable with identifying these alternative predictions.

Are patients formulating a plan of action for exposure?

Patients learned to lay out a plan for proceeding with each exposure prior to conducting it. During the review of exposures, therapists should assess how patients are doing with this.

If patients are not complying with this guideline to their detriment, then compliance might be improved through some of the same methods described above for facilitating compliance with prediction testing. Those include recording the plan on a card or audiotape, or involving the coach in the process. If necessary, the therapist and patient can lay out the behavioral goals of upcoming exposures during the preceding session until the patient can do this unassisted. As with formal prediction testing, if patients demonstrate repeated noncompliance over a few sessions but are improving anyway, then compromise may be the best course. Fortunately, most patients rapidly develop the ability to formulate a plan for exposures once they are faced with doing them, and appreciate the benefit of doing so.

Clinical Vignette

Bob's exposures involve a routine plan with which he has grown familiar. The therapist reinforces its use.

Therapist: Bob, before you get into an exposure, are you thinking about how you're going to proceed? You know, laying out a plan of action?

Bob: Yeah, in general, I am. It's pretty much the same for each exposure.

Therapist: How so?

Bob: Well, it's like I was saying, I usually know what parts of the exposure are going to be hard. So I break them down in ways that let me do them one at a time. That way I can think about how I'm going to handle them. Handling them is pretty much the same though. You know—breathing, talk myself through.

Therapist: How does this differ from the way you used to approach these situations?

Bob: Oh, it's very different. I didn't use to think about how I was going to deal with it, other than to hope that I didn't lose it. I might have planned how to get out of there, if things began to look bad.

Therapist: So do planning and rehearsing what you want to do help?

Bob: Oh yeah, they help.

Therapist: Good, I think you've made a very positive change here, one that you want to try to keep doing.

Are coping strategies being done correctly and used appropriately?

Patients are asked to demonstrate their coping strategies if a misunderstanding of how to do them is suspected. Problems are corrected on the spot.

The appropriate use of coping strategies refers to managing fearful thinking and bodily sensations of fear in an effort to accomplish the behavioral goals of the exposure. As discussed previously, patients may inappropriately attempt to use the coping strategies as a means to avoid feared sensations. This problem is suspected when patients describe using their coping strategies to fight or block anxious feelings. Interoceptive techniques can be used to address fears of sensations. Options include doing formal sensation induction exercises as described in Chapter 5 or, preferably, intentionally inducing and recovering from feared sensation during object or situational exposures. Again, a graduated approach may be necessary under these circumstances.

As discussed previously, patients are discouraged from expecting that their coping strategies will stop sensations. They are urged instead to expect some level of fear, and to try to ride it out while focusing on accomplishing the present exposure task. It is expected that patients will need some time until they feel comfortable doing this. So, therapists usually allow patients to overfocus on managing sensations early in therapy, and then gently encourage them away from that and toward mastering the encounter as therapy progresses. Most patients can make this transition after a few successful exposures. Those who remain fearful and overfocused on feared sensations may benefit from the more direct interoceptive interventions recommended.

Clinical Vignette

Bob has found that the feeling of "weakness" he gets in his legs provokes a fear of collapsing. Although Bob's coping strategies help manage the sensation, shifting his weight has proved more reassuring, probably because it helps confirm the fear-countering belief that his balance is intact and controllable. The therapist checks to see if an interoceptive exposure adjunct may help, but finds that Bob is unable to induce fear of the sensation apart from the phobic situation. Therefore, the therapist encourages continued situational exposure.

Therapist: Bob, you've said that the sensations you feel in your legs frightens you most. How are you doing with it?

Bob: Better. Even though I know it's coming, it still bothers me at first.

Therapist: What specifically are you doing to help you overcome your fear of it?

Bob: Well, usually I'm taking my deep breath and just riding it out, but it helps a lot to move around, you know, test my balance a little bit. Sometimes when I get that feeling, I feel like I'm actually losing my balance, like when I feel I'm being pulled over the edge. But when I move around a little bit and see that I'm okay, I feel better. It also helped to read that it's part of the flight or fight reaction—that it might be because I'm so tense in the situation. That lets me know to relax a little. So I do.

Therapist: It sounds as if you've come up with an approach that's working well for you. I think with continued exposure we can expect to see that feeling fade, as well as your concern about it. I was wondering, though, were there any exercises that you did during your self-therapy last week that created that weak feeling in your legs?

Bob: No, it only comes when I'm in a high situation.

Therapist: So our only opportunity to practice overcoming it is in that situation.

Bob: Yeah, it seems so.

Therapist: Well, it seems to me that you're doing a good job with it. I like the idea that you're moving around. That shows that you're starting to challenge your fear of that feeling rather than trying to leave the situation or sit down. Do you think that's helping?

Bob: Yeah, I'm getting better at believing that it will be all right. I'm expecting it now, too, so it's not a surprise. That helps.

Therapist: Great. Let's look at another challenge. What if weakness occurs in a situation where you can't move around, like when you're walking up a ladder? How do you think you'll handle that situation?

Bob: Yeah, I've been thinking about that. My thought was that if I need to stop and try to regroup I will. I think what I'll probably do is stop, then just try to keep going a step at a time, when I'm ready. If I stop too long, I might get caught up in it.

Therapist: That sounds like a good plan, Bob. So take it at your pace, but try to keep going?

Bob: Yeah.

Are exposures long enough to optimize their therapeutic benefit?

One of the most important guidelines for exposure is that patients stay for a duration sufficient to test their fears, experience some fear reduction, and gain a sense of control, predictability, and mastery in managing the encounter. Although fear reduction per se is a goal of any particular exposure, it is too restrictive to use as a sole index for judging the success of an exposure. In part, that is because fear reduction can result from a therapeutic gain or from safety-seeking actions of one form or another. Therefore, it is necessary to assess *how* patients are achieving fear reduction, and if it seems related to overcoming fear rather than dodging it.

The Exposure Record Form provides information useful in assessing how fear reduction is achieved during an exposure such as anxiety ratings, the duration of the exposure, why the exposure ended, and how patients faced challenges. Discussion of those data can help determine whether a patient is staying and benefiting or escaping. If patients show a propensity to escape, subtly or obviously, then the fear prompting escape is identified. If possible, that fear is then made an explicit target of future exposures. Those exposures may need to be gradated, or even therapist-assisted, if they seem excessively challenging. For example, a patient fearful of enclosed places may be showing fear reduction during exposure because they are adept at distracting themselves from the situation. They may need to go back into a larger area, with the goal of attending to its fearful features and coping with their reactions until they become more comfortable. Other considerations for managing problems related to within-session fear reduction are discussed in the sections Overcoming Potential Obstacles and Avoidant versus Adaptive Coping later in this chapter.

Are exposures frequent enough to optimize their therapeutic benefit?

For the same reasons patients are asked to do prolonged exposures, they are asked to do exposures to the same object or situation repeatedly. The conventional method for assessing between-session fear reduction is to track, at least, the patient's rating of "highest anxiety" across exposures. Exposures are repeated until those ratings wane. As mentioned above, therapists should also be sensitive to how that fear reduction is being achieved and, in particular, to whether patients are developing a pattern of subtle avoidance.

Typically, therapists have to be persistent in encouraging repeated exposure. The most common reasons why patients do not return to an exposure are that they have mastered it quickly, are avoiding it, misunderstand the importance of repeated exposure, or find it impractical. Therapists will need to sort through these possibilities to determine the appropriate focus of their intervention. Considerations and specific strategies for overcoming obstacles related to between-session fear reduction are discussed further in Overcoming Potential Obstacles later in this chapter.

Clinical Vignette

Bob did not repeat this exposure frequently enough to maximize its therapeutic benefit. Although aware that this may represent avoidance, Bob's therapist treats it for now as the misunderstanding Bob portrays it to be. Bob's repeated noncompliance may indicate a different intervention. That question will be revisited if the present plan fails.

Therapist: Bob, I notice that you did the exposure to sitting on your roof only a few times. I was wondering why you didn't do it more frequently?

Bob: There was no need to. I was doing fine with it.

Therapist: All right, but fine in what sense?

Bob: Well, my anxiety went away fairly quickly both times.

Therapist: Good. Yes, from your Exposure Record Form, it looks as if your highest anxiety was up around a four and went to a one during the first exposure. The second time was the same—a four that went to a one. You're saying that it went to one more quickly the second time?

Bob: Yeah, the second time it dropped quicker—like after a few minutes.

Therapist: That's good. It's nice when the length of time the alarm is on gets shorter. Why do you think it was shorter the second time?

Bob: I'm not sure, maybe because I'd done it before.

Therapist: That's likely, the more you do it the better it will get. You know one of our goals is that you feel more confident about your ability to do the exposure. Do you feel that way about climbing the ladder and getting on your roof?

Bob: Yeah, I guess. It's not as bad as some of the other exposures I'm going to be doing.

Therapist: Well, I think it's a good sign that your fear came down more quickly during the second exposure. But I'm concerned that you haven't repeated this exposure frequently enough to build some real confidence in doing it, confidence that you could take to other, more challenging exposures later.

Bob: Well, we said that I should expect some nervousness in some situations. Couldn't this be one of them?

Therapist: Yes, that's a good point. Some situations will be like that, as we've said. I'm just not so sure we can tell yet whether this is one of them. How might we tell when you've done this enough?

Bob: I don't know.

Therapist: Well, let's look at how uncomfortable you were at the beginning of each of them. In both exposures, your highest SUDs rating was four. Since both times were a four, we can't really tell if the four level is what this situation will always be. It might get lower. The only way to really know is to do it again, enough times to see where it levels off. For example, if you did it 3 more times and went to a two and stayed there a few times, then that may be as low as it's going to go. At that level you may feel that you really have a handle on this situation, whereas now it's a four. But we don't know about this one yet, because you've only done it twice.

Bob: I see. So I need to do these things a lot—until I'm comfortable.

Therapist: I think it will help you get closer to your goals. What do you say that if you have the opportunity, then try to take it? If you can, try to create it, by giving yourself a long enough time to do the exposures over and over, including even going back later, maybe another day, to do it some more. Does that seem possible?

Bob: Yeah, I don't think I understood that, but now I do.

Therapist: Can you foresee anything that would prevent you from doing this?

Bob: No, not really. I've just got to make more time.

Therapist: Is that possible?

Bob: Yeah.

Therapist: Okay. If you run into an obstacle, even if it's that you've become reluctant, I hope you'll bring that back to the session so we can work it out.

Placing an emphasis on compliance with the guidelines for exposure throughout the educational, preparatory, and early exposure phases of the therapy can help circumvent many of these problems. It is not unusual (and always nice) when this review requires therapists to do little more than praise patients for work well done.

KEY CONCEPTS AND CLINICAL CONSIDERATIONS FOR ACCOMPLISHING GOAL #2—ENCOURAGING ADAPTIVE VERSUS AVOIDANT COPING

While reviewing completed exposures, therapists help patients identify and replace safety-seeking with coping that encourages personal efficacy in managing encounters. To the extent that safety signals and other avoidant coping methods are present during exposures, patients' success can become contingent on them, particularly if that success is attributed to those factors. Patients reliant on safety-seeking are at risk for setbacks when those means for coping are blocked or otherwise unavailable.

A recent study demonstrated this process in patients whose agoraphobic avoidance was treated successfully with combinations of exposure plus placebo or exposure plus an active medication (Basoglu et al. 1994). After eight weeks of exposure, all pills, active or not, were discontinued. Patients were monitored to see who maintained their gains or began relapsing. These investigators found that patients who had more strongly attributed their therapeutic gains during exposure to their pills than to themselves were more likely to relapse. Thus, the continued success of patients who attributed gains to pills, active or inactive, appeared contingent on the presence of those pills. After those pills were discontinued, patients were more likely to relapse. Although it may not be the sole determinant of long-term recovery, patients who believe that they possess within themselves effective means for overcoming fears are more likely to maintain their gains unassisted. Therefore, it is important for therapist to identify and minimize reliance on factors to which patients can attribute their success at the expense of personal efficacy. Those factors include the presence of safety signals, protective measures, other subtle avoidant coping strategies, and even medication (see Chapter 10).

When avoidance is identified, therapists and patients develop a plan to remove it, gradually or otherwise, during subsequent exposures. One thing this does is create an explicit test of whether the avoidant coping strategy is instrumental in the patient's success. Even if safety-seeking actions are not tested explicitly, though, the process of identifying and removing them increases the likelihood that patients will develop their own skills for mastering phobic encounters and attribute successes to these efforts. Of course, removing avoidance may increase discomfort temporarily. Therefore, means for managing it (e.g., reviewing coping, therapist or coach assistance) should be considered.

In sessions to come, one subtle safety cue that is intentionally removed is the formal practice of rehearsing exposures that had been encouraged throughout the initial stage of therapy. As discussed previously, rehearsal is important early in therapy as patients attempt to acquire new ways of managing phobic encounters and resist their well-entrenched avoidant methods. However, unexpected (i.e., unrehearsed) encounters with phobic objects and situations can occur during or after treatment and be high-risk times for setbacks. Therefore, as patients show evidence of success and express some degree of readiness, they should attempt some spontaneous exposures. Planning spontaneity (not really an oxymoron) can be done in a few ways. For example, patients can schedule a time for exposure, but not be informed of what it will entail until immediately before conducting it. The therapeutic coach, a phone call, or a note that patients agree not to read until the time of the exercise can communicate the nature of the exposure. As always, graduating these tasks should be considered.

Clinical Vignette

In this exchange, the therapist enlists Lucy's aid in helping Bob overcome his tendency to avoid subtly by diverting his attention.

Therapist: Bob, one of the ways in which you're prone to avoid subtly is by looking away from the ground or otherwise diverting your attention from the things that trigger your fear alarm during exposure. Do you remember?

Bob: Yeah, we picked up on it when I did the exposure here at your office.

Therapist: Right. We set the goal of trying to look at those things and cope with whatever feelings you have when you do that. How have you been doing with that?

Bob: You know, I really forgot about that. I'm not sure whether I'm still doing it or not.

Lucy: I noticed that he does that during the exposures that we've done together. I didn't know if I should say anything about it because I thought he may need to do it for a while until he gets more comfortable.

Therapist: That's a good observation, Lucy. It may help if you two work together on this goal since, Bob, you're so used to it and have a hard time recognizing it, while Lucy sees it easily. What do you think about making that a part of each exposure?

Bob: That will probably help. I think it's just a habit I've developed.

Lucy: I might be wrong, but I think Bob might have a hard time changing it. He does it whenever he gets close to a drop-off.

Therapist: I think you're right, Lucy. This is probably going to be challenging. We're going to need to pay special attention to it. Bob, how do you want Lucy to point this out during exposures?

Bob: Just say when I'm doing it.

Therapist: Can I suggest also that, since Lucy might be able to predict when it's likely to happen, she and you try to identify it before it does? Then you can get a jump on it before it does you.

Bob: Okay, that makes sense. So you want me to try to catch it. But if I don't, then Lucy will point it out?

Therapist: Yes. Lucy, are you comfortable with that?

Lucy: Yeah, I think I can do that.

Therapist: Good, let's go with that plan. Why don't we write this goal on the Exposure Record Forms, so it's right there in front of you when you get to the exposure.

Bob: That's a good idea, 'cause I'll forget.

Therapist: Bob, we can expect that you might get a stronger alarm reaction when you start looking toward the ground. How do you want to manage that?

Bob: The same way I've been doing it, I guess. If I know ahead of time, I can probably get calmed down and ready before I do it. If not, I'll just do my best.

Therapist: Why don't we practice this now in imagination, using an exposure that you're going to be doing in the weeks to come.

Bob and Lucy: Okay.

Another safety cue that should be targeted for eventual removal is the presence of the therapeutic coach. The therapist discovers that Bob has already been doing this and has some understanding of why it is important. The therapist also checks to see if Bob is forgoing Lucy's assistance because he fears watching her do the exposures (a form of avoidance).

Therapist: Bob, have you tried exposures where Lucy doesn't accompany you?

Bob: Yeah, there are times when she can't come with me, so I just do them by myself. Same thing at work, you know, she's not there.

Lucy: Also, when I'm there, I might stay with Bob when we first start the exposure, but then later he always does them by himself.

Therapist: That's great. Bob, you seem to appreciate the importance of trying to do these things by yourself as you get more comfortable.

Bob: Well, I'm going to have to do them by myself eventually, aren't't I?

Therapist: Yeah, in a nutshell, that's it. Lucy, how has Bob seemed when he's watching you do exposures?

Lucy: Well, at first he was kind of a pain—always telling me to watch out for this or that. But we talked about it, and I think he's gotten better at not worrying so much. I think he sees that I'm all right now.

Therapist: Bob, how do you feel you're coming with that?

Bob: I think a lot better. I know we said I wasn't going to do that, but I just felt Lucy was going to lose it somehow or another, kind of like I do with myself. But she's pretty good at it, so I'm not as worried as I used to be.

KEY CONCEPTS AND CLINICAL CONSIDERATIONS FOR ACCOMPLISHING GOAL #3—CONTINUING PATIENT EDUCATION

As in every session, the therapist attempts to advance the patient's understanding of the phobia, its maintenance, and treatment. Although it may seem redundant to revisit educational concepts, doing so is natural and can help consolidate patients' learning. As patients progress in therapy and shift from an abstract to an experiential understanding of its principles and practices, they often better appreciate them and are more likely to retain them permanently. In this sense, education can facilitate longer-term recovery. Since these concepts have been presented and reviewed previously, they will not be again here.

KEY CONCEPTS AND CLINICAL CONSIDERATIONS FOR ACCOMPLISHING GOAL #4— PROBLEM-SOLVING POTENTIAL OBSTACLES

Therapists spend much of this and later sessions problem-solving potential obstacles to therapeutic change. To the degree that patients can also learn this skill, they improve their chances of overcoming potential setbacks after therapy. Since much of the remainder of therapy involves problem-solving, problems commonly encountered during exposure therapy and considerations for overcoming them, drawn from material presented thus far, are presented in this section.

Problem-solving is the primary therapeutic intervention used to address potential obstacles. Table 7–1 outlines the primary procedural steps to problem-solving.

Addressing Common Problems

The problems below are presented in a format that invites readers to entertain their own considerations for addressing each problem before proceeding to the ones suggested.

Problem 1: "My anxiety isn't coming down during exposures."

This very common concern can be thought of as a failure to attain fear reduction within the session, discussed previously. There are a few possibilities to consider:

First, the duration of exposure may not be long enough. Scheduling more time for exposure or changing to a less feared situation, if time is limited, may help.

Second, exposures may be too infrequent. Some exposures by their nature are short in duration (e.g., driving across a feared bridge), so increasing their duration is not an option. In those cases, scheduling enough time to allow repeated exposures should be considered. Over time, anxiety during the exposure should decrease.

Third, it is possible that patients are leaving the exposure too soon. If so, this may reflect the patient's misunderstanding of that guideline, and suggests a brief educational intervention. More often, it reflects escape behavior. In escape, patients often use their feelings of

Table 7-1: Problem-Solving Procedures

Problem solving is the conventional therapeutic intervention for address-ing obstacles to progress. Its primary procedural steps are:

1. *Define the problem*
Some problems are identified by therapists who observe impediments to the patient's progress. Others come in the form of questions or concerns expressed by the patient. Identified problems should be defined specifi-cally and operationally (i.e., translated into specific, doable, and mea-surable actions). For example, a problem introduced as, "my exposure is not working well" may end up being redefined as "my anxiety is not com-ing down during the exposure session." Asking patients for examples of their problems can help specify and operationalize their definitions.

2. *Formulate working hypotheses based on the therapeutic model*
This step involves developing likely reasons why the obstacle is present. For example, the obstacle may represent a situation where the patient is not in compliance with a guideline for exposure, is subtly avoiding, or holding unrealistic expectations about the nature of therapeutic change. Multiple hypotheses should be generated.

3. *Choose a hypothesis and generate a plan for overcoming the obstacle*
From the working hypotheses developed in Step 2, choose the formulation that is best supported and plan a specific strategy for overcoming the obstacle. For example, if it is hypothesized that the presence of a safety cue, such as a therapeutic coach, is an obstacle to the patient's develop-ment of confidence, then an indicated plan would involve gradually remov-ing the therapeutic coach during subsequent exposure exercises. Plans may involve multiple goals, such as patient education, cognitive restructur-ing, or skills development. They may be delivered didactically or, prefera-bly, in the form of a performance-based self-therapy exercise. It is important to consider plans with which the patient is most likely to comply.

4. *Enact the chosen plan*

5. *Reevaluate the plan*
After the plan has been implemented as intended and given sufficient time to work, it should be reevaluated. If it has been ineffective, then other formulations and plans should be tested.

surging fear as a signal to stop the exposure rather than focusing on behavioral goals designed to keep them in the situation. As indicated previously, the general therapeutic plan for overcoming escape should involve the following primary steps:

1. Try to identify fears prompting the escape.
2. Develop an exposure exercise that tests the fears. If the fears cannot be identified, encourage patients to set behavioral goals that keep them in the presence of the phobic object or situation, managing its challenges until their anxiety wanes and confidence grows.
3. Develop a coping plan for managing those challenges that encourages mastery of the exposure task.

Therapists can supplement this intervention with education, cognitive restructuring, or coping skills training as necessary. The therapist may have to join the patient on these exposures if they continue to be an obstacle.

Fourth and finally, the anxiety the patient reports may be appropriate to the situation. Sometimes anxiety decreases across repeated exposure, but does not go away completely. Patients may describe this as a failure of exposure to decrease anxiety. If so, they may be holding the unrealistic expectation that exposure will *eliminate* discomfort. In that case, therapists should reemphasize that some level of anxiety is appropriate to that particular experience. Rather than trying to eliminate it, patients are helped to accept those feelings as a natural part of the encounter.

Problem 2: "I did well during my initial exposures, but got very anxious during later ones."

This concern arises frequently, but is a natural part of the therapeutic change process. It relates to the course of between-session fear reduction discussed previously. There are several considerations in addressing it:

First, although anxiety reduction is the eventual goal of treatment, it is not likely to occur in a linear fashion from exposure to exposure. One reason for this is that any of a multitude of factors that can increase the fearfulness of an encounter may have been absent from an early exposure, then present during a subsequent one. This should be expected as exposures become more challenging. It can also occur unexpectedly, though. For example, a feared animal might be more active during a subsequent exposure; a storm may have contained stronger winds. Patients should be helped to expect some unexpected feelings during exposures and encouraged to cope with them as practiced.

Second, it is possible that the patient has been using subtle avoidance sporadically, in this case perhaps during initial exposures but not subsequent ones. Consequently, the later exposures would be more difficult. An appropriate intervention would help patients to recognize the subtle avoidance, work to abandon it, and cope as planned with any temporary rise in anxiety.

Third, tantamount to those interventions is that patients are encouraged to adopt a bigger picture and more realistic expectations of the course of their improvement. Although they can expect a trend toward general improvement over the course of exposures, there may be ups and downs. It is often very effective to show patients their actual course of recovery by graphing data from their exposure records. It will usually reveal these ups and downs in the context of a trend toward improvement. Otherwise, this point can be made through other examples and reemphasized as continued exposure reveals it.

Fourth and finally, this concern suggests that patients may be defining success during exposures as the absence of anxiety, rather than the accomplishment of their behavioral goals. This tendency is common and understandable but counterproductive because, as discussed above, anxiety is likely to fluctuate from exposure to exposure even as patients improve. Those fluctuations can shake the confidence of patients who define success based on how much anxiety they experience. As urged throughout therapy, patients should be helped to focus on accomplishing their session-by-session behavioral goals of completing exposure tasks, developing adaptive coping strategies, and testing fears, rather than tracking whether exposure number three produced more or less anxiety than exposure number two. Even though it is often difficult for patients to believe early in therapy, their fear will decrease by focusing their efforts on behavioral goals.

Problem 3: "I didn't get anxious during the exposure."

This happens frequently in exposure therapy and may reflect positive change or a problem, depending on the following considerations:

First, if the exposure was not expected to elicit strong anxiety (e.g., if it is low on the Fear and Avoidance Hierarchy), then moving on to a more challenging exposure is indicated.

Second, sometimes a safety signal or some other form of subtle avoidance may be precluding exposure to the phobic cue. Common examples include the presence of the therapist, therapeutic coach, or medication. Identifying those and targeting them for removal, gradually or otherwise, is indicated.

Third, this concern suggests that patients may have been expecting, possibly overestimating, the likelihood that anxiety would be present—their anticipatory fears were strong, but the exposure itself was uneventful. If this seems to be the case, then it represents another piece of therapeutic evidence disconfirming patients' fearful predictions.

Problem 4: "I only do exposures on my 'good days.'"

This problem refers to some patients' tendency to conduct exposures only when they feel capable of accomplishing them. They usually do not recognize this as a problem, but it represents another form of subtle avoidance.

Although everyone can relate to having good and bad days, when patients use them to determine when they will do exposure, it reflects their fearful assumption that they will succeed only under certain circumstances. As with any safety signal, if that assumption remains unchallenged, then self-confidence gained through exposure will be conditional (i.e., if it's a good day, then I can do it; if not, I can't). As discussed, this leaves patients vulnerable to setbacks if, for example, they unexpectedly encounter the phobic object or situation on a bad day. Scheduling a series of exposures so that some are likely to fall on bad days or targeting exposures for the next bad day may help.

Problem 5: "I was confident before the exposure, but still felt very anxious when I did it."

This experience is more common later in the course of therapy, after patients have had some success with exposure, and can be disheartening to the patient who is trying to build confidence. In the language of the treatment model, the patient should be helped to recognize that their phobic fears have been strongly bound to the phobic cue and to a degree remain state dependent (i.e., called up more readily in an anxious than calm state). Sensing threat, feeling sensations of anxiety, and having the urge to flee can occur in an instant, outside of patients' awareness and despite the increasingly confident frame of mind with which the patient may be anticipating a phobic encounter.

As with Problem 2, patients should be helped to expect that their anxiety reaction can come on in this sudden and unexpected manner, even during the course of their general improvement. Although unexpected, its presence is as much a false alarm as when it is anticipated. Patients should plan to cope with these challenges as they would any expected fears.

Problem 6: "How come I can see my phobic fears are unrealistic, but still feel as if I'm back to square one during exposure?"

Although a common variation of the previous problem, it is slightly different, and can be quite demoralizing to patients, reducing their motivation and jeopardizing the treatment's credibility. As in Problem 5, these seemingly contradictory beliefs that patients show inside versus outside a phobic encounter reflect the state-dependent nature of the phobia. The gap between what patients know while outside the phobic situation and what they feel while inside it will take time and frequent exposure to close.

It helps to reassure patients that the disparity they feel is an expected part of the change process. Whether well informed or highly motivated, no one begins the process of overcoming fear with confidence that its outcome will be positive. Indeed, patients should expect *not* to feel confident during early exposures. They are more likely to feel as if they are faking it to a degree, acting as if the situation is safe and manageable during a time when they feel it is not. With repeated exposure, however, their once-intellectual appreciation of safety will become more convincing. Examples of how patients have overcome fears of other situations in their lives may help demonstrate these points, but repeated exposure will be needed to prove them.

Problem 7: "I didn't get around to doing my exposures."

Fear, poor time management, a change in motivation, or other factors can lead to noncompliance. As discussed in Chapter 6, there are several options for approaching noncompliance motivated by fear. The most common include starting with low-challenge exposures or using "crutches" initially. Measures such as scheduling a specific time for exposure, asking patients to commit to their therapeutic coach, or doing therapist-assisted exposure until compliance is established may initiate or reinitiate compliance. Making exposures high-priority items, making them more convenient, or tying them to routine activities may help as well. Operant strategies such as response costs, where a patient loses something of value (e.g., money, a privilege) if noncompliant, and positive reinforcement for completed exposures may help establish and maintain compliance; negotiating with patients what those costs and reinforcements will be is important. Finally, asking patients to recall what motivated them to enter treatment may reenergize those incentives. Issues related to facilitating treatment compliance are given special attention in Chapter 10.

Some patients, despite previous efforts and time invested, may be too frightened to begin exposure. Under those circumstances, medication assistance is an option. Options for managing medication within the context of exposure can be found in Chapter 10.

Finally, a small proportion of patients will not realize that they are unwilling to do exposure until faced with it. Alternative treatment options or termination, if desired by patients, should be considered. Therapist should help patients to adjust to this likely disappointment and facilitate their transition into whatever option they next chose. Patients may eventually want to return to exposure and should be given a standing invitation to do so.

Problem 8: "I've done exposure repeatedly, but I'm still not convinced that [my fears] aren't going to happen."

This concern, discussed previously in this chapter, is common to later therapy after patients have made progress but not to the degree they had hoped. Consider the following possibilities.

As indicated previously, therapists should rule out the hypothesis that avoidance is precluding fear reduction. If so, removing it and repeating exposures are indicated. A therapist should also consider the possibility that previous exposures were not valid tests of a patient's fears. Creating valid (usually more challenging) exposures is indicated. The primary goal of either of these interventions is that patients conduct exposures in ways that truly test their fears. As discussed previously, some of the most effective exposures are those wherein patients risk making themselves vulnerable to feared outcomes. It is not uncommon for patients who are struggling to have been doing exposure in ways that subtly circumvent challenging fears. These patients reach a pivotal point in their progress, where improvement stalls unless they can transition from doing exposures in a somewhat guarded, cautious, semi-safe manner to one that truly tests their fears. Until exposures take this form, therapists cannot know whether treatment has failed or been applied suboptimally. If therapists have difficulty in session identifying what kinds of experiences are likely to challenge patients' fears or what types of safety-seeking may be precluding that challenge, then they should accompany patients to a high-fear exposure, observe, and intervene accordingly.

If these options have been exhausted, therapists focus their efforts on helping patients refine their abilities to cope with encounters (i.e., overcome secondary fears of not being able to cope) while helping patients to tolerate the probabilistic nature of catastrophic outcomes, as discussed previously. The message here is that patients may not be able to eliminate their doubts about the feared outcome, but they can learn to tolerate and manage encounters that are necessary to function.

SELF-THERAPY EXERCISE

Throughout this session, therapists will have encouraged patients' therapeutic progress and problem-solved obstacles to it. The final step in this process is to develop exposure exercises that help accomplish goals identified during the session. As reviewed above, most of these exercises will aim to increase patients' compliance with the guidelines for exposure, remove another layer of subtle avoidance, and move up the hierarchy to more challenging exposures. These self-therapy exposures are best developed during the course of this session as part of a problem-solving plan or as the next step in building upon successes. It is recommended that the next session be scheduled some weeks from this one, allowing patients time to accumulate exposures and begin the process of separating from formal therapeutic contact. After addressing questions, the next session is scheduled.

8

Treatment Session 7— Maintaining Gains and Preventing Relapse

SESSION OUTLINE

As with all sessions later in therapy, patients' most recent exposure exercises are reviewed. While continuing to facilitate gains and problem-solve obstacles, therapists place increased emphasis on strategies designed to encourage the maintenance of those gains. As time permits, relapse prevention strategies are introduced as well. Self-therapy exercises that support these goals are scheduled at the conclusion of the session. Since this session addresses issues involving posttreatment recovery, patients may benefit from having all or part of it recorded on a card, audiotape, or videotape for later reference.

SESSION GOALS

1. To review previous exposures, emphasizing the maintenance of developing treatment gains, problem-solving obstacles, and fostering patients' personal efficacy.
2. To introduce relapse prevention strategies.

KEY CONCEPTS AND CLINICAL CONSIDERATIONS FOR ACCOMPLISHING GOAL #1—REVIEWING EXPOSURES

The general approach to reviewing patients' most recent exposure exercises is the same as the previous session. It involves encouraging patients' compliance with the guidelines for exposure, helping them exchange avoidant for nonavoidant coping strategies, and problem-solving obstacles to change with them. As patients show progress in these areas, they are encouraged to advance through the hierarchy to establish more firmly their new approach to feared encounters. Soon, they should begin targeting their most feared situations. Those efforts may require some initial assistance by the coach or therapist. Depending on the outcome of this review, interventions including education, cognitive restructuring, skills development, or the assignment of specific self-therapy exercises are conducted.

Fostering Independence

As the end of therapy draws nearer, increasing emphasis is placed on encouraging the development of patients' independence and personal efficacy in managing their recovery. To the extent that patients have been empowered with a model for understanding and overcoming their phobias, the groundwork for these changes has been laid. Moreover, to the degree that patients have been successful in shifting from a reliance on avoidant to more adaptive coping, the development of personal efficacy has been encouraged. As therapists see some evidence that patients are developing confidence in their new approach to phobic encounters and that it is resulting in effective gains, they should begin encouraging the patients' independence more directly.

Making this shift to independence requires patients, in a general sense, to take on the duties of the therapist. So far, however, patients have had to rely on the therapist's expertise in evaluating progress and problems and determining an appropriate course of action. To the degree that this endeavor has been collaborative, patients will be ready to take it on themselves. It helps, in judging patients' degree of readiness, to assess to what degree they can accomplish the following tasks by themselves:

1. recognizing and complying with the guidelines for exposure
2. recognizing and overcoming avoidant coping tendencies
3. problem-solving these and other obstacles to continued improvement

Formal or informal role reversal is a useful technique for both assessing and strengthening these skills. Regardless of the method used, however, patients are encouraged to take the lead in evaluating the plusses and minuses of their own progress and in developing appropriate next steps in their recovery.

Clinical Vignette

For the most part, Bob demonstrates the ability to recognize when he is in compliance with the guidelines for exposure. An informal role reversal helps him to see that his tendency not to do exposures repeatedly, identified last session, is a form of avoidance. That obstacle is then problem-solved.

Therapist: [while reviewing past exposures] Bob, you've spent a lot of time learning how to do exposures in ways to get the most out of them. In what ways have you been doing exposures within these guidelines that we've discussed?

Bob: Well, I'm staying in and riding out my anxiety. I'm not looking to escape as much as I used to.

Therapist: Good. How are you doing that?

Bob: Mostly talking myself through it. You know, telling myself that I'm going to be okay.

Therapist: So you're using your coping strategies to stay in the situation. It also seems as if you're giving yourself enough time to do this.

Bob: Yeah, I usually give myself at least an hour.

Therapist: How has staying in the situation helped you?

Bob: Well, I'm getting a little more confident that I can. I'm not as afraid of just losing it completely.

Therapist: So some of your big concerns aren't as strong as they used to be?

Bob: Yeah, it's coming along.

Therapist: So you're staying in the situation long enough, and finding some of your fears less believable. You're also using your coping strategies effectively—to help you do that.

Bob: Yes, I think I've gotten pretty good at those things.

Therapist: Is Tape 2 becoming more believable?

Bob: Yeah, I guess I'm not as afraid of falling, but I'm still not as confident as I'd like to be about how it's going to go.

Therapist: You still have strong concerns before you start exposures?

Bob: Yeah, at times.

Therapist: What do you think will help you build your confidence?

Bob: Time, I guess.

Therapist: Just time, you think?

Bob: Time and more experience.

Therapist: Do you feel as if you're repeating exposures enough to become more comfortable and confident in them?

Bob: Well, I don't know if I'm doing them a lot.

Therapist: Why, do you think, you're not repeating exposures the way we had planned?

Bob: I don't know. I do them. It's kind of like once I've done it a few times then . . . I don't know, you know, it's like it's over, you've done it, move on.

Therapist: Bob, let's switch places as we've done and let me ask you this: It's okay if I don't do more exposures, isn't it? It might rock the boat to do them again.

Bob: No, that's probably not good.

Therapist: Why do you say that?

Bob: It's avoiding, isn't it?

Therapist: Yeah, I'm glad you're recognizing it and being honest with yourself about it. I know it's difficult, but this is one of the few guidelines that you've had trouble with. And it's not just you. Everyone has to deal with this as they get closer to really facing their fears. It sounds as if you've been getting your feet wet, but you haven't been ready to swim.

Bob: Yeah, I have done some exposures a lot—the ones I do at work. But I might as well come clean here. It's the bad ones that I talk myself out of doing.

Therapist: What are you saying to yourself about why you shouldn't go back in again?

Bob: Well, it's like you said. I just feel like I'd be pushing my luck.

Therapist: So in the back of your mind you feel that the more you do it, the more likely it is that something bad's going to happen [lottery logic]?

Bob: Yeah, I guess. It doesn't make much sense, does it?

Therapist: Well, it's understandable even though it sounds like you recognize that if it was true, the more you played the lottery the more likely it would be that you would win.

Bob: Yeah, if only that were true. I guess it's just fear.

Therapist: Yes, it's Tape 1 again. Recognizing that is the first step. You seem to see what it is.

Bob: Yeah, but it's a lot easier to give good advice than to take it.

A common therapeutic stumbling block is identified in Bob's concern that he can give advice, but has difficulty taking it. Role reversal and other techniques can often help patients see what they need to do. Of course, doing it is another thing. The next step for patients is to translate their advice into specific self-therapy exercises, while being sensitive to barriers that could affect their compliance. This is a skill that will be important to their long-term recovery and worth taking time to develop.

Therapist: Yeah, that's true, Bob. A lot of times pretending that we're advising someone else helps us to see what might be best for us. And this is something you do very well. It's an ability that will help you long after therapy. You're also right in recognizing that after you've figured out what to do, the next question is how to do it. How should we proceed?

Bob: Well, I know that I just gotta do it. It's like I talk myself out of it, though. I put it off, or lie to myself that it's okay to quit.

Therapist: Okay, let's come up with a plan for tackling this, knowing that you're likely to try to talk yourself out of it again. Go with me here for a second. You're the therapist again.

Therapist: [acting as patient] I know I need to do this exposure some more, but my fear, my Tape 1, is going to try to talk me out of it.

Bob: [acting as therapist] Well, don't get into a debate with it. Just do it.

Therapist: But, what can I do to not listen to it and "just do" exposures repeatedly?

Bob: I don't know. Just set them up. Schedule them. Or give yourself time to do a bunch in one day—to try to get on a roll.

Therapist: Bob, you're not only good at giving advice, you're good at figuring out how to act on it. I would have said the same thing. What do you think?

Lucy: I can help him with this.

Therapist: How, Lucy?

Lucy: Well, I could watch the kids or get a babysitter if he needs me there. That would free up some time for him.

Therapist: Bob, what do you think?

Bob: Well, if I know that Lucy is bending over backwards to help, I feel some pressure to do this.

Therapist: Is that bad?

Bob: No, it's just realizing that I'm really going to have to do it. It's like, now I've really got to face it. I can't hide.

Therapist: Would anything else help you to go through with your plan besides Lucy's support and scheduling time for them?

Bob: I can't think of anything.

Therapist: Do you want me to join you, as we did earlier?

Bob: No, I think I can do it. Maybe if it doesn't work out, we can try it like when we started. But I think it's time to just do it.

Therapist: Okay. So you two give it a try. Then next session we can see how it's coming along and go from there.

Exposure, Exposure, Exposure

The most important activity patients can do to extend and maintain their gains is to continue exposure after acute treatment. Toward that end, patients have been discouraged from seeing acute treatment as terminal, as, for example, antibiotic therapy is for an infection. From the antibiotic model, acute treatment aims to eliminate the infection. It is a cure. When the cure is achieved, treatment is finished. From the first session, exposure therapy is described as an incremental change process that continues after acute treatment ends, becoming a permanent way to approach the phobic object and situation.

To facilitate this process, patients not only begin tackling their most feared objects or situations, but begin extending exposures beyond those areas that cause the most direct functional impairment. For example, it is not uncommon for patients, after making initial gains, to restrict their exposures only to the objects or situations that they are forced to encounter (e.g., an immunization, the elevator at work, the road to the grocery store). Of course, these types of exposures are not discouraged. However, going beyond them prevents gains from being restricted only to certain situations and is another step toward eliminating avoidance. This intervention involves asking patients to scheduling specific, out-of-the-ordinary exposures, as well as going a little out of their way to create exposures out of everyday opportunities that they may have passed up previously.

Clinical Vignette

Bob's therapist encourages him to take everyday opportunities to do exposures, and to extend exposures into areas where he is not required to do them. The importance of planning high-fear exposures beyond those at work is highlighted as well.

Therapist: Bob, in addition to doing exposures repeatedly, you've progressed to a point where we should begin working exposures into your everyday activities. This means taking everyday opportunities to go to high places, rather than pass them up.

Bob: I already do that. I have to do it as part of my job.

Therapist: Good. Then you're doing exposures to things that you have to do. Are you also going into high places that you really don't have to go?

Bob: Like what?

Therapist: Well, for example, you talked about that walkway near your office modules that overlooks the ground floor. You tackled that one some time ago. Do you walk *next* to that railing whenever possible?

Bob: Well, I walk down that aisleway, but I don't necessarily walk *next* to the railing.

Therapist: Well, that's one example of creating an opportunity to do an exposure as part of your everyday life. It might be something that you really don't think about, but if you walk nearer to the railing, it helps serve some of the purposes that your other exposures are serving.

Bob: Hmm, I never thought about that.

Therapist: Yes, it's about making opportunities, going a little out of your way to create everyday exposures. The more you do this, the more natural it will become for you. And this activity will help you make stronger and more enduring progress. This is true for things apart from work, too, like when you're out and about, or on vacation—things like that. It means just creating the opportunity to go into high places even if it's a little out of the way. Like taking the McCluggage Bridge (a high bridge Bob has avoided) to go to town rather than the easier ones.

Bob: It makes sense.

Therapist: This will be easy to forget, because it requires you to break your routine. How can we make this easier for you to do?

Lucy: I can remind him of some of those.

Therapist: Good, that will help when you're there, Lucy. Besides Lucy's help, what else might remind you, Bob, especially at work?

Bob: I could put a few little notes on my desk.

Therapist: Is your desk cleaner than mine, where you'll see the notes?

Bob: No offense, but yes. You know, when I need to remember to pick something up on my way home, I'll put a rubber band on my watchband. I always check my watch. So it's like a string on my finger, to remind me. Do you think that might help?

Therapist: Yes, I like the way you're thinking about this. I think that's a good idea. So, you want to try it?

Bob: Yeah.

Later in the session, the therapist discusses the importance of doing high-fear exposures.

Therapist: Bob, I see that you've begun doing exposures to the eights, nines, and tens at work. And our plan is to repeat them more frequently. Have you thought about eights, nines, and tens apart from work?

Bob: Well, we've been planning a trip down to St. Louis in a month or so. I thought I'd see if I felt like tackling some of the things that Lucy and the kids have always wanted to do, but that I've never done.

Therapist: That sounds like a good idea. What do you have in mind?

Bob: Well, they want to go to Six Flags [an amusement park]. They'll want to ride the ferris wheel. You know, it's the kind that's like a cage the whole family can sit in. I knew we'd be doing this eventually. That's why I put it on my list [hierarchy] when we began.

Therapist: Oh, that would be a particularly good exposure for you, partly because it's high and partly because the whole family would be there.

Bob: Tell me about it. I know they'll want to go up in the St. Louis Arch too, but I haven't decided about that yet.

Therapist: These sound like good, challenging exposures for you, Bob. And it doesn't take a trained therapist to see that you're hesitant.

Bob: Oh, yeah. In fact, up until today, I was kind of thinking about how I might get out of it some way or another.

Therapist: But now that's different?

Bob: Well, like we said a minute ago, it's time to do these things. If I can do the tough ones at work, these shouldn't be too bad, I hope.

Therapist: Up until now it sounds as if you haven't made a specific plan to do them. Is there a reason for not planning them?

Bob: No, I thought I'd decide when I got there.

Therapist: Bob, a little while ago, you were advising me that it's probably better to just schedule challenging exposures, rather than to wait and possibly get into a debate between Tape 2 and Tape 1. Do you want to take that back?

Bob: I knew you were going to say that.

Lucy: Well, Bob, you were saying the same thing the other day.

Bob: [joking] I know. Must have been a moment of weakness.

Therapist: It seems you've already seen the potential problem here.

Bob: Yeah, if I wait, Tape 1 is going to be playing at full volume. I know.

Therapist: Bob, it's up to you. You can see the plusses and minuses. What do you want to do?

Bob: Let's just set it up and do it. It'll be better for me to just set my mind to doing these things and stick with it. I work better that way.

Therapist: Bob, I think you're making some very tough but positive decisions today. And I know this is going to be a challenge for you. Hang in there. If you want you can give me a call anytime between now and next session, do that. Let's talk about how much time we'll need to give you before that next session.

KEY CONCEPTS AND CLINICAL CONSIDERATIONS FOR ACCOMPLISHING GOAL #2—PREVENTING RELAPSE

If time permits, therapists can introduce relapse prevention strategies this session. Concepts and considerations for preventing relapse are overviewed in Chapter 10 under Preventing Relapse.

An important first step in relapse prevention is defining relapse for patients and showing them how it differs from other setbacks that may occur during the natural course of their recovery. For example, patients often mistakenly believe that relapse occurs "all of a sudden" and out of their control. One day they are doing fine, then suddenly the phobia returns. Left unchallenged, that misconception can foster relapse by making any future setback seem like the reemergence of the entire phobia. Under those circumstances, patients may be more likely to give in to old phobic habits than attempt to over-come the setback.

Relapse is described as a shift back into the avoidance-based phobic cycle that characterized the patient's ways of handling phobic objects or situations prior to treatment. To help patients understand this, it may help to have them recall how avoidance dominated their approach to phobic objects or situations prior to treatment and contrast that to the way they approach those same situations now. Relapse is a return to those old ways, a return that requires patients to choose to begin avoiding again. Once relapse is defined with this emphasis on choosing to avoid, therapists can then discuss circumstances during which patients are vulnerable to making that choice. This approach reframes future challenges as potential obstacles to be overcome by patients rather than as a relapse overcoming them. Therapy is then spent planning how to manage those moments of vulnerability.

High-Risk Times

One set of circumstances during which patients are vulnerable to relapse includes times when they have a bad experience during a phobic encounter, a setback. A setback can involve a moment when patients experience unexpected fear, escape, or avoid an encounter after having not done so for a while. For example, one of the patient's previous fears may happen to some degree, such as being involved in an automobile accident, being scratched or bitten by a dog, or fainting during an injection. Setbacks are likely to occur when patients face objects or situations to which they were unable to do exposure during treatment. This is one reason why patients are encouraged to broaden exposures to many objects and situations before treatment ends. Setbacks, however, can occur in response to familiar objects or situations as well.

Overcoming setbacks ultimately involves continued reexposure to the phobic object or situation. Patients are encouraged to do this in the same way that they have overcome any setback or challenge during therapy, either by graduated exposure or, preferably, by returning to the scene of the setback. Either way, patients should begin reexposures as soon after a setback as possible, as it often becomes more difficult to do the longer they wait. If the setback occurs in response to an object or situation to which exposure is inconvenient (e.g., flying in an airplane), then patients are encouraged to approach that problem as they have other inconvenient exposures, by doing exposure in imagination, through simulation, or other means until the next opportunity arrives to do it in vivo.

Another high-risk time for relapse is when patients are feeling stressed. Stressors can include daily hassles, a physical illness, or a challenging life situation like a new job, a change in health status, or the death of a loved one. If an encounter with a previously feared object or situation occurs in the context of those stressors, it can easily be seen by patients as an overwhelming demand, the "straw that broke the camel's back." Although patients always have the option to avoid phobic encounters until stressful times have passed, they are encouraged not to do so. Instead, they are urged to focus their energies on managing the stressors themselves, while dealing with any phobic encounters as they have learned to do during treatment.

This approach does not usually necessitate giving patients a full course in stress management. Reviewing general approaches to managing stresses while discouraging avoidance is usually sufficient. Patients may have shown the ability to manage stressful challenges throughout their lives, and can be shown that those strengths are not likely to have changed. However, if patients have shown serious deficits managing stressors, then some form of adjunctive stress management training should be considered.

To help patients prepare for managing high-risk times, they and their therapists rehearse probable challenges and strategies for managing them. If possible, they start this exercise during this session. If not, this session's self-therapy exercise asks the patient to identify high-risk times for this purpose next session.

Insidious Avoidance

Although setbacks or stressors present challenges to long-term recovery, perhaps the most difficult form of relapse to prevent is the gradual and insidious slide back into avoidant behavior that occurs over time, not in response to any identifiable precipitant. Patients may tell themselves, for example, that "it's just not convenient for me to do this now," or "skipping one time won't hurt." Soon, avoidance becomes more pervasive and the vulnerability to relapse more likely, especially if unexpected encounters occur.

Effective relapse prevention sensitizes patients to these seemingly innocuous decisions. It urges them to routinely challenge any inkling of fear that may creep up by opting to approach rather than avoid it. Making exposure a routine part of daily life is one of the most effective means by which patients can prevent insidious avoidance. For example, a patient formerly afraid of enclosed spaces can make a habit of using the previously avoided elevator at work. Someone overcoming fear of a specific animal might consider purchasing one as a pet. A person previously afraid of a specific food should consider making it a routine part of their diet.

Clinical Vignette

Bob and his therapist briefly review some high-risk times for relapse, to which they will return next session.

Therapist: [after introducing the concept of high-risk times in relapse prevention] Bob, we'll do some more of this next session after you've had time to think about them, but right now can you think of a future situation that may be a challenge to you, in the sense that you might opt to start avoiding again?

Bob: Well, of the things we've talked about, I think if I have a bad experience, a setback, that would be tough.

Therapist: Can you think of an example of how that might occur?

Bob: Well, I can see it happening if I'm in a situation where I haven't been before, like maybe going up in the St. Louis Arch or that ferris wheel. If I have a bad time, that could be hard.

Therapist: Well, let's go through that situation for a second and talk about how you would try to handle it. What could happen when you visit the Arch that could potentially set you back?

Bob: I could get, well, big-time fear, like I haven't felt for some time.

Therapist: And what are you concerned could happen if that occurs?

Bob: Well, actually, I'm not as concerned about some of the old things. I mean, I don't think I'm going to completely lose it and freak out. But I hate that old feeling, the real bad one. I think it would be more of a downer than anything—that it was back again.

Therapist: So you don't want it to ever happen. And if it did. . . what then?

Bob: I don't know. I might feel like I'm never going to get better.

Therapist: I can see how it would be easy to feel that way if that happened. Can you see yourself then feeling that it would be no use—that you might as well start avoiding it again?

Bob: Kind of, but kind of not. I mean, if I panicked or something in a high situation, that doesn't mean I'll give up. It just might feel that way.

Therapist: So even though you've known that panic could happen during the course of your recovery, if it did, you still might feel disappointed?

Bob: Yeah, that's it. I know I should expect a bad time here or there like we said. It would just be disappointing, or even frustrating, at the moment.

Therapist: Well, I think that's very insightful, Bob. This would be a challenging moment for you. How would you try to overcome that feeling and not fall back into avoidance?

Bob: I don't know for sure.

Therapist: Bob, if you have moments like this in the future, when you're not sure how to proceed, consider turning it around as we've done throughout this therapy. As I've said, you're good at solving these problems when you do this. Let's try it. Let's say someone you care about has made progress through exposure therapy. But then they have a bad experience with an exposure and start feeling as if they might as well quit because it's too much work or they'll never get better anyway. How would you advise this person?

Bob: Well, I'd tell them they shouldn't act on the feeling. Just because you're feeling that way doesn't mean it's true.

Therapist: What should they act on?

Bob: Well, what has helped—just to try to go back into situations.

Therapist: [acting as hypothetical advisee] Well, doesn't having a panic attack in this high situation prove that more exposure isn't going to help me? I've done lots of exposure, and yet I still got a panic attack.

Bob: That's a good question.

Therapist: What do you think?

Bob: Well, you just had a setback. It doesn't mean all is lost or that if you go back, it's going to be the same.

Therapist: But when it happens, I feel as if all is lost.

Bob: Yeah, but don't act on that feeling like I said.

Therapist: But what if I don't want to go back into the Arch, or I can't?

Bob: Hmm. Well, just sleep on it. Then come back and try it again.

Therapist: How do I get the strength to do that, though?

Bob: Maybe talk with someone about it. Remember that you've done it before. Think about how to do it again.

Therapist: Do you hear yourself, Bob?

Bob: Yeah, again, I'm just giving advice.

Therapist: Right. But that's a necessary step—to see a problem and come up with a plan for solving it. You're very good at this when you force yourself to answer your own concerns as you would a loved one's. You've done the next step too—put a plan together. For example, you knew to schedule exposures rather than wait until you got to St. Louis and Six Flags.

Bob: That's true. That's the bottom line too, isn't it—get back in there.

Therapist: Yes, it is.

In sum, relapse prevention helps patients to recognize and overcome times when they are vulnerable to begin avoiding again. These times may include setbacks, stressors, as well as those subtle, everyday moments when patients face the decision to approach or avoid previously avoided activities. To prevent relapse, patients are urged to make exposure an everyday activity. If they find themselves feeling fear or the urge to seek safety from something for whatever reason, they are encouraged to draw upon their resources, personal and social, and face the feared object or situation as they have throughout therapy. This includes the possibility of structuring some formal exposure exercises well after they have left therapy.

SELF-THERAPY EXERCISE

At the conclusion of this session, patients identify the next set of exposures they will do. They also set the goal of taking opportunities to do more everyday exposures. Finally, patients are assigned an exercise that asks them to list potential high-risk times for relapse. The results of these exercises will be reviewed next session.

To facilitate a review of patient progress that will be conducted next session, the therapist asks the patient to complete, immediately prior to the next session, three forms used to assess the major dimensions of their specific phobia: (1) the items selected as treatment goals from the Fear and Avoidance Hierarchy, (2) the Phobic Thoughts Questionnaire, and (3) the Phobic Sensations Questionnaire.

As with last session, the next therapy session should be scheduled some weeks from this one, allowing patients time to complete their exercises and gain more personal successes as formal therapeutic contact wanes.

9

Treatment Session 8— Toward Independence

SESSION OUTLINE

As in recent sessions, patients' latest exposures are reviewed. Relapse prevention is revisited, including coping with high-risk times. Termination issues are addressed. Finally, patients' progress throughout therapy and their plans for posttreatment are discussed.

SESSION GOALS

1. To review exposure with continued emphasis on extending and maintaining gains and encouraging patients' self-sufficiency.
2. To review and rehearse relapse prevention strategies.
3. To facilitate the transition from acute therapy to posttreatment.
4. To evaluate patients' progress and review their plans for the future.

KEY CONCEPTS AND CLINICAL CONSIDERATIONS FOR ACCOMPLISHING GOAL #1—REVIEWING EXPOSURES

Picking up from last session, therapists continue to assist patients in developing the skills needed to continue their progress after therapy. Particular attention is paid to a patient's ability to evaluate previous exposures and plan future exercises that will extend therapeutic gains and overcome potential obstacles. As was suggested last session, patients may benefit from having information from this session recorded on a card, audiotape, or other easily accessible resource for later use.

Continued use of the Exposure Record Form or a similar form after therapy is urged because it directs patients to continue practicing those skills that encourage long-term recovery. For example, it directs patients to test predictions, lay out a plan for the exposure, evaluate whether they are in compliance with the guidelines for exposure, identify areas of strength and weakness, and create self-therapy exposures that facilitate positive change. As therapists assess and encourage the development of these same skills during this session, they want to see that patients are clearly showing fear reduction and a growing sense of mastery in managing phobic encounters before any decision to terminate treatment is made.

Clinical Vignette

Last session's review revealed that Bob was not repeating exposures as frequently as desired. This session's review shows that he is on his way to overcoming that problem.

Therapist: Bob, from your Exposure Record Form you seem to be developing the ability to identify what you're doing well during exposure and where you could improve.

Bob: Yeah, it helps to do the form, to have it all written down.

Therapist: Do you think you could remember these questions [points to form] if you forgot the form sometime?

Bob: Probably. I've used it enough.

Therapist: I encourage you to continue using the form. Maybe, every once in a while, you might try not using it and see how well you remember what to do.

Bob: All right. I think I know it pretty well.

Therapist: Yes, I think you do, too. Last session you identified the need to do exposures repeatedly. How successful have you been in accomplishing that goal?

Bob: Not bad. I started setting off enough time to do them more than once or twice at a time.

Lucy: You also went back other days and did some of them again.

Therapist: Yes, it looks like, from your exposure records, that when you've repeated exposures during the same day, your highest anxiety rating for each exposure comes down. Did you notice that?

Bob: Yeah, it definitely gets easier the more you do it. I did notice, when I went back Thursday to the roof of the power plant, that I felt pretty nervous again at first. That took me off guard a little.

Therapist: Yeah, your anxiety rating on the first exposure Thursday was actually higher than when you did that exposure previously. What do you make of that?

Bob: I know!! I wasn't expecting that. I think it was because this time I knew I was going to have to really face it and do it over and over. Last time, I can see now that I was kind of in then out. I was really avoiding it in a way. This time it was now or never.

Therapist: It sounds like this time you did a "real" exposure—you really faced it, and because of that it made you more nervous. Did you get anything out of it?

Bob: Yeah, even though I got a strong jolt the first few times, by the fourth time I felt like I really knew what was going to happen. I was getting used to it. I think that helps. It makes you more sure that you can do it.

Therapist: The situation became more predictable. That made it easier?

Bob: Yeah. But I feel more confident than I have before. I know better what's going to happen, and that makes me feel better. I have to tell you, at first, I wasn't really sure if I was going to be able to do that one on the roof. That was where this all started. But I feel a lot better about it now—kind of charged up. I even did it when my supervisor was there.

Lucy: He asked his supervisor to go with him.

Bob: Yeah. I told him I wanted him to check my work on the circuit box. But really I wanted him to see that I could go up there. I think I was actually better at it than him. I noticed that he was a little nervous himself. So I'm feeling a lot better about it.

Therapist: That's great. I'm glad you're starting to feel a real change. It's one thing that we've talked about it, but it's another to experience it. Is it more believable to you that continuing exposure is the key to overcoming this?

Bob: Yeah, I just needed to keep doing it. When we first started this, I was cautious, which was okay because I wasn't really ready to face it. But now I see that you really have to go after it to feel more sure that it's all right.

Therapist: I think you've just hit the nail on the head, Bob. Let me ask you a tough question. Knowing that you want to keep facing your old fears as you've been doing, what could prevent you from continuing what you've started over the last month or so?

Bob: Just me not wanting to make the effort, I guess. But I'm feeling better, and that makes me want to do this now.

Therapist: Does this experience give you a good idea of how you should try to do exposures?

Bob: Yeah, not only how often, but how to do them, too. You've got to really face your fear.

KEY CONCEPTS AND CLINICAL CONSIDERATIONS FOR ACCOMPLISHING GOAL #2—REVISITING RELAPSE PREVENTION

The discussion of relapse prevention continues during this session. The primary goal here is that patients leave with the idea that continuing exposure and resisting avoidance are the keys to preventing relapse. If desired, therapists can review the primary pathways to relapse discussed in the last session. These include insidious avoidance, in which patients begin opting out of one situation then another, and deliberate avoidance, often occurring in response to high-risk times.

Between sessions, patients were asked to conduct a self-therapy exercise in which they identified personal high-risk times for relapse. Those situations are reviewed, emphasizing how relapse could occur and how it can be prevented. Regarding insidious avoidance, therapists review relevant examples from the patient's everyday life, discussing how the decision to avoid or approach a previously feared object or situation could either snowball into the redevelopment of a phobic cycle or facilitate continued recovery, respectively.

Clinical Vignette

Last session, Bob indicated that a potentially high-risk situation for him would be if he had strong fear during an exposure after having not felt that for some time. He thought that this would be most likely in high-fear situations to which he had done little previous exposure, a common high-risk situation for patients. Since he remains concerned about some upcoming exposures, his therapist first reviews evidence gained throughout therapy that demonstrates to Bob that he has managed these types of challenges in the past. The discussion then shifts to how Bob could manage future challenges similarly.

Therapist: [after hearing Bob describe the high-risk situation] Yes, it sounds as if you're still a little concerned about what could happen on that ferris wheel.

Bob: Yeah, sometimes I'll be sitting there and drift off into a daydream about being on that thing and getting panicked. It's not like it used to be where I'm stuck on it, but it does make me nervous.

Therapist: Well, let's talk about your track record for a second. It might help remind us what's likely to happen in the future. Can you think of times during therapy where you've had to deal with exposures that involved strong fear, and especially where the strong fear surprised you?

Bob: Well, yeah, of course.

Lucy: Tell about the baseball game, Bob.

Bob: But that went well. This is supposed to be hard ones.

Lucy: Well, it was hard at first, remember?

Bob: You're right. That's a good example.

Therapist: So what happened there?

Bob: Well, we went to the Cubs game in Chicago. The company gave out some tickets. Of course, they were in the "nosebleed" seats.

Lucy: Our seats were way up in the stadium, in the second tier.

Bob: Anyway, I felt real unsteady when we were climbing the steps to get to them.

Lucy: It surprised you too, didn't it?

Bob: Yeah, I knew it was high, but because it was steps and not a ladder, I really didn't expect to be that nervous. But it hit me. In fact, my first thought was just to leave. I hadn't had that sneak up on me like that for a while.

Therapist: So what did you do?

Bob: Well, at first I sat down, you know, got my bearings. Then I noticed that if I looked across the stadium in a certain way, that's what made me feel nervous. You know, getting that view where you can't really tell how high you are, but you know you're way up there. Just like the very first exposure we did here. Remember?

Therapist: Yeah, I remember. So what happened at the stadium?

Bob: Well, I just kept doing that, you know. I treated it like an expo-sure—looking up until I was used to it. I hadn't really been doing that up until this last month or so—you know, really challenging it while you're in the middle of it, like you've said.

Therapist: Great. So you challenged it. What happened?

Bob: Well, it became no big deal after a while. I just forgot about it later and watched the game.

Lucy: You did more than that, Bob. You got us hot dogs [laughing].

Bob: Oh, yeah. I went to the concession stand just to prove to myself that I could climb those damn stairs back up to the seats.

Lucy: You also changed your seat later.

Bob: Yeah, that's right. After a while, we got up and sat in some empty seats that were closer to the edge of the terrace that we were sitting in.

Therapist: You did that to feel safer?

Bob: No! We were in the second tier of seats way above the seats below us. We moved to the edge of that.

Therapist: Don't tell me that in the middle of this situation, you actu-ally made it harder for yourself—twice?

Lucy: It was Bob's idea, too. He got mad that his phobia was happening at a ball game—you know, interfering with his first love, the Cubs.

Bob: Now, now, dear, I love you too. But it's true. I was getting upset. But I thought about what we said, and used my anger to help me kind of push my limits.

Therapist: So you used your frustration to give you strength?

Bob: Yeah. We went over and sat in those seats just to prove that we could, that I could.

Therapist: So, Bob, how does this example speak to what you would do if you felt unexpected, strong fear in a high place in the future?

Bob: Hmm, that's kind of tricky of you. But you're right, it makes me feel better.

KEY CONCEPTS AND CLINICAL CONSIDERATIONS FOR ACCOMPLISHING GOAL #3—ADDRESSING TERMINATION

As the end of treatment draws near, termination issues come to the fore. In addition to the issues related to ending a meaningful therapeutic relationship, patients ending a directive therapy for specific phobias, like other patients, often fear that they might not be able to carry on independently. As indicated previously, the therapist aims throughout treatment to make termination a natural outgrowth of the patient's developing self-efficacy. To the degree that therapists are successful in doing that, patients will be better able to adjust. Of course, formal therapy should not end until the therapist believes that the patient has acquired the knowledge and skills necessary to continue independently.

Just as exposure can test patients' phobic fears, it can also test their fears of deteriorating after therapy ends. By scheduling therapy sessions further and further apart, patients have begun this test. Their progress between sessions speaks to the likelihood of continued progress after therapy ends. Discussing this evidence can help boost patients' confidence that they can continue to do well.

Some studies support the benefit of scheduling a "booster session" of treatment after acute therapy. In light of this, therapists and patients may want to schedule such a session some months after acute treatment to assess and support the patient's progress, and to maintain the patient's focus on working to overcome the phobia.

There are other methods that can make helpful therapeutic information available to patients after formal treatment, and thus support their efforts. Self-help manuals and books are an example. If used, it is important that these materials are consistent with an exposure-based treatment approach, or inconsistencies can erode the treatment's credibility and patients' confidence. In addition, handouts outlining, for example, guidelines for exposure, problem-solving steps, or procedures for evaluating and planning exposures can be developed throughout therapy to be used as a resource after it. Finally, as has been suggested, video or audio recordings of all or part of patients' therapy sessions can be particularly useful as resources after or, for that matter, during treatment (Macaskill 1996). Of course, appropriate informed consent should be obtained before recording any patient's therapy.

Ultimately, proof that a patient will attain long-term recovery can only come with time. Just as support may have helped patients tackle other fears, they are reassured that it remains available if needed while they move toward independence.

Clinical Vignette

Bob, Lucy, and the therapist discuss Bob's concerns about leaving formal therapy. They discuss Bob's sources of support and evidence of his personal efficacy.

Therapist: Bob, how do you feel about carrying on after this session?
Bob: Well, okay, I guess. I hope I can.
Therapist: Do you have any concerns about that not happening?
Bob: Oh, not beyond what we've discussed with the Arch and ferris wheel, which are probably going to go all right. I guess I worry whether I can do this without coming here.
Therapist: Have you thought about how not coming here could cause you to start avoiding heights again?
Bob: A little. If nothing else, it's been helpful just to hear the messages over and over again. I kind of knew what to do, but it has helped to hear it. I think I'm just going to miss that more than anything. But I wonder in the back of my mind if I'll *need* it.
Therapist: Well first, Bob, I'm going to miss it, too. I've watched you battle and overcome this thing. You've worked so hard and done so well. Overcoming a phobia takes a lot of courage.
Bob: Thanks. I couldn't have done it without you.
Therapist: Well, thank you. We've all been a good team, haven't we? Bob, I believe in the last month that you've reached the top of the mountain and are now on the downhill side. I also feel confident that you're going to continue to improve. You have shown the kind of changes that I've seen in others who keep progressing. In fact, I've been very impressed during the times when you've reversed roles with me during our exercises. I think, in a sense, you've become a good therapist for yourself. How do you feel about your ability to listen to the therapist in you?
Bob: Pretty good. I feel like I understand what's going on now. That makes a big difference. I also feel like I'm starting to beat it. And now that I'm feeling better, it kind of makes me want to go on.
Therapist: I'm confident you'll continue to do that. In a second I'd like to talk with you about some of the things you plan to do in the near future, but first I want to talk about how we can keep some of the therapeutic messages in front of you. Even though you know these things, you can take the [self-help manual, handouts, audiotapes, or videotapes] with you if you want.

Bob: Yeah, I'd like to do that.

Therapist: Plus, Bob, it goes without saying, but if you ever want to come back in or give me a call, you're always welcome.

Bob: Okay. That's good to know.

Therapist: Another thing is that you and Lucy have done so well working together. I know you've said you don't want to burden her, but there's nothing wrong with asking for her support if you feel you might need it.

Lucy: Yes, Bob, it makes me feel like I'm important to you, too.

Bob: I know. You are. And you're right.

Lucy: Bob has done so well thus far. I know he'll make it if he keeps up what he's started.

Therapist: Yes, he has. That's a good point, too, Lucy. We've been saying it a lot lately—keeping up what you've started. Bob, do you feel as though you've changed the way you approach heights?

Bob: Yes, I don't look for an out, like I used to. I'm facing them now.

Therapist: I think you're well on your way to making it a permanent way to deal with heights.

Bob: I hope so.

Therapist: You've said you wondered if you'll be able to continue doing the things you've learned. I don't know if you've noticed, but the time between the last few therapy sessions has gotten longer and longer. How have you done over that time?

Bob: Pretty good. Real good, actually. But you know, the thing is, I always knew I was coming back. Now, I'm not. Like I said, I'm not obsessing about it, but I'm not sure if that will make a difference either.

Therapist: Well, it probably has helped in some ways. As you said, it's good to know that support is there. The support is still there, too, not only in Lucy, but as I said, if you want, you can come in any time you want.

Bob: That's true.

Therapist: Bob, do you think that knowing you were coming back was the critical difference that helped you manage the situations you've conquered over the last few weeks?

Bob: Probably not, really. It's not like I was thinking that and that's what did it. It was just me dealing with it the way I've learned how to.

Therapist: And you really have done well. But I understand that you really won't feel the confidence you're looking for until you actually continue to do it and see that you can.

Bob: Yeah, time will tell. It'll probably go okay.

Therapist: You know, Bob, you were faced with a similar question at the beginning of therapy, in that you were worried about whether you were going to be able to do exposure. How has that turned out?

Bob: Yeah, that's true. I *was* worried. I guess anticipating it is always worse than what actually happens.

Therapist: That can be your new your motto.

Bob: Yes, I can testify to that one.

Therapist: Why don't we look once more at some of the improvements that you've made and where you're going from here.

KEY CONCEPTS AND CLINICAL CONSIDERATIONS FOR ACCOMPLISHING GOAL #4—REVIEWING PROGRESS AND FUTURE DIRECTIONS

Before the session ends, the patients' progress throughout therapy is reviewed. Therapists will need to prepare for this review by gathering the patients pre- and post-treatment Fear and Avoidance hierarchies, Phobic Sensations Questionnaires, and Fearful Thoughts Questionnaires, as well as any other records therapists desire. Developing charts that depict patients' progress toward their treatment goals often helps encourage patients to carry on (for more information on assessing outcomes for these and other purposes see Outcomes Management in Chapter 10).

Patients improve on various dimensions of their phobias at different rates. For example, by the end of treatment, patients typically report that their understanding of the phobia, its maintenance, and treatment have improved greatly. Although increased knowledge per se does not ensure a change in symptoms or functioning, it empowers and often comforts patients and is likely to increase their chances of continuing independently.

Most patients show significant decreases in avoidance behavior by treatment's end. The degree of this change will be reflected in the difference between pre- and post-treatment avoidance ratings of selected items on patients' Fear and Avoidance Hierarchies. Change in avoidance behavior typically precedes changes in cognitive domains; consequently, cognitive change may not be as complete at this time. Ratings of fear (and confidence, if collected) of targeted hierarchy items, as well as ratings on the Phobic Thoughts Questionnaires can show the degree of change in those cognitive domains. Change in physical sensation reactivity and fear of sensations may not be as complete as changes in avoidance either. The extent of those changes will be seen in patients' pre- versus post-treatment ratings on the Phobic Sensations Questionnaires. Figures 9–1 through 9–3 show Bob's pre- and post-treatment ratings on the various scales discussed.

Although patients have heard that their therapeutic gains will not be complete by the end of acute treatment, realizing it may raise some concerns. Typically, patients will show greater improvement in situations to which they have done more exposure. That evidence can support the reassurance that gains will continue as exposure does. Areas of incomplete change also suggest targets for future exposures. Before leaving the review, therapists ask patients to lay out their general plan for exposures over the course of the next few months.

Figure 9–1: Bob's Fear and Avoidance Hierarchy (Pre- to Post-treatment Change in Treatment Goal Targets—Fear, Avoidance, Confidence)

Targeted Item	Pre-Treatment			Post-Treatment		
	F	A	C	F	A	C
Occupational Goals						
Circuit box top of processing plant (item 1)	10	10	1	3	0	8
Catwalks (item 5)						
(outside)	8	7	3	2	0	8
(inside)	6	5	3	1	0	10
Freight Elevator (item 6)						
(>2 stories)	6	10	4	2	0	10
Social Goals						
Ferris wheel (item 2)	10	10	1	5	0	7
Climbing ladder to roof (item 8)	3	3	6	0	0	10

F = fear (0–10)
A = avoidance (0–10)
C = confidence (0–10)

Figure 9–2: Bob's Fearful Thoughts Questionnaire
(Pre-to-Post-Treatment Change)

	Pre-Treatment		Post Treatment	
	How Often (0–10)	Belief (0–10)	How Often (0–10)	Belief (0–10)
I could fall (can't maintain balance).	10	9	3	1
I could faint.	6	5	0	0
I could jump (lose judgment).	4	5	0	0
I could be embarrassed (can't cope with this).	7	7	2	2
My legs could give out.	9	9	2	1
I will be pulled off edge.	6	8	1	1
I will slip.	4	6	1	1
I will flip over rail.	4	6	0	0
Structures will break—rails.	7	6	2	2
Others will fall—family.	9	9	3	1

Figure 9–3: Bob's Phobic Sensations Questionnaire
(Pre-to-Post-Treatment Change)

	Pre-Treatment		Post Treatment	
	Inten-sity (0–10)	Fear (0–10)	Inten-sity (0–10)	Fear (0–10)
Heart beats faster	8	2	3	1
Heart pounds hard	8	2	1	0
Breathing is faster	6	0	1	0
Breathing is difficult	7	2	0	0
Feel faint, dizzy, unsteady (Have you ever fainted? yes___ no ✓)	6	7	0	0
Weakness (Have you ever collapsed? yes___ no ✓)	10	10	3	3
Other things seem unreal	4	6	0	0
Sweating	3	0	0	0
Other (specify) __muscle tension__	7	0	2	0

Clinical Vignette

Bob's therapist finds that Bob has plans for continued exposure after treatment.

Therapist: Bob, what are your plans for the near future?

Bob: Besides doing the things I'm doing at work, the arch in St. Louis and the ferris wheel at Six Flags are the big ones.

Therapist: Right. How about everyday opportunities?

Bob: Well, I'm doing the walkway thing at work, like we'd talked about. Are there others, Lucy?

Lucy: We've been walking by the balcony rail at the mall, too. Oh, and Bob uses the McCluggage Bridge now.

Therapist: Fantastic. Bob, are you using the freight elevator at work frequently?

Bob: Not a lot. But that's because I really don't have a need to.

Therapist: Does it still cause you some concern when you need to use it?

Bob: Just a little. . . . All right, so I'll do it some more.

Therapist: Bob, you didn't even give me a chance to say it first.

Bob: You don't need to anymore.

10

Special Issues

Topics of special interest discussed in this chapter include the management of medications within the context of exposure-based treatments of specific phobia, monitoring the outcomes of treatment, facilitating treatment compliance, and preventing relapse. The first topic supplements material described in previous chapters; each of the other topics overviews issues and strategies presented throughout previous chapters.

MANAGING MEDICATION

Most outcome studies evaluating pharmacotherapeutic agents indicated for anxiety disorders (e.g., tricyclic antidepressants, benzodiazepines, beta blockers, selective serotonin reuptake inhibitors) have found them more effective for disorders other than specific phobias. Indeed, there is near unanimous consensus that pharmacotherapy for specific phobia is a second-line consideration behind exposure-based treatment. Despite this, many patients seeking exposure-based treatment arrive either already on medication or requesting it.

Benefits and Risks

Of patients arriving on medication, most have been prescribed a low-potency benzodiazepine such as lorazepam (Ativan), diazepam (Valium), or, less often, a high-potency benzodiazepine such as alprazolam (Xanax). Most of those patients are using their medication on a p.r.n. (as needed) schedule, usually just prior to phobic encounters. The benzodiazepines are used most frequently with specific phobias, partly because they have a quicker onset of action and fewer side effects than alternative medications that typically take weeks to effect change. Taken 20 minutes to one hour before an exposure, a benzodiazepine can effectively attenuate the anxiety engendered by it. They are used routinely to help anxious patients undergo necessary medical procedures without undue distress.

The primary rationale for using a benzodiazepine in combination with exposure presumes that excessive anxiety may slow patients' progress, foster noncompliance, or lead to attrition; attenuating that anxiety should minimize those risks. Studies examining whether benzodiazepines actually mitigate any of these problems report mixed results, though. For example, one study found that a low, waning dose of a benzodiazepine (i.e., taken four hours before exposure) helped patients proceed through their exposure hierarchies more quickly than patients whose exposures were unassisted by medication (Marks et al. 1972). Other studies, however, have reported that benzodiazepine-assisted exposure has had no significant affect, for example, on attrition compared to unassisted exposure (Marks et al. 1993, Wardle et al. 1994).

Weighing against the potential benefits of benzodiazepine assistance is the risk that it may interfere with the maintenance of therapeutic gains after the drug is discontinued. For example, several studies show that benzodiazepines can interfere in a dose-dependent relationship with the acquisition and retention of new information (Barbee et al. 1992, Curran 1986, Tata et al. 1994). A benzodiazepine may alter the way information is stored in memory such that information acquired in the presence of the drug may be less retrievable after it has been discontinued. That effect, called *state dependent learning*, has been invoked to explain why patients who achieved fear reduction during benzodiazepine-assisted exposure have been more likely to relapse after drug discontinuation than patients who undergo unassisted exposure (Marks et al. 1993, Sartory 1983).

Although this state dependent interference appears more pronounced following a standing dose schedule than a p.r.n. schedule (see Wardle 1990 for review), any use of medication during exposure raises other concerns. For example, like any safety signal, medication may interfere with exposure-based treatments at motivational or attributional levels, by reducing patients' incentive to learn alternative coping strategies or undermining their sense of self-efficacy (see Spiegel and Bruce 1997 for review). As discussed previously, to the extent that patients attribute their gains to safety cues such as pills, their post-treatment recovery can be jeopardized when those safety cues are then taken away (Basoglu et al. 1994).

Finally, patients on standing doses of benzodiazepines may also face a withdrawal syndrome upon taper that can make discontinuation of the medication difficult. Fortunately, few patients with specific phobias are on standing dose regimens of benzodiazepines, although it is common to see this regimen prescribed for patients with comorbid anxiety or other disorders.

Despite the recognized advantage of unassisted exposure-based treatment, patients continue to be treated initially with benzodiazepines for a variety of reasons. These include inaccessibility to exposure therapy, patients' fear of doing unassisted exposure, and lack of knowledge about the effectiveness of exposure as a first-line intervention among patients and providers. The physician also may feel pressured to prescribe to the patient who presents in a phobic crisis immediately before a pending encounter with the phobic object or situation (e.g., an upcoming plane trip), despite recognizing that exposure is a better long-term solution. For whatever reasons patients present to exposure therapy on or requesting medication, it is clear that they do. Consequently, therapists will continue to face tough decisions about how best to manage medication in the context of exposure therapy.

Specific Recommendations

Since exposure-based therapies for specific phobias have demonstrated efficacy as a first-line intervention, it is recommended that if the therapist does not need to introduce the risks associated with medication assistance then they should not. If discomfort or attrition are concerns, then therapists are advised to consider making exposure tasks more manageable by graduating them, employing therapist assistance, or using other easily removable aids to make initial exposures easier.

The "as required" Schedule

If patients are using medication on an as-needed basis to assist exposure, then it is recommended that the treatment plan for managing the medication is guided by the exposure-based model. Accordingly, the medication is handled as a potential safety signal that is targeted for removal (gradual or not) soon after initial medication-assisted exposures have been mastered. The unassisted exposures can serve as tests of patients' fearful predictions that they will be unable to manage without their medication. It makes common sense clinically then for therapists to try to arrange those initial unassisted exposures in ways that maximize patients' chances of completing them successfully and with minimal distress.

The "standing" Schedule

Patients with specific phobias are rarely prescribed a standing dose regimen, although standing dose regimens are not unusual for patients who are receiving concurrent psychopharmacotherapy for comorbid conditions, but seeking treatment for a specific phobia.

If patients enter treatment on standing dose regimens *prescribed for their specific phobia*, as opposed to another comorbid condition, then initiating a drug taper after initial successes but during therapy (not afterward) is recommended based on recent discontinuation studies reporting success with that approach (see Spiegel and Bruce 1997 for review). If the medication is a benzodiazepine, that taper schedule should be slow and flexible to reduce possible withdrawal symptoms that could complicate discontinuation. Success has been found with decreasing decrement taper schedules, where 25 to 33 percent of the current dose is reduced approximately weekly to biweekly (Spiegel et al. 1994). Providers without prescription privileges will have to work in concert with the prescribing provider to coordinate the taper with exposure.

Again, from an exposure-based therapeutic model, each step down on the taper schedule serves as an exposure that tests patients' fears and doubts about managing their fears while on less and less medication. At the same time, the taper reduces taper-emergent symptoms such as withdrawal symptoms. The first and last dose steps typically are the most feared, and may require extra temporary support. It is recommended that the taper be initiated as soon into therapy as possible and ended before therapy ends, so patients have the opportunity to gain some experience with exposure while medication-free. Tapering during therapy also allows patients the opportunity to shift attribution of gains from the medicine to personal efforts, a shift that has predicted resistance to relapse. Providers should also consider using a taper in conjunction with exposure even if the medication does not require a taper for pharmacologic reasons (e.g., BuSpar). Tapering in this fashion is designed to serve as a graded hierarchy for exposure, not a means to reduce taper-emergent symptoms. Throughout the taper procedure, therapists should encourage patients to shift from reliance on the medication to using their newly learned coping strategies and attributing gains to those efforts.

Other Conditions

Finally, if patients are on standing doses of medications *for conditions other than a specific phobia*, then the exposure treatment may need to be conducted in the presence of that medication. If the agent is a benzodiazepine, then the possibility of switching to an agent with fewer risks for complicating exposure-based procedures (e.g., a tricyclic or SSRI antidepressant) should be explored with the prescribing physician. If discontinuation is the goal of the concurrent pharmacotherapy, then coordinating it within the context of the exposure, as described above, may increase patients' chances of discontinuing it successfully and without acute relapse of the phobia. If discontinuation is not planned until after treatment of the specific phobia, then consideration should be given to reestablishing therapeutic contact at the time of discontinuation, if patients appear at risk or fear relapse of the specific phobia.

MONITORING OUTCOMES

In the advent of healthcare reform and the growing trend toward managing the costs of psychotherapeutic services, quality of care has become a key issue for third-party payers, mental health delivery system planners, and treatment providers. As third-party purchasers and payers have increased pressure on cost containment, concerns about compromising the quality of care have grown. One of many consequences of these movements is that service providers are routinely being required to demonstrate the value of their services to purchasers of mental health care. Indeed, many require demonstration of clinical improvement toward selected treatment goals in exchange for reimbursement. Thus, it is becoming necessary for therapists to develop a system for monitoring the outcomes of their interventions if they are going to survive in what is becoming an increasingly cost-restrictive and competitive clinical environment.

To create an outcomes monitoring plan, therapists are being asked to document formally what they already monitor informally. Therapists already continuously assess the impact of their treatments on patients and use that data to direct the ongoing course of therapy, provide feedback to patients, and make decisions about the need for continued service. The seemingly burdensome task of developing a monitoring plan that is sensitive to relevant clinical change, useful to the provider and patient, easy to use, and applicable to third party payer requirements can actually be done for this exposure-based treatment for specific phobia with a little preplanning.

An outcomes monitoring plan should track the major dimensions of patients' problems and the impact they have on patients' lives. This usually requires measuring symptom status (distress) and social and occupational disability. More comprehensive systems may also assess corollary areas such as quality of life, burden on social systems such as the family, or other relevant domains. Most third-party payers require practitioners to assess symptom status and disability prior to acute treatment (baseline) and at periodic points throughout treatment.

As described in the preceding chapters, monitoring the outcome of the treatment described in this volume can be accomplished by using data from the rating forms that are recommended for use as a routine part of the treatment. The conventional method (described in this volume) involves tracking patients' fear and avoidance ratings of selected items on the Fear and Avoidance Hierarchy. Items selected should be those that are indicated as primary treatment goals and that account for the majority of patient's distress and disability.

Ratings from the Exposure Record Forms can also be used for monitoring outcomes. Although more time consuming, this method can reduce some of the biases inherent to the retrospective global ratings made of hierarchy items. In addition, the data gained from exposure records can be used to provide patients and providers with feedback of progress, lending some clinical utility to the measure. Practitioners who want to assess other relevant dimensions (e.g., fear of sensations, confidence, social support) can attach these ratings to either form. The choice of plans is up to providers (for now).

Current trends in outcome management are emphasizing the use of standard measures whose psychometric properties have been established through conventional methods. Clearly, this goal is worthwhile. To date though, difficulties exist in identifying measures that show adequate reliability and validity, are specific to diagnostic categories, and satisfy the other criteria of a good outcome measure, discussed above, such as sensitivity to clinical change, relevance to the clinician, and ease of use in routine practice. Attempts to identify such measures are beginning to appear (e.g., Fischer and Corcoran 1994). And although some measures have been developed for certain specific phobias (usually in conjunction with research projects), no standard measure meeting all of the above criteria can be recommended.

Despite this, some third-party payers require the use of particular measures. The most prevalent of those is the Global Assessment of Functioning Scale (Endicott et al. 1976, Luborsky 1962). It is a clinician-rated, 0–100 scale used to assess different degrees of general symptom severity and functional disability. Readers might recognize the scale as the one used to assess global functioning on Axis V in the *DSM-IV*. Thus, it behooves clinicians to check with third-party payers to see if particular scales are required or to secure approval for measures the clinician wants to use to monitor outcomes. Further information about outcomes assessment can be found in several recent volumes on the topic (e.g., Ogles et al. 1996, Sederer and Dickey 1996).

FACILITATING TREATMENT COMPLIANCE

Few things are more disappointing than witnessing a patient fail to benefit from a potentially beneficial treatment due to noncompliance. Practicing clinicians know that this potential problem presents with each new patient. Fortunately, research on treatment compliance has developed to the point where guidelines for facilitating it can be offered. This section reviews practices and procedures designed to help patients do what will help them.

One of the most effective means for preventing noncompliance involves considering how it could occur with each therapeutic recommendation. In this way compliance is monitored continuously. Many of the warning signs that signal nonadherence are missed when we as providers focus on treating a specific phobia instead of the person with the specific phobia, their resources, and their circumstances. Therapists need to consider therapeutic requests from the patients' perspective, looking for specific obstacles that could prevent patients from carrying out those requests. For example, therapists should ask themselves: Does my request consider the patient's knowledge, attitude, and life circumstances? How will it affect the patients' self-concept? How could personality factors interfere with accomplishing these actions? How will my request affect the patient's social systems? In general, involving patients in the process of planning treatment and identifying treatment goals can reveal concerns, priorities, and resources that could affect compliance with those plans. Specifically, asking patients routinely what could prevent them from accomplishing any given therapeutic request and then collaboratively solving those problems can circumvent potential obstacles on an ongoing basis.

Facilitating compliance requires therapists to be flexible and to negotiate solutions to possible noncompliance. As Meichenbaum and Turk (1987) point out, "An acceptable regimen that is carried out appropriately is better than an ideal one that is ignored" (p. 247). As readers know, sometimes patients and therapists have to make do the best they can.

An often overlooked but critical aspect of facilitating compliance involves helping patients feel that their provider is accessible to them. This involves inviting patients' questions and concerns and clarifying misunderstandings. Whether assigning a therapeutic exercise, scheduling an appointment, or even returning a phone call, when therapists communicate to patients that their time and effort are respected and appreciated compliance is more likely.

Finally, gentle repetition and persistence in communicating what patients need to know is critical to facilitating compliance. This involves not giving up on difficult patients too soon. It may mean reemphasizing key concepts in anticipation that understanding may take time or fade over time. Making review a routine part of each session and taking opportunities when they arise to revisit important points are practices that can improve patients' understanding and compliance. Communicating concepts through examples and methods with which the patient is familiar can make it more likely they will be understood and used. The sensitive use of memory prompts, such as notes or other reminders, can make compliance more likely with patients who may forget for various reasons.

Treatment can work only when patients do it. It is hoped that by integrating these treatment compliance practices in to the application of this therapy, patients will be given a fighting chance to see that what has been an effective approach to overcoming phobias for others can be an effective approach for them as well.

MAINTAINING GAINS AND PREVENTING RELAPSE

It is well established that patients who do exposure to phobic objects and situations are likely to make significant therapeutic gains toward overcoming their fear and avoidance. Patients who can continue exposure after treatment increase their chances of maintaining those gains and preventing relapse.

Doing this, however, is no easy task. In part, it requires patients to enter therapy as novices and leave equipped to take over the responsibility of managing their own progress. As discussed previously, helping patients prevent relapse begins in the first session of treatment. Strategies designed to help patients achieve long-term recovery have been incorporated throughout the description of the present therapy. In this section, key concepts guiding those specific recommendations are reviewed.

Collaborative Relationship

Relapse prevention efforts begin with the establishment of a collaborative therapeutic relationship that facilitates a shift from a healthy therapeutic dependence to independence. Collaboration in this sense is not static. It involves helping patients to adopt the evidence-based therapeutic practices described while accommodating their changing needs, capacities, and resources.

During the educational and skills-building phases of early treatment, interventions emphasize simple, straightforward concepts and tasks applied with support and sensitivity to the process of these interventions. For example, if patients like to read, supplemental reading material may help assist the intervention. However, if patients have difficulty reading or do not like to do it, the same assignment can be countertherapeutic. Modeling a coping exercise, for example, without sensitivity to process might be informative and facilitative for one patient, or demeaning, for instance, to another. Similarly, before patients begin showing improvement, their confidence may be low, their knowledge and skills lacking. They may be embarrassed and minimizing, or histrionic and overembellishing. Some patients may need more structure, education, and reassurance. Others may need sober but supportive challenging. Sensitivity to these issues early in therapy can foster the confidence and growth that underpin later independence.

As patients progress, the collaboration shifts. Therapists begin supportively encouraging patients to assume more responsibility for deciding therapeutic actions and for managing the consequences of those actions. Several means for facilitating this shift were described throughout the treatment. They include interactive teaching methods, self-therapy exercises and their review, mutual treatment planning and goal setting, role reversal, and use of questions that encourage patients' self-learning and mastery. These techniques place patients' eventual self-sufficiency as a superordinate goal. When used throughout therapy they set the stage for making termination of this relationship a natural outgrowth of patients' developing independence.

Collaboration in this larger sense also involves managing social supports that can accommodate and encourage patients' progress. When patients' change can be assimilated into the existing social systems, long-term recovery is more likely. Using a therapeutic coach or bringing family or others into therapy for these purposes are examples.

Self-Management Skills

Since part of maintaining therapeutic gains requires patients to manage the demands of continuing exposure, therapy helps patients acquire the knowledge and skills necessary for those activities. Accordingly, emphasis is placed on helping patients understand the factors maintaining their phobias and the role of exposure in changing them. Patients are empowered when they know why they are doing what they are doing. Ultimately, though, they need to know how to do it. Therefore, the guidelines for exposure, how to plan for it, how to cope with its challenges, and how to build on successes are taught throughout therapy.

Understanding Relapse

The road to recovery is rarely smooth and straight. When patients anticipate that, it increases their chances of navigating it successfully. As discussed in previous chapters, some of the more common challenges patients face after treatment are setbacks. Part of mitigating the effects of a setback involves helping the patient reframe it not as a failure or indicator of pending relapse, but as a natural and expected part of the recovery process. Discussing a setback as a natural part of recovery encourages patients to adopt flexible expectations that can help them adapt to its ups and downs. Left unchanged, rigid and unrealistic expectations can lead patients to interpret anything less than a problem-free course of recovery as a failure, and serve to precipitate relapse. Patients need to know how to manage these challenges as well. Therefore, they are taught how to identify high-risk situations and rehearse planned ways of coping with them. They are also oriented to the seemingly innocuous but pivotal role that the everyday decision to avoid or approach plays in determining their long-term recovery.

Enhancing Self-Efficacy

Self-efficacy (Bandura 1977) refers not only to patients' beliefs that their actions will effect the change they want, but also that they are capable of those actions. The fact that exposure is by its nature a performance-based learning experience makes it fertile ground for the growth of self-efficacy. Part of enhancing self-efficacy also occurs when therapists encourage patients to attribute their therapeutic gains to themselves. Although discussing that may help, arranging exposures to prove it is a much more powerful intervention. A critical step in that process is the identification and removal of various forms of safety-seeking to which success can be attributed. These include safety signals such as the therapist or coach, medication, or any factor outside the patients' abilities that they feel accounted for their success during an exposure. Exposures done without reliance on unnecessary supports help patients learn that *they* possess and can master the skills necessary to manage and overcome their fears in the long run. Therapeutic support can help them reach this goal. It is our hope that this volume helps you in providing that support to your patients.

REFERENCES

Bandura, A. (1969). *Principles of Behavior Modification*. New York: Holt, Rinehart & Winston.

———— (1977). Self-efficacy: Toward a unifying theory of behavioral change. *Psychological Review* 84:191–215.

———— (1986). *Social Foundations of Thought and Action: A Social Cognitive Theory*. Englewood Cliffs, NJ: Prentice-Hall.

Bandura, A., Jeffery, R. W., and Gajdos, E. (1975). Generalizing change through participant modeling with self-directed mastery. *Behaviour Research and Therapy* 13:141–152.

Bandura, A., Jeffery, R. W., and Wright, C. (1974). Efficacy of participant modeling as a function of response induction aids. *Journal of Abnormal Psychology* 83:56–64.

Barbee, J. G., Black, F. W., and Todorov, A. A. (1992). Differential effects of alprazolam and buspirone upon acquisition, retention, and retrieval processes in memory. *Journal of Neuropsychiatry* 4:308–314.

Barlow, D. H. (1988). *Anxiety and Its Disorders*. New York: Guilford.

Barlow, D. H., ed. (1981). *Behavioral Assessment of Adult Disorders*. New York: Guilford.

Barlow, D. H., Leitenberg, H., Agras, W. S., and Wincze, J. P. (1969). The transfer gap in systematic desensitization: an analog study. *Behaviour Research and Therapy* 7:191–196.

Barlow, D. H., and Mavissakalian, M. (1981). Directions in the assessment and treatment of phobia: the next decade. In *Phobia: Psychological and Pharmacological Treatment*, eds. M. Mavissakalian and D. H. Barlow. New York: Guilford.

Basoglu, M., Marks, I. M., Kilic, C., et al. (1994). Alprazolam and exposure for panic disorder with agoraphobia: attribution of improvement to medication predicts subsequent relapse. *British Journal of Psychiatry* 164:652–659.

Beck, A. T., and Emery, G. (1985). *Anxiety Disorders and Phobias: A Cognitive Perspective*. New York: Basic Books.

Blanchard, E. B. (1970). Relative contributions of modeling, informational influences, and physical contact in extinction of phobic behavior. *Journal of Abnormal Psychology* 76:55–61.

Bruce, T. J., Spiegel, D. A., Gregg, S. F., and Nuzzarello, A. (1995). Predictors of alprazolam discontinuation with and without cognitive behavior therapy in panic disorder. *American Journal of Psychiatry* 152:1156–1160.

Cerny, J. A., Barlow, D. H., Craske, M., and Himadi, W. G. (1987). Couples treatment of agoraphobia: a two-year follow-up. *Behavior Therapy* 18:401–415.

Chambless, D. L. (1990). Spacing of exposure sessions in treatment of agoraphobia and simple phobia. *Behavior Therapy* 21:217–229.

Clark, D. M., Salkovskis, P. M., Hackmann, A., et al. (1994). A comparison of cognitive therapy, applied relaxation, and imipramine in the treatment of panic disorder. *British Journal of Psychiatry* 164:759–769.

Cobb, J. P., Mathews, A. M., Childs-Clarke, A., and Blowers, C. M. (1984). The spouse as co-therapist in the treatment of agoraphobia. *British Journal of Psychiatry* 144:282–287.

Curran, H. V. (1986). Tranquillizing memories: a review of the effects of benzodiazepines on human memory. *Biological Psychology* 23:179–213.

Denny, D. R., Sullivan, B. J., and Thiry, M. R. (1977). Participant modeling and self-verbalization training in the reduction of spider fears. *Journal of Behavior Therapy and Experimental Psychiatry* 8:247–253.

deSilva, P., and Rachman, S. (1984). Does escape behaviour strengthen agoraphobic avoidance? A preliminary study. *Behaviour Research and Therapy* 22:87–91.

Diagnostic and Statistical Manual of Mental Disorders. (1994). 4th ed. Washington, DC: American Psychiatric Association.

Dombeck, M. J., and Ingram, R. E. (1993). Cognitive conceptions of anxiety. In *Psychopathology and Cognition*, eds. K. S. Dobson and P. C. Kendall. San Diego, CA: Academic.

Emmelkamp, P. M. G., and Wessels, H. (1975). Flooding in imagination vs. flooding in vivo: a comparison with agoraphobics. *Behaviour Research and Therapy* 13:7–15.

Endicott, J., Spitzer, R. L., Fleiss, J. L., and Cohen, J. (1976). The global assessment scale: a procedure for measuring overall severity of psychiatric disturbance. *Archives of General Psychiatry* 33:766–771.

Fischer, J., and Corcoran, K. (1994). *Measures for Clinical Practice*, vol. 1 and vol. 2, New York: Free Press.

Foa, E. B., Blau, J. S., Prout, M., and Latimer, P. (1977). Is horror a necessary component of flooding (implosion)? *Behaviour Research and Therapy* 15:397–402.

Foa, E. B., and Kozak, M. S. (1985). Treatment of anxiety disorders: implications for psychopathology. In *Anxiety and the Anxiety Disorders*, eds. A. H. Tuma and J. D. Maser. Hillsdale, NJ: Erlbaum.

——— (1986). Emotional processing of fear: exposure to corrective information. *Psychological Bulletin* 99:20–35.

Foa, E. B., Jameson, J. S., Turner, R. M., and Payne, L. L. (1980). Massed vs. spaced exposure sessions in the treatment of agoraphobia. *Behaviour Research and Therapy* 18:333–338.

Hegel, M. T., Ravaris, C. L., and Ahles, T. A. (1994). Combined cognitive-behavioral and time-limited alprazolam treatment of panic disorder. *Behavior Therapy* 25:183–195.

Jansson, L., and Ost, L. G. (1982). Behavioral treatments for agoraphobia: an evaluative review. *Clinical Psychology Review* 2:311–336.

Jerremalm, A., Jansson, L., and Ost, L. G. (1986). Individual response patterns and the effects of different behavioural methods in the treatment of dental phobia. *Behaviour Research and Therapy* 24:587–596.

——— (1977). Physiological assessment of anxiety and fear. In *Behavioral Assessment: New Directions in Clinical Psychology*, eds. J. D. Cone and R. A. Hawkins, pp. 178–195. New York: Brunner/Mazel.

Kazdin, A. E., and Wilcoxon, L. A. (1976). Systematic desensitization and nonspecific treatment effects: a methodological evaluation. *Psychological Bulletin* 83:729–758.

Lang, P. J. (1968). Fear reduction and fear behavior: problems in treating a construct. In *Research in Psychotherapy*, vol. 3, ed. J. M. Shlien, pp. 90–103. Washington, DC: American Psychological Association.

Leitenberg, H. (1976). Behavioral approaches to treatment of neuroses. In *Handbook of Behavior Modification and Behavior Therapy*, ed. H. Leitenberg, pp. 124–167. Englewood Cliffs, N.J.: Prentice-Hall.

Leitenberg, H., and Callahan, E. J. (1973). Reinforced practice and reduction of different kinds of fears in adults and children. *Behaviour Research and Therapy* 11:19–30.

Luborsky, L. (1962). Clinicians' judgments of mental health. *Archives of General Psychiatry* 7:407–417.

Macaskill, N. D. (1996). Improving clinical outcomes in REBT/CBT: the therapeutic uses of tape-recording. *Journal of Rational-Emotive & Cognitive-Behavior Therapy* 14:199–207.

Marks, I. M. (1975). Behavioral treatments of phobic and obsessive-compulsive disorders: a critical appraisal. In *Progress in Behavior Modification*, vol. 1, ed. R. Hersen, R. M. Eisler, and P. M. Miller, pp. 66–158. New York: Academic.

—— (1978). Behavioral psychotherapy of adult neurosis. In *Handbook of Psychotherapy and Behavior Change*, ed. A. E. Bergin and S. Garfield, pp. 493–547. New York: Wiley.

—— (1981). Space "phobia": a pseudo-agoraphobic syndrome. *Journal of Neurology, Neurosurgery, and Psychiatry* 44:387–391.

Marks, I. M., Swinson, R. P., Basoglu, et al. (1993). Alprazolam and exposure alone and combined in panic disorder with agoraphobia: a controlled study in London and Toronto. *British Journal of Psychiatry* 162:776–787.

Marks, I. M., Viswanathan, R., Lipsedge, M. S., and Gardner, R. (1972). Enhanced relief of phobias by flooding during waning diazepam effect. *British Journal of Psychiatry* 121:493–505.

Marshall, W. L., Gauthier, J., Christie, M. M., et al. (1977). Flooding therapy: effectiveness, stimulus characteristics, and the value of brief in vivo exposure. *Behaviour Research and Therapy* 15:79–87.

Mavissakalian, M., and Barlow, D. H., eds. (1981). *Phobia: Psychological and Pharmacological Treatment*. New York: Guilford.

McNally, R. J. (1987). Preparedness and phobias: a review. *Psychological Bulletin* 101:283–303.

Meichenbaum, D. H. (1971). Examination of model characteristics in reducing avoidance behavior. *Journal of Personality and Social Psychology* 17:298–307.

—— (1977). *Cognitive-Behavior Modification: An Integrative Approach*. New York: Plenum.

Meichenbaum, D., and Turk, D. C. (1987). *Facilitating Treatment Adherence: A Practitioner's Guidebook*. New York: Plenum.

Mineka, S. (1985). Animal models of anxiety based disorders: their usefulness and limitations. In *Anxiety and the Anxiety Disorders*, eds. A. H. Tuma, and J. D. Maser, pp. 199–244. Hillsdale, NJ: Erlbaum.

Mineka, S., Gunnar, M., and Champoux, M. (1986). Control and early socioemotional development: infant rhesus monkeys reared in controllable versus uncontrollable environments. *Child Development* 57:1241–1256.

Mowrer, O. H. (1947). On the dual nature of learning: a reinterpretation of "conditioning" and "problem solving." *Harvard Educational Review* 17:102–148.

Munby, J., and Johnston, D. W. (1980). Agoraphobia: the long-term follow-up of behavioural treatment. *British Journal of Psychiatry* 137:418–427.

Ogles, B. M., Lambert, M. J., and Masters, K. S. (1996). *Assessing Outcome in Clinical Practice*. Boston: Allyn and Bacon.

Ost, L. G., and Hugdahl, K. (1981). Acquisition of phobias and anxiety response patterns in clinical patients. *Behaviour Research and Therapy* 19:439–447.

——— (1983). Acquisition of agoraphobia, mode of onset, and anxiety response patterns. *Behaviour Research and Therapy* 21:623–631.

Ost, L. G., Johansson, J., and Jerremalm, A. (1982). Individual response patterns and the effects of different behavioural methods in the treatment of claustrophobia. *Behaviour Research and Therapy* 20:445–460.

Ost, L. G., Lindahl, I. L., Sterner, U., and Jerremalm, A. (1984). Exposure in vivo vs. applied relaxation in the treatment of blood phobia. *Behaviour Research and Therapy*, 22:205–216.

Ost, L. G., and Sterner, U. (1987). Applied tension: a specific behavioural method for treatment of blood phobia. *Behaviour Research and Therapy* 25:25–30.

Otto, M. W., Pollack, M. H., Sachs, G. S., et al. (1993). Discontinuation of benzodiazepine treatment: efficacy of cognitive behavioral therapy for patients with panic disorder. *American Journal of Psychiatry* 150:1485–1490.

Pavlov, I. P. (1927). *Conditional Reflexes* (G. Anrep, Trans.). New York: Oxford University Press.

Rachman, S. J. (1977). The conditioning theory of fear acquisition: a critical examination. *Behaviour Research and Therapy* 15:375–387.

——— (1978). *Fear and Courage*. San Francisco: Freeman.

——— (1984). Agoraphobia: a safety-signal perspective. *Behaviour Research and Therapy* 22:59–70.

——— (1985). The treatment of anxiety disorders: a critique of the implications for psychopathology. In *Anxiety and the Anxiety Disorders*, eds. A. H. Tuma, and J. D. Maser, pp. 453–461. Hillsdale, NJ: Erlbaum.

Rachman, S. J., Craske, M., Tallman, K., and Solyom, C. (1986). Does escape behavior strengthen agoraphobic avoidance? A replication. *Behavior Therapy* 17:366–384.

Rimm, D. C., and Mahoney, M. J. (1969). The application of reinforcement and participant modeling procedures in the treatment of snake-phobic behavior. *Behaviour Research and Therapy* 7:369–376.

Ritter, B. (1968). The group treatment of children's snake phobias, using vicarious and contact desensitization procedures. *Behaviour Research and Therapy* 6:1–6.

——— (1969a). Treatment of acrophobia with contact desensitization. *Behaviour Research and Therapy* 7:41–45.

——— (1969b). The use of contact desensitization, demonstration-plus-participations, and demonstration alone in the treatment of acrophobia. *Behaviour Research and Therapy* 7:157–164.

Rosenthal, T. L., and Bandura, A. (1978). Psychological modeling: theory and practice. In *Handbook of Psychotherapy and Behavior Change: An Empirical Analysis*, eds. S. L. Garfield, and A. E. Bergin, 2nd ed., pp. 621–658. New York: Wiley.

Sartory, G. (1983). Benzodiazepines and behavioral treatment of phobic anxiety. *Behavior Psychotherapy* 11:204–217.

Sederer, L. I., and Dickey, B., eds. (1996). *Outcomes Assessment in Clinical Practice*. Baltimore: Williams and Wilkins.

Seligman, M., and Hager, J. (1972). *The Biological Boundaries of Learning*. New York: Appleton-Century-Crofts.

Selye, H. (1956). *The Stress of Life*. New York: McGraw-Hill.

—— (1976). *The Stress of Life*, revised ed. New York: McGraw-Hill.

Spiegel, D. A., and Bruce, T. J. (1997). Benzodiazepines and exposure-based cognitive behavior therapies for panic disorder: conclusions from combined treatment trials. *American Journal of Psychiatry* 154:773–781.

Spiegel, D. A., Bruce, T. J., Gregg, S. F., and Nuzzarello, A. (1994). Does cognitive behavior therapy assist slow-taper alprazolam discontinuation in panic disorder? *American Journal of Psychiatry* 151:876–881.

Stern, R., and Marks, I. (1973). Brief and prolonged flooding: a comparison in agoraphobic patients. *Archives of General Psychiatry* 28:270–276.

Tata, P. R., Rollings, J., Collins, M., et al. (1994). Lack of cognitive recovery following withdrawal from long-term benzodiazepine use. *Psychological Medicine* 24:203–313.

Thorpe, G., Hacker, J., Cavallaro, L., and Kulberg, G. (1987). Insight versus rehearsal in cognitive-behaviour therapy: a crossover study with sixteen phobics. *Behavioural Psychotherapy* 15:319–336.

Wardle, J. (1990). Behavior therapy and benzodiazepines: allies or antagonists? *British Journal of Psychiatry* 156:163–168.

Watson, J. P., Mullett, G. E., and Pillay, H. (1973). The effects of prolonged exposure to phobic situations upon agoraphobic patients treated in groups. *Behaviour Research and Therapy* 11:531–545.

Williams, S. L., and Zane, G. (1989). Guided mastery and stimulus exposure treatments for severe performance anxiety in agoraphobics. *Behaviour Research and Therapy* 27:237–245.

—— (1997). Guided mastery treatment of phobias. *The Clinical Psychologist* 50:13–15.

Wolpe, J. (1958). *Psychotherapy by Reciprocal Inhibition*. Stanford, CA: Stanford University Press.

Zane, G., and Williams, S. L. (1993). Performance-related anxiety in agoraphobia: treatment procedures and cognitive mechanisms of change. *Behavior Therapy* 24:625–643.

APPENDICES

APPENDIX 1

Bibliography of Selected Studies Supporting the Efficacy of the Treatment

Agras, W. S., Leitenberg, H., Barlow, D. H., and Thomson, L. E. (1969). Instructions and reinforcement in the modification of neurotic behavior. *American Journal of Psychiatry* 125:1435–1439.

Bandura, A. (1969). *Principles of Behavior Modification*. New York: Holt, Rinehart & Winston.

Bandura, A., Blanchard, E. B., and Ritter, B. (1969). The relative efficacy of desensitization and modeling approaches for inducing behavioral, affective, and attitudinal changes. *Journal of Personality and Social Psychology* 13:173–199.

Bandura, A., Jeffery, R. W., and Gajdos, E. (1975). Generalizing change through participant modeling with self-directed mastery. *Behaviour Research and Therapy* 13:141–152.

Bandura, A., Jeffery, R. W., and Wright, C. (1974). Efficacy of participant modeling as a function of response induction aids. *Journal of Abnormal Psychology* 83:56–64.

Barrett, C. L. (1969). Systematic desensitization versus implosive therapy. *Journal of Abnormal Psychology* 74:587–592.

Blanchard, E. B. (1970). Relative contributions of modeling, informational influences, and physical contact in extinction of phobic behavior. *Journal of Abnormal Psychology* 76:55–61.

Boulougouris, J. C., Marks, I. M., and Marset, P. (1971). Superiority of flooding to desensitization as a fear reducer. *Behaviour Research and Therapy* 9:7–16.

Denney, D. R., Sullivan, B. J., and Thiry, M. R. (1977). Participant modeling and self-verbalization training in the reduction of spider fears. *Journal of Behavior Therapy and Experimental Psychiatry* 8:247–253.

D'Zurilla, T. J., Wilson, G. T., and Nelson, R. (1973). A preliminary study of effectiveness of graduated prolonged exposure in the treatment of irrational fear. *Behavior Therapy* 4:672–685.

Emmelkamp, P. M. G., and Wessels, H. (1975). Flooding in imagination vs. flooding in vivo: a comparison with agoraphobics. *Behaviour Research and Therapy* 13:7–15.

Foa, E. B., Blau, J. S., Prout, M., and Latimer, P. (1977). Is horror a necessary component of flooding (implosion)? *Behaviour Research and Therapy* 15:397–402.

Gelder, M. G., Marks, I. M., Wolff, H. E., and Clarke, M. (1967). Desensitization and psychotherapy in the treatment of phobic states: A controlled inquiry. *British Journal of Psychiatry* 113:53–73.

Kirsh, I., Tennen, H., Wickless, C., et al. (1983). The role of expectancy in fear reduction. *Behavior Therapy* 14:520–533.

Lazarus, A. (1961). Group therapy of phobic disorders by systematic desensitization. *Journal of Abnormal and Social Psychology*, 63:504–510.

Leitenberg, H. (1976). Behavioral approaches to treatment of neuroses. In *Handbook of Behavior Modification and Behavior Therapy*, ed. H. Leitenberg, pp. 124–167. Englewood Cliffs, N.J.: Prentice-Hall.

Leitenberg, H., Agras, W. S., Allen, R., Butz, R., and Edwards, J. (1975). Feedback and therapist praise during treatment of phobia. *Journal of Consulting and Clinical Psychology* 43:396–404.

Leitenberg, H., Agras, S., Edwards, J. A., et al. (1970). Practice as a psychotherapeutic variable: an experimental analysis within single cases. *Journal of Psychiatric Research* 7:215–225.

Leitenberg, H., and Callahan, E. J. (1973). Reinforced practice and reduction of different kinds of fears in adults and children. *Behaviour Research and Therapy* 11:19–30.

Marks, I. M. (1975). Behavioral treatments of phobic and obsessive-compulsive disorders: A critical appraisal. In *Progress in Behavior Modification*, vol. 1, ed. R. Hersen, R. M. Eisler, and P. M. Miller, pp. 66–158. New York: Academic.

––––––– (1978). Behavioral psychotherapy of adult neurosis. In *Handbook of Psychotherapy and Behavior Change*, ed. A. E. Bergin and S. Garfield, pp. 493–547. New York: Wiley.

Marshall, W. L., Gauthier, J., Christie, M. M., et al. (1977). Flooding therapy: effectiveness, stimulus characteristics, and the value of brief in vivo exposure. *Behaviour Research and Therapy* 15:79–87.

Meichenbaum, D. H. (1971). Examination of model characteristics in reducing avoidance behavior. *Journal of Personality and Social Psychology* 17:298–307.

––––––– (1977). *Cognitive-Behavior Modification: An Integrative Approach*. New York: Plenum.

Ost, L. G. (1978). Fading vs. systematic desensitization in the treatment of snake and spider phobia. *Behaviour Research and Therapy* 16:379–389.

Ost, L. G., Salkovskis, P. M., and Hellstrom, K. (1991). One-session therapist-directed exposure vs. self-exposure in the treatment of spider phobia. *Behavior Therapy* 22:407–422.

Rimm, D. C., and Mahoney, M. J. (1969). The application of reinforcement and participant modeling procedures in the treatment of snake-phobic behavior. *Behaviour Research and Therapy* 7:369–376.

Rimm, D. C., and Masters, J. C. (1979). *Behavior Therapy: Techniques and Empirical Findings*, 2nd ed. New York: Academic Press.

Ritter, B. (1969a). Treatment of acrophobia with contact desensitization. *Behaviour Research and Therapy* 7:41–45.

––––––– (1969b). The use of contact desensitization, demonstration-plus-participations, and demonstration alone in the treatment of acrophobia. *Behaviour Research and Therapy* 7:157–164.

Stern, R., and Marks, I. (1973). Brief and prolonged flooding: a comparison in agoraphobic patients. *Archives of General Psychiatry* 28:270–276.

Watson, J. P., Gaind, R., and Marks, I. M. (1971). Prolonged exposure: a rapid treatment for phobias. *British Medical Journal* 1:13–15.

Watson, J. P., Mullett, G. E., and Pillay, H. (1973). The effects of prolonged exposure to phobic situations upon agoraphobic patients treated in groups. *Behaviour Research and Therapy* 11:531–545.

APPENDIX 2

Phobic Types Questionnaire

This questionnaire asks you to indicate which type of phobia you would like treated and, if you indicate more than one, the order in which you would like to work on them.

INSTRUCTIONS (please see questionnaire on page 230 while reading instructions):

1. Listed below are different types of phobias. Please indicate which phobia(s) you would like to have treated by placing an X in the column labeled *Check*. Feel free to comment on the phobia in the space provided. If the type of phobia from which you suffer is not listed, please describe it in the space marked "Other." Leave all other spaces blank. (Please see the sample below.)

2. If you have marked more than one phobia, please rank the order in which you prefer to have them treated in the column marked *Rank*. Use the following scale to rank phobias: 1= treat first, 2=treat second, etc. Again, leave all other spaces blank. (Please see the sample below.)

Please note that some phobias can be treated together. Others may be better treated before others. Although you are asked to rank these phobias, the final decision of how and when to treat them can be made between you and your therapist.

When you have finished this form, please complete the Phobic Objects, Situations, and Activities Questionnaires.

Sample

Check	Rank	Type of Phobia
_____	_____	Animals
X	2	Insects - Spiders
X	1	Heights
_____	_____	Storms
_____	_____	Water

Phobic Types Questionnaire

Check	Rank	Type of Phobia
_____	_____	Animals (list) _____
		_____
_____	_____	Insects (list) _____
		_____
_____	_____	Heights _____
_____	_____	Storms _____
_____	_____	Water _____
_____	_____	Blood _____
_____	_____	Needles _____
_____	_____	Dental work _____
_____	_____	Seeing a doctor _____
_____	_____	Bridges _____
_____	_____	Driving _____
_____	_____	Enclosed places _____
_____	_____	Flying _____
_____	_____	Elevators _____
_____	_____	Choking _____
_____	_____	Vomiting _____
_____	_____	Getting a disease _____
_____	_____	Other _____

When you have finished this form, please complete the Phobic Objects, Situations, and Activities Questionnaire.

APPENDIX 3

Phobic Objects, Situations, and Activities Questionnaire

For each phobia a person has, there may be one or several objects, situations, or activities that they fear or avoid to different degrees. For example, a person fearful of enclosed spaces (claustrophobia) may have a mild fear of going into their basement, but do not avoid doing so; they may have a moderate fear of going into a small room, but will do so occasionally; and they may have a strong fear of caves, and avoid them completely. This questionnaire asks you to indicate the different types of objects, situations, and activities you fear and avoid because of your phobia.

INSTRUCTIONS (please see questionnaire on page 232 while reading instructions):

1. Write the name of your primary phobia in the space labeled *Type of Phobia.*

2. List the types of objects, situations, and activities that you fear and avoid in the column labeled *Objects, Situations, or Activities.* List as many as come to mind.

3. For each object, situation, or activity listed, please rate how fearful it is to you, under the column labeled *Fear (0–10)* using the 0–10 *fear* scale at the top of the questionnaire.

4. Finally, for each object, situation, or activity listed, please rate how much you avoid that item under the column labeled *Avoidance (0–10)* using the second 0–10 *avoidance* scale at the top of the questionnaire (please see sample below).

Sample

Type of Phobia: Enclosed places		
Object or Situation	**Fear (0–10)**	**Avoidance (0–10)**
Caves	10	10
Small Room (e.g., closet)	5	3
Basement	2	0

Phobic Objects, Situations, and Activities Questionnaire

Type of Phobia _____

Please use the following scale to make your rating of *fear*:

```
0-------1-------2-------3-------4-------5-------6-------7-------8-------9-------10
No Fear       Mild Fear         Moderate        Strong        Severe
```

Please use the following scale to make your rating of *avoidance*:

```
0-------1-------2-------3-------4-------5-------6-------7-------8-------9-------10
   No          Some            Often          Mostly         Always
Avoidance    Avoidance         Avoid          Avoid          Avoid
```

Objects, Situations, or Activities	Fear (0–10)	Avoidance (0–10)

After completing this form, please complete the Methods of Coping Questionnaire.

APPENDIX 4

Methods of Coping Questionnaire

It is natural to try to cope with phobic objects or situations in some form or another. This questionnaire asks you to indicate the various ways you have found yourself trying to cope with your phobic object or situation.

INSTRUCTIONS (please see questionnaire on page 234 while reading instructions):

1. Write the name of your primary phobia in the space labeled *Type of Phobia*.
2. Place an X next to each method of coping that you have used when faced with encountering the phobic object or situation. Leave all other spaces blank (please see sample below).

Please feel free to list other methods you have used that are not listed by writing them in the space marked "Others."

Also feel free to make any other comments that might help us understand how you try to cope with the phobia.

Sample

Check	Method of seeking safety
__X__	Avoid situation completely
__X__	Escape
_____	Keep my distance
__X__	Look away

Methods of Coping Questionnaire

Type of Phobia _____

Check Method of coping

_____ Avoid it _____

_____ Escape _____

_____ Keep my distance while in its presence _____

_____ Avert my attention _____

_____ Wear protective garments _____

_____ Have a safe person with me (who?)_____

_____ Have a safe object with me (what?)_____

_____ Talk to myself (what?) _____

_____ Pray_____

_____ Prepare for encounters (how?) _____

_____ Freeze or stand still _____

_____ Take medicine/alcohol/drugs (specify) _____

_____ Try to be informed/read/learn about object or situation _____

_____ Fight off feelings _____

_____ Try to relax _____

_____ Others _____
                _____
                _____

After completing this form, please complete the Fearful Thoughts Questionnaire.

APPENDIX 5

Fearful Thoughts Questionnaire

Everyone has had fearful thoughts or images about what they think could happen during an encounter with a phobic object or situation. For example, we may fear that the phobic object, situation, or our own reactions could harm us in some way. Some individuals have a few fears; others have many. Likewise, some fearful thoughts may occur rarely; others may be present with each encounter. Finally, some fearful thoughts are very believable at the moment we are thinking them; others are less believable.

This questionnaire asks you to list what you have feared could happen during phobic encounters, then rate how often the thought has occurred and how believable it has been.

INSTRUCTIONS (please see questionnaire on page 236 while reading instructions):

1. Write the name of your primary phobia in the space labeled *Type of Phobia*.

2. List all fearful thoughts or images that you can remember having had regarding phobic encounters under the column labeled *Fearful Thought*.

3. For each thought listed, rate how frequently it has occurred under the column labeled *How Often (0–10)* using the 0–10 *how often* scale at the top of the questionnaire (please see sample below).

4. Finally, rate how believable each thought has been (at its most) under the column labeled *Belief (0–10)* using the 0–10 *how believable* scale at the top of the questionnaire (please see sample below).

Sample: Animal Phobia

Fearful Thought:	How often (0–10)	Belief (0–10)
I will get bitten, stung	10	10
I could die	7	3
I could catch disease	4	3
I could faint	2	6
I could go crazy	3	4
I could be embarrassed	9	10

Fearful Thoughts Questionnaire

Type of Phobia _____

Please use the following scale to to rate *how often* the feared thought has occurred:

0-------1-------2-------3-------4-------5-------6-------7-------8-------9-------10
Never   Seldom   Half the Time   Often   Always

Please use the following scale to rate *how believable* the thought has been:

0-------1-------2-------3-------4-------5-------6-------7-------8-------9-------10
No belief   Mildly   Moderately   Strongly   Completely

Fearful Thought	How Often (0–10)	Belief (0–10)
_____	_____	_____
_____	_____	_____
_____	_____	_____
_____	_____	_____
_____	_____	_____
_____	_____	_____
_____	_____	_____
_____	_____	_____
_____	_____	_____
_____	_____	_____
_____	_____	_____

After finishing this questionnaire, please complete the Phobic Sensations Questionnaire.

APPENDIX 6

Phobic Sensations Questionnaire

When people encounter a phobic object or situation, they often feel certain physical sensations (feelings). Some sensations are strong and stand out; others are milder. Some sensations can be frightening; others are not.

This form asks you to indicate which sensations you have experienced during phobic encounters, how strong they usually are, and how much they have frightened you.

INSTRUCTIONS (please see questionnaire on page 238 while reading instructions):

1. Write the name of your primary phobia in the space labeled *Type of Phobia.*

2. Please place an X next to each sensation that you have experienced during a phobic encounter under the column labeled *Check.*

3. For each sensation checked, rate how strong that sensation usually has been under the column labeled *Intensity (0–10)* using the scale at the top of the questionnaire.

4. Finally, for each sensation checked, rate how frightening that sensation has been under the column labeled *Fear (0–10)* using the same scale at the top of the questionnaire (please see sample below).

Sample

Feelings (Sensations)	Intensity (0–10)	Fear (0–10)
Heart beats faster	8	0
Heart beats harder	2	2
Breath quickens	7	0
Short of breath	0	0
Feel unsteady	2	5
Faintness	0	0

Phobic Sensations Questionnaire

Type of Phobia _____

Use this scale to rate the *intensity (strength)* and your *fear* of each
sensation marked:

0-------1-------2-------3-------4-------5-------6-------7-------8-------9-------10
None   Mild   Moderate   Strong   Severe

Check	Feelings (Sensations)	Intensity (0–10)	Fear (0–10)
_____	Heart beats faster	_____	_____
_____	Heart pounds harder	_____	_____
_____	Breathing is faster	_____	_____
_____	Breathing is difficult	_____	_____
_____	Chest feels tight	_____	_____
_____	Feel faint, dizzy, unsteady (Have you ever fainted? yes___ no___)	_____	_____
_____	Vision changes (how?_____)	_____	_____
_____	Weakness (Have you ever collapsed? yes___ no___)	_____	_____
_____	Shaky or trembling	_____	_____
_____	Numbness/tingling	_____	_____
_____	Chills or hot flushes	_____	_____
_____	Feeling detached from oneself	_____	_____
_____	Other things seem unreal	_____	_____
_____	Feeling of choking	_____	_____
_____	Sweating	_____	_____
_____	Nauseous or other stomach distress (Have you ever vomited? yes___ no___)	_____	_____
_____	Other (specify) _____	_____	_____

APPENDIX 7

Behavioral Assessment Form

During this self-therapy exercise, you are asked to approach the feared object or situation that you and your therapist discussed. The purpose of this exercise is to learn more about your reactions to these encounters. Your goal is to approach the chosen object or situation and record your reactions to it using the attached form as your guide. You do not have to suffer through this exercise, and can stop it whenever you want.

INSTRUCTIONS:

Please describe the exposure: _____

_____

_____

Immediately before the encounter, please complete these questions:

1. What are you fearing could happen during this encounter (list all fears)?

2. What physical sensations (feelings) are you experiencing?

3. Which (if any) of those sensations frighten you?

4. Do you have any urges to avoid? yes ___ no ___ If yes, how?

5. How are you planning to cope when you start this encounter?

Other comments?

Now approach the object or situation. Monitor what is happening to you, your thoughts, feelings, how you find yourself behaving. End the encounter when you want. Then finish completing the rest of this form.

Immediately after the encounter, complete these questions:

1. Did any of the things you feared happen?

2. Did any other fears come up during the encounter?

3. What physical sensations did you experience during this encounter?

4. Did any of those sensations frighten you?

5. How did you try to cope with the encounter (list all ways)?

6. Why did you stop the exercise?

Other comments?

APPENDIX 8

Exposure Record Form

Immediately Before the Exposure Please Complete the First Page of this Form

1. Date/Time: _____

2. Briefly describe the exposure task and whether this is the first, second, etc., time you have done it. _____

3. Please rate your anxiety level right now (0-10): _____

4. How confident are you that you can manage this exposure 0-10? __

5. Before doing the exposure, imagine doing it. As you do that, briefly list (one or two words) what you fear could happen during this encounter. List each and all fears that come to mind. Then rate how believable each fear *feels* on the following scale:

   0-------1-------2-------3-------4-------5-------6-------7-------8-------9-------10
   No   Mildly   Moderately   Strongly   Completely
   Belief

   Predicted fears and rated belief (0–10)

6. Now reimagine the encounter. However, this time instead of listing the feared events, list the most likely challenges you will face (being objective) and how you intend to cope with those. Remember to include that you might feel fear or doubt if that is most likely, but also how you plan to manage those feelings. Briefly describe this alternative prediction below. Finally, rate how believable it *feels* using the above 0-10 scale.

Alternative Prediction and rated belief (0–10)

7. Now, lay out your plan for doing the exposure, breaking it down into steps if you wish.

If a coach is with you, discuss with him or her how you want to carry out the plan and cope with each step.

8. Conduct the exposure, keeping the suggestions below in mind. Afterward, please finish the rest of this form.

Remember: go at your own pace. Stay in the present. Focus on step-by-step coping. Use your coping strategies. Try to stay with the exposure until you feel more comfortable being in the situation. Look for ways you might be subtly avoiding and change those.

Immediately After the Exposure, Complete the Following Section:

1. What was your highest anxiety during the exposure (0–10) _____?

2. What was your lowest anxiety during the exposure (0–10) _____?

3. When did each of those occur?

4. What prominant fearful thought(s) did you have during the exposure (list briefly)?

5. What physical sensations did you have? Did any of them frighten you?

6. How long did the exposure last?

7. Why did you decide to end it?

8. What were your biggest challenges during the exposure?

9. What coping strategies were most helpful?

10. Did you find yourself subtly avoiding? If yes, how?

11. What would you do differently next time?

12. Have you repeated this exposure frequently enough (so you are confident about managing it)?

13. What exposures should you do next time?

14. Please go through each predicted fear listed under #5 and #6 on the first page and indicate whether that prediction occurred or did not using Yes for those that occurred and No for those that did not.

Please bring this form to your next appointment.

APPENDIX 9

Sensation Exposure Record

INSTRUCTIONS (please read all instructions before beginning this exercise; see Recording Form on page 247 while reading instructions): This procedure involves 4 steps: exercise, recover, record, and repeat.

Exercise: From the list provided, select an exercise that will induce physical sensations (feelings). Next, do the exercise until you begin to feel the sensations, continue a few seconds longer (for example, 5, 10, up to 30 seconds), then stop.

Recover: When you stop, you will feel the sensations. Use your coping strategies (breathing, relaxation, self-talk) to regroup and calm yourself. Take as long as you need.

Record: On the form provided, indicate which sensations you felt by rating how intense they were using the 0–10 scale at the top of the form. Then make the last rating, which asks how frightening the feelings were during or after the exercise.

Repeat: After recovering and recording, repeat the procedure of exercise, recover, and record as follows: if you experienced no anxiety during the first cycle, then you need only repeat it 2 more times. If you continue to experience no anxiety, then please move on to another exercise. If you do experience anxiety during an exercise, then repeat the procedure of exercise, recover, record as many times as necessary for your anxiety ratings to lower and level off.

Exercises (have your therapist demonstrate these and other exercises):

Rapid Breathing: Inhale through mouth deeply and rapidly, then exhale through mouth forcefully. Do this rapidly, about one cycle (one inhale/one exhale) each second.

Spinning: Spin in a chair or stool.

Holding Breath: Hold your breath as long as you can.

Muscle Tension: Tense all muscles in your body; hold as long as you can.

Run in Place: Hop or run in place.

Restricted Breathing: Breathe through a straw, plastic pen container, or into your fist so that breathing is restricted.

Head Shaking: Shake your head from side to side (not too forcefully).

Sensation Exposure Record (Recording Form)

Name _____   Date _____

After each exercise, record which sensations you experienced and how frightening they were using the scale below:

0-------1-------2-------3-------4-------5-------6-------7-------8-------9-------10
Not at all   Mild   Moderate   Strong   Severe

Exercise (see attached list): _____

Sensations:	Sample	1st cycle	2nd	3rd	4th	5th	6th	7th	8th
Dizziness, unsteady feelings, or faintness	3								
Hard heartbeat or faster heart rate	4								
Shortness of breath, smothering sensations, or couldn't get enough air									
Hot flashes or chills	1								
Weakness									
Trembling or shaking									
Sweating	1								
Nausea or stomach distress									
Numbness or tingling sensations									
Self or surroundings seemed strange or unreal									
Chest pain or discomfort									
Choking									
Lump in throat									
Other									
How frightening were the feelings	3								

APPENDIX 10

Developing Your Coping Strategies

In learning coping strategies for managing the physical sensations (feelings) you experience in phobic situations, it helps to know where they come from and why the techniques you are about to learn are recommended.

When we sense possible trouble or harm in a phobic situation, a branch of our nervous system, the sympathetic nervous system, becomes active. This system is what produces the physical sensations you feel when you encounter a phobic object or situation. Those feelings are part of our body's natural alarm reaction, termed the *flight or fight response*. The flight or fight response prepares us to flee or fight when we sense that harm is possible.

Scientists believe that the flight or fight response is probably a holdover from the days of early humankind, when our ancestors faced threats to their lives from animals, insects, and the natural environment (common phobic objects and situations) on a daily basis. Although the feelings this alarm produces may seem scary, think for a second how the changes occurring to the body during the flight or fight response may have helped our ancestors to survive everyday, life-threatening situations. For example, under threat, the adrenal glands increase adrenaline secretion. This serves as the chemical switch for the flight or fight reaction. Our respiratory and heart rates increase; muscles tense; we sweat; vessels of the cardiovascular system constrict at surface areas. Although these feelings may seem scary or even make us feel as if real harm could happen during phobic encounters, they are actually there to help us flee or fight, as they did our forebearers. For example, they bring more blood and oxygen to the large muscles, where it is needed to help us run faster or fight more vigorously. Sweating made our ancestors slippery—easier to escape the grasp of predators. Although vessel constriction at the surface of our skin may make us feel cold, look pale, and even produce numbness or tingling sensations, it served to reduced the risk of blood loss in our ancestors in case a predator cut or scratched them. The flight or fight reaction made it more likely that our ancestors survived threats and passed this system on to us. Those whose bodies were not as well equipped did not survive.

It is important to understand that the sympathetic nervous system does not know if the harm we sense during phobic encounters is likely or not. It simply reacts to what we sense. If we sense harm, it activates; if we don't, it remains at rest. When a situation is actually harmful, the flight or fight reaction is valuable, because it helps us to escape that harm. However, during phobic encounters, we have learned to sense harm where its risk is actually low or more manageable than it seems. In those situations, the flight or fight reaction is a "false alarm," because it is alarming us to flee harm that is unlikely or manageable. Unfortunately, this false alarm gives us such a strong and convincing feeling that harm is actually present that it often interferes with our ability to learn that harm is actually unlikely and that we can manage the encounter. Even though the feelings we experience during a false alarm are not harmful to us, it is easy to misinterpret them that way. For example, the shortness of breath we may feel during this reaction occurs because our respiratory rate increases while our chest muscles are tightening. Although it may be more difficult to breathe, we still can, especially if we do it in a particular way that you will learn in a moment. But when we're fearful, it is easy to misinterpret that change in breathing as a sign of trouble, even though it is not. If you have any concerns like these about sensations you experience, you should discuss them with your therapist.

Fortunately, the body is also equipped with another branch of the nervous system, called the parasympathetic system, that reverses the effects of the flight or fight reaction, that is, it relaxes us and restores calm. You may have noticed that when you leave a phobic situation your body calms. This is the work of the parasympathetic system. You will find at times, if you already haven't, that if you stay in the phobic situation and face fears that the flight or fight reaction does not run indefinitely. Eventually the parasympathetic system will activate and restore balance.

So how can we use this knowledge to help us? Some aspects of the sympathetic and parasympathetic systems can be controlled voluntarily. Those under the most direct control are the muscular and respiratory systems. To the degree that you can become skilled in calming these two systems, the flight or fight response will become more manageable. This will help you to be able to stay in the phobic situation so you can find that it is more manageable and less threatening than it seems. As it becomes less threatening, the sense of harm that triggers the flight or fight reaction grows weaker and you begin to regain a long-lost feeling—confidence.

THE PACED, DIAPHRAGMATIC BREATHING AND RELAXATION EXERCISE

The first step in developing your coping skills is to get your body used to doing them. Therefore, until your next appointment you should practice the following exercise at least once, but preferably more than once, each day. During a later session, your therapist will show you how a briefer version of this exercise can be used to cope during phobic encounters.

The first step in the coping exercise involves diaphragmatic breathing. Diaphragmatic breathing is commonly known as stomach or belly breathing. Think about breathing for a second. Our lungs sit in the chest in a space that is surrounded on the top and sides by the rib cage and on the bottom by the diaphragm. The diaphragm is a sheet of muscle that bows upward under the lungs like a dome. It separates the lung space from the abdominal cavity, which contains the stomach and intestines.

As we breathe in, we have to increase this lung space. We can do this in several ways: (1) by expanding the rib cage (chest breathing), (2) by pulling down or flattening the diaphragm (diaphragmatic breathing), or (3) by doing both of these actions. Chest (or thoracic) breathing requires more effort than diaphragmatic breathing. It is particularly difficult when we are anxious because the muscles of our chest and shoulders are tightening. That struggle can make us feel as if our breathing is labored, which can make us even more anxious. Therefore, as part of coping in anxious situations, you are asked to do diaphragmatic or stomach breathing.

Some people are naturally good at diaphragmatic breathing; others have to practice it for a while. To see what it feels like to breathe diaphragmatically, lie on a bed or the floor on your stomach with your arms crossed under you head. Relax your stomach muscles and breathe normally, inhaling through your nose. In this position you are most likely to breathe diaphragmatically. If so, you'll notice a slight pressure on your stomach as you inhale. Try this for a few minutes until you have the feel of it. Then practice it as follows: sit in a comfortable chair with both feet on the floor. Loosen any restrictive clothing. If you like, you can place one hand lightly on your chest and the other on your stomach just above your navel. Now breathe slowly through your nose, relaxing your stomach and using only your diaphragm. Inhale as deeply as is comfortable and then exhale through pursed lips as if you are blowing through a straw. Exhale at least as long as it took you to inhale. This is called paced breathing. When you're breathing correctly, your belly will swell outward as you breathe in, and slowly fall back inward as you breathe out.

When you have gotten the paced diaphragmatic breathing down, add one more component to this exercise. After you've taken a few breaths, mildly contract the muscles of your face and neck and then let them go limp during the next most convenient exhale. Take a few more diaphragmatic breaths, then tense your shoulder muscles, relaxing them during the next most convenient exhale. After a few more diaphragmatic breaths, tense your back muscles, then relax. Do you see where we're going? You're coordinating your breathing, stretching, and relaxing, moving down through the major muscle groups of your body. Do this until you feel all major muscle groups are relaxed. You may have to do some of the more tense groups (for example, your neck or back) a few times before they unwind.

After you have this procedure down, do this exercise for approximately 15–30 minutes at least once, and preferably more than one time, a day. Begin the exercise with approximately 5 minutes of paced diaphragmatic breathing. Then do approximately 10 to 20 minutes of combined paced diaphragmatic breathing and muscle stretching and relaxing, followed by 5 more minutes breathing. During those last 5 minutes allow your breathing to become slower and slower, your muscles more and more heavy. Drift away and enjoy the quiet calm.

THE COPING STRATEGY

Diaphragmatic breathing and relaxation can also be used as a coping strategy to manage anxiety before or during exposures.

To begin coping, take a deep diaphragmatic breath through your nose. Hold it for a second or so, then exhale slowly through pursed lips. This starts the exercise. Next, begin paced diaphragmatic breathing with the goal of gradually slowing your rate of breathing. This may not be easy at first. Don't panic. Just begin extending your exhale, taking a deep breath here and there, or even holding your breath for moments. Eventually, you will be able to slow your breathing.

As you are slowing your breathing rate, begin stretching and relaxing major muscle groups. Also, move around a little. This breaks up the natural inclination to "freeze" when anxious. As you proceed, relax the muscles of your face, neck, and shoulders in unison with an exhale every now and then. The idea is to stretch, breath diaphragmatically and paced, and relax rather than tense up, freeze, and labor through chest breathing. This allows you to regroup and cope. No need to rush, either. Take it at your own pace.

It is also helpful to focus your thoughts while you ride out your anxious feelings. Talk with your therapist about how to use coping self-statements and other coping strategies with this exercise.

It is important to use your coping strategies appropriately. Even though you will be tempted, try not to use the strategies simply to stop your feelings of anxiety. Why? First, because those feelings will not usually just stop, and finding that out will probably make you more uncomfortable. But, more importantly, you really don't need to stop the feelings of flight or fight. They will not harm you. Your goal is to cope, allowing them to run their course. One way to think of this is as you would riding out an ocean wave. You allow it to pick you up, then set you back down. You don't try to stop it, fight it, or run from it. As you get better at coping with it (and you will with practice), it will become less and less frightening and begin to go away.

APPENDIX 11

Applied Tension

Fainting or near-fainting experiences can occur during exposure to blood, injection, or injury, especially if they have happened routinely in the past. They occur because of a temporary drop in heart rate and blood pressure that decreases the flow of blood to the brain. This is not a harmful reaction, but the possibility that it could happen can make exposure seem more frightening. The exercise and coping strategy described in this section will help reduce the likelihood that you will faint during exposure or reduce your recovery time if you do.

It may be helpful to understand why fainting sometimes occurs in response to the sight of blood, injury, and injections. Scientists believe that fainting, like the flight or fight reaction, is a holdover from the days of early humankind when our ancestors were faced with threats to their lives on a daily basis. Think for a second about how the tendency to faint may have spared the lives of our ancestors, allowing them to pass this tendency on to us (some gift, huh?). Fainting in response to the sight of blood or injury was adaptive because it slowed the loss of blood from an incurred injury. If one did not faint, the accelerated heart rate and blood pressure that accompanies the flight or fight response might have produced more blood loss and increased the risk of death. It is interesting to note also that some predators in the animal kingdom (e.g., bears) actually become less aggressive when their prey feigns deaths or becomes immobile. Unfortunately, the kinds of present-day situations where we see blood or injury (e.g., a television show, having our blood drawn) are not life-threatening, but can still produce this near-fainting or fainting reaction.

As you go through exposure to overcome your phobia, it will be useful for you to have a strategy that reduces the likelihood that you will faint, or decrease your recovery time if you do. This technique, developed and tested by Swedish psychologist Lars-Goran Ost, is called applied tension. It requires you to use your the ability to detect the first signs of feeling faint and then tense specific muscles of the body to increase blood pressure to the brain. Here's how you do it:

Sit in a comfortable chair with both feet on the floor. Imagine feeling the signs of faintness. At that moment, begin tensing the muscles of your neck, shoulders, chest, back, and legs, leaving your stomach relaxed so that you can breathe diaphragmatically. Hold this tension tightly until you feel warmth in your face. This usually takes anywhere from 10–30 seconds. After you feel flushed in your face, relax your body and breath normally and diaphragmatically for approximately 30 seconds. Then repeat this cycle of tensing until warm in the face, then relaxing.

Try to accomplish approximately 30 cycles of tension and relaxation per day, either all at one time or divided into two or three separate exercises. Of course, more than that is fine. Practice this exercise until your next appointment. Then, you and your therapist can practice using the technique during exposures.

Please note that when you do this exercise, you are asked to tense muscles tightly; however, if you begin developing a headache or other pain, decrease the intensity of your muscle tension until it is more comfortable. As you practice, try to find a level of tension that works for you.

If you want, you can produce some feelings of unsteadiness or lightheadedness and then practice using applied tension to calm them. Talk with your therapist, who can show you what exercises will produce these feeling safely.

As you become more comfortable with your exposures, fainting or near-fainting will start to go away. As that time nears, you should begin trying exposure without using the applied tension technique. You and your therapist can work out when it's best to begin that transition. If you have any questions or concerns about using applied tension, please bring them up with your therapist.

INDEX